GERMAN

Phrase Book
&Dictionary

Philippa Goodrich
Language Consultant: Sabine Heidelbach

Educational Publishers LLP trading as BBC Active
Edinburgh Gate, Harlow, Essex CM20 2JE

BBC logo © BBC 1996. BBC and BBC ACTIVE are trademarks of the British
Broadcasting Corporation

copyright © Philippa Goodrich and BBC Worldwide Ltd 2005

Published 2005. Reprinted 2006.

Based on the BBC German Phrase Book by Carol Stanley and Philippa
Goodrich,
copyright © Carol Stanley and Philippa Goodrich 1990

ISBN-10: 0-5635-1919-3
ISBN-13: 9-780563-519195

Managing Editor: Joanna Kirby
Project Editor: Josie Frame
Index Editor: Paula Peebles
Designer: Elizabeth Burns
Concept design: Pentacor Book Design
Illustrations copyright © Joanna Kerr @ New Division 2005
Cover design: Two Associates
Cover photo copyright © archivberlin Fotoagentur GmbH/ALAMY
Senior Production Controller: Man Fai Lau

Printed and bound in China
CTPS/02
The Publisher's policy is to use paper manufactured from sustainable forests.

Other languages available:
French | Greek | Italian | Portuguese | Spanish

how to use this book

This book is divided into colour-coded sections to help you find the language you need as quickly as possible. You can also refer to the **contents** on pages 4–5, the contents lists at the start of each section or the **index** on page 221.

Along with travel and language tips, each section contains:

 YOU MAY WANT TO SAY...
language you'll need for every situation

 YOU MAY SEE...
words and phrases you'll see on signs or in print

 YOU MAY HEAR... questions, instructions or
information people may ask or give you

On page 12 you'll find **essentials**, a list of basic, all-purpose phrases to help you start communicating straight away.

Many of the phrases can be adapted by simply using another word from the dictionary. For instance, take the question Wo ist das Stadtzentrum? (Where is the town centre?). If you want to know where the *station* is, just substitute der Bahnhof (station) for das Stadtzentrum to give Wo ist der Bahnhof?.

The **pronunciation guide** is based on English sounds, and is explained on page 6. If you want some guidance on how the German language works, see **basic grammar** on page 143. The **dictionary** is separated into two sections: English–German (page 151) and German–English (page 195).

We welcome any comments or suggestions about this book, but in the meantime, have a good trip – Gute Reise!

contents

pronunciation guide

✳ pronunciation

● You don't need perfect pronunciation to be able to communicate – it's enough to get the sounds approximately right and stress words in the correct place.

● German pronunciation is very regular – you can tell how a word is pronounced from the way it's written, once you know what each letter (or group of letters) represents.

Long words in German are often a combination of several shorter words, so it may help with pronunciation to split the long word into its individual parts.

A pronunciation guide is given with the phrases in this book – the system is based on English sounds, as described below.

● Many German consonants are pronounced in a similar way to English.

● The final 'e' on a word is always pronounced. For the German alphabet, see page 9.

✳ stress

● In this book a stressed syllable is shown in the pronunciation guide by bold type: *problaym*, *keelomayter*

✳ vowels

GERMAN VOWELS	APPROX ENGLISH EQUIVALENT	SHOWN IN BOOK AS	EXAMPLE	
a	**a in 'cat'**	*a*	danke	*danke*

	or	a in 'car'	aa	Abend	aabent
ai and ay		i in 'pile'	iy	Kaiser	kiyzer
au		ow in 'cow'	ow	Raucher	rowker
ä		e in 'let'	e	Geschäft	gesheft
	or	ay in 'pay'	ay	spät	shpayt
äu		oy in 'boy'	oy	Kohlensäure	kohlenzoyre
e		e in 'let'	e	essen	essen
	or	ay in 'pay'	ay	gehen	gayen
ei and ey		i in 'pile'	iy	Bein	biyn
eu		oy in 'boy'	oy	heute	hoyte
i		i in 'hit'	i	bitte	bitte
	or	ee in 'meet'	ee	ihn	een
ie		ee in 'meet'	ee	dieser	deezer
o		o in 'lot'	o	Woche	voke
	or	o in 'bone'	oh	Monat	mohnaat
ö		er in 'fern'	er	können	kernnen
u		oo in 'book'	oo	Butter	bootter
	or	oo in 'room'	ooh	Zuschlag	tsoohshlaag
ü		ew in 'dew'	ew	für	fewr
y		ew in 'dew'	ew	typisch	tewpish

✳ consonants

GERMAN VOWELS		APPROX ENGLISH EQUIVALENT	SHOWN IN BOOK AS	EXAMPLE	
b		b in 'but'	b	Bad	baat
	or	p in 'pencil'	p	abholen	aphohlen
c		c in 'cat'	k	Café	kaffay
ch		k in 'kit'	k	brauche	browke

	or	sh in 'shut'	*sh*	ich	*ish*
	or	k in 'can'	*k*	Charakter	*ka**rak**ter*
d		d in 'dog'	*d*	Dame	***daa**me*
	or	t in 'tin'	*t*	und	*oont*
f		f in 'feet'	*f*	fünf	*fewnf*
g		g in 'got'	*g*	grün	*grewn*
ḥ		h in 'hard'	*h*	Hand	*hant*
j		y in 'you'	*y*	ja	*yaa*
l		l in 'look'	*l*	lang	*lang*
m		m in 'mat'	*m*	Mutter	***moo**tter*
n		n in 'not'	*n*	Name	***naa**me*
p		p in 'pack'	*p*	Person	*per**zohn***
qu		k+v	*kv*	Quittung	***kvi**ttoong*
r		roll at the back of the mouth	*r*	Rücken	***rew**ken*
s		s in 'set'	*s*	…	…
	or	z in 'zoo'	*z*	Sie	*zee*
	or	sh in 'shut'	*sh*	Stunde	***shtoon**de*
sch		sh in 'shut'	*sh*	schnell	*shnell*
ß		ss in 'stress'	*ss*	heiß	*hiyss*
t		t in 'tin'	*t*	Tag	*taag*
v		f in 'feet'	*f*	vier	*feer*
	or	v in 'voice'	*v*	Ventil	*ven**teel***
w		v in 'voice'	*v*	wo	*voh*
x		x in 'taxi'	*ks*	Taxi	***tak**see*
z		ts in 'hits'	*ts*	zeigen	***tsiy**gen*

8

✳ the German alphabet

● The umlaut means that there are three extra vowels in German: ä ('a' umlaut), ö ('o' umlaut) und ü ('u' umlaut).

● The ß symbol represents a double 'ss' and is called 's z' or 'scharfes s'

● **How is it spelt?**   Wie schreibt man das?   *vee shriybt man das*

LETTER	PRONOUNCED	LETTER	PRONOUNCED
A	*aa*	O	*oh*
Ä	*ay*	Ö	*er*
B	*bay*	P	*pay*
C	*tsay*	Q	*koo*
D	*day*	R	*ayr*
E	*ay*	S	*es*
F	*ef*	ß	*es tset/sharfes es*
G	*gay*	T	*tay*
H	*haa*	U	*oo*
I	*ee*	Ü	*ew*
J	*yot*	V	*fow*
K	*kaa*	W	*vay*
L	*el*	X	*iks*
M	*em*	Y	*ewpsilon*
N	*en*	Z	*tset*

pronunciation guide

● If you book accommodation or a restaurant over the phone, you'll probably be asked to spell your name. Here's what the Germans say for each letter of the alphabet. (For example, to spell the name 'Goodrich' you can say: Gustav, Otto, Otto, Dora, Richard, Ida, Caesar, Heinrich).

LETTER	NAME	LETTER	NAME
A	Anton	O	Otto
Ä	Ärger	Ö	Ökonom
B	Berta	P	Paula
C	Caesar	Q	Quelle
D	Dora	R	Richard
E	Emil	S	Samuel
F	Friedrich	Sch	Schule
G	Gustav	T	Theodor
H	Heinrich	U	Ulrich
I	Ida	Ü	Übermut
J	Julius	V	Viktor
K	Kaufmann	W	Wilhelm
L	Ludwig	X	Xanthippe
M	Marta	Y	Ypsilon
N	Nordpol	Z	Zacharias

the basics

*essentials

Hello.	Hallo!	*hal*lo
Good morning.	Guten Morgen.	*gooh*ten morgen
Good afternoon.	Guten Tag.	*gooh*ten tag
Good evening.	Guten Abend.	*gooh*ten *aa*bent
Good night.	Gute Nacht.	*gooh*te nakt
Goodbye.	Auf Wiedersehen.	owf *vee*derzayen
Yes.	Ja.	yaa
No.	Nein.	niyn
Please.	Bitte.	*bit*te
Thank you (very much).	Danke schön.	*dan*ke shern
You're welcome.	Bitte schön.	*bit*te shern
I don't know.	Ich weiß nicht.	ish viyss nisht
I don't understand.	Ich verstehe nicht.	ish fer*shtay*e nisht
I don't speak much German.	Ich spreche nur ein bisschen Deutsch.	ish *shpre*ke noor iyn *biss*yen doytsh
Do you speak English?	Sprechen Sie Englisch?	*shprek*en zee *eng*lish
Pardon?	Wie bitte?	vee *bit*te
Could you repeat that please?	Noch einmal, bitte.	nok *iyn*mal *bit*te
Could you speak more slowly, please?	Langsamer, bitte.	*lang*zaamer *bit*te
How do you say it in German?	Wie sagt man das auf Deutsch?	vee zaagt man das owf doytsh

Excuse me.	Entschuldigung.	*entshooldigoong*
I'm sorry.	Es tut mir Leid.	*es toot meer liyt*
OK, fine.	Ist in Ordnung.	*ist in ortnoong*
It doesn't matter.	Es macht nichts.	*es maakt nishts*
Cheers!	Prost!	*prost*
What's your name?	Wie heißen Sie?	*vee hiyssen zee*
How are you?	Wie geht's dir?	*vee gayts deer*
Pleased to meet you.	Sehr angenehm.	*zayr angenaym*
I'd like...	Ich möchte...	*ish mershte...*
Is/Are there (any)...?	Gibt es...?	*gipt es...*
Do you have...?	Haben Sie...?	*haaben zee...*
What's this?	Was ist das?	*vas ist das*
How much is it?	Was kostet es?	*vas kostet es*
Can I/we...?	Kann man...?	*kan man...*
Where is/are...?	Wo ist/Wo sind...?	*voh ist/voh zint...*
How do I/we get to...?	Wie kommt man nach/zu...?	*vee kommt man naak/tsoo...*
Can you show me on the map?	Können Sie mir das auf der Karte zeigen?	*kernnen zee meer das owf der karte tsiygen*
Can you write it down?	Können Sie es aufschreiben?	*kernnen zee es owfshryben*
Help!	Hilfe!	*hilfe*
It's an emergency!	Es ist ein Notfall!	*es ist iyn nohtfall*

* numbers

0	null	*nooll*
1	eins	*iyns*
2	zwei	*tsviy*
3	drei	*driy*
4	vier	*feer*
5	fünf	*fewnf*
6	sechs	*zeks*
7	sieben	***zee**ben*
8	acht	*akt*
9	neun	*noyn*
10	zehn	*tsayn*
11	elf	*elf*
12	zwölf	*tsverlf*
13	dreizehn	***dry**itsayn*
14	vierzehn	***feer**tsayn*
15	fünfzehn	***fewnf**tsayn*
16	sechzehn	***zek**tsayn*
17	siebzehn	***zeeb**tsayn*
18	achtzehn	***akt**sayn*
19	neunzehn	***noyn**tsayn*
20	zwanzig	***tsvan**tsig*
21	einundzwanzig	***iynoon**tsvantsig*
22...	zweiundzwanzig...	***tsviy**oontsvantsig...*
30	dreißig	***driy**ssig*
40	vierzig	***feer**tsig*
50	fünfzig	***fewnf**tsig*
60	sechzig	***zek**tsig*
70	siebzig	***zeeb**tsig*
80	achtzig	***akt**sig*
90	neunzig	***noyn**tsig*
100	hundert	***hoon**dert*
101	hunderteins	***hoon**dertiyns*

102...	hundertzwei...	*hoondert**tsviy***
200	zweihundert	*tsviyhoondert*
250	zweihundertfünfzig	*tsviyhoondert-**fewnftsig***
500	fünfhundert	***fewnf**hoondert*
1,000	tausend	*tow**zent***
100,000	hunderttausend	*hoondert**towzent***
one million	eine Million	*iyne mill**yohn***
one and a half	eineinhalb	*iyn**iynhalp***
million	Millionen	*mill**yohnen***

✳ ordinal numbers

first	erster (m), erste (f), erstes (n)	***erster, erste, erstes***
second	zweiter (m), zweite (f) zweites (n)	***tsviyter, tsviyte, tsviytes***
third	dritter etc.	***dritter***
fourth	vierter	***feerter***
fifth	fünfter	***fewnfter***
sixth	sechster	***zekster***
seventh	siebter	***zeepter***
eighth	achter	***akter***
ninth	neunter	***noynter***
tenth	zehnter	***tsaynter***

✳ fractions

quarter	ein Viertel	*iyn **feertel***
half	ein halb	*iyn halp*
three-quarters	drei Viertel	*driy **feertel***
a third	ein Drittel	*iyn **drittel***
two-thirds	zwei Drittel	*tsviy **drittel***

the basics

15

✳ days

Monday	Montag	*mohntaag*
Tuesday	Dienstag	*deenztaag*
Wednesday	Mittwoch	*mittvok*
Thursday	Donnerstag	*donnerztaag*
Friday	Freitag	*friytaag*
Saturday	Samstag	*zamstaag/zonnaabent*
Sunday	Sonntag	*zonntaag*

✳ months

January	Januar	*yanoo-ar*
February	Februar	*faybroo-ar*
March	März	*merts*
April	April	*ahpril*
May	Mai	*miy*
June	Juni	*yoohnee*
July	Juli	*yoohlee*
August	August	*owgoost*
September	September	*zeptember*
October	Oktober	*oktohber*
November	November	*november*
December	Dezember	*detsember*

✳ seasons

spring	Frühling	*frewling*
summer	Sommer	*zommer*
autumn	Herbst	*herpst*
winter	Winter	*vinter*

✳ dates

YOU MAY WANT TO SAY...

What day is it today?	Welchen Tag haben wir heute?	*vel*shen Taag *haa*ben veer *hoy*te
What date is it today?	Welches Datum haben wir heute?	*vel*shes *daa*toom *haa*ben veer *hoy*te
What date is...	Wann...	*vann*...
your birthday?	hast du Geburtstag?	hast dooh ge*boort*stag
Easter?	ist Ostern?	ist *oh*stern
(It's) the fifteenth of April.	(Wir haben) den fünfzehnten April.	(veer *haa*ben) den *fewnft*saynten *a*pril
On the fifteenth of April.	Am fünfzehnten April.	am *fewnft*saynten *ah*pril

✳ telling the time

● To say that it is 'half past....' in German you have to say that it's half way round to the next hour. So 'half past five' is halb sechs, because it's half way round to six; 'half past two' is halb drei, because it's half way to three o'clock. You may also hear viertel zwei, which means 'a quarter past one', and dreiviertel zwölf, which is 'a quarter to twelve'.

● In timetables the 24-hour clock is used. In spoken language, people may also say um zehn Uhr morgens, meaning '10am', or um drei Uhr nachmittags, which is '3pm'.

time phrases

What time is it?	Wie spät ist es?	vee shpayt ist es
What time does it...	Um wie viel Uhr...	oom vee feel oohr...
open/close?	öffnet/schließt es?	erffnet/shleesst es
begin?	fängt es an?	fengt es an
finish?	ist es zu Ende?	ist es tsooh ende
It's...	Es ist...	es ist...
ten o'clock	zehn Uhr	tsayn oohr
half past ten	halb elf	halp elf
midday	Mittag	mittaag
midnight	Mitternacht	mitternakt
At...	Um...	oom...
quarter past nine	Viertel nach neun	feertel naak noyn
quarter to ten	Viertel vor zehn	feertel fohr tsayn
twenty past ten	zwanzig nach zehn	tsvantsig naak tsayn
twenty-five to ten	fünf nach halb zehn	fewnf naak halp tsayn
in...	in...	in...
ten minutes	zehn Minuten	tsayn minoohten
an hour	einer Stunde	iyner shtoonde

* time phrases

today	heute	hoyte
tomorrow	morgen	morgen
the day after tomorrow	übermorgen	ewbermorgen
yesterday	gestern	gestern

the day before yesterday	vorgestern	*fohrgestern*
this morning	heute Morgen	*hoyte morgen*
this afternoon	heute Nachmittag	*hoyte naakmittaag*
this evening	heute Abend	*hoyte aabent*
tonight	heute Abend	*hoyte aabent*
on Friday	am Freitag	*am friytaag*
on Fridays	freitags	*friytaagz*
every Friday	jeden Freitag	*yayden friytaag*
for a week	eine Woche lang	*iyne voke lang*
for two weeks	zwei Wochen lang	*tsviy voken lang*
next week	nächste Woche	*nekste voke*
next month	nächsten Monat	*neksten mohnaat*
next year	nächstes Jahr	*nekstes yaar*
last night	gestern Abend	*gestern aabent*
last week	letzte Woche	*letste voke*
a week ago	vor einer Woche	*fohr iyner voke*
a year ago	vor einem Jahr	*fohr iynem yaar*
since ...	seit...	*ziyt...*
last week	letzter Woche	*letster voke*
last month	letztem Monat	*letstem mohnaat*
last year	letztem Jahr	*letstem yaar*
I've been here for a month.	Ich bin seit einem Monat hier.	*ish bin ziyt iynem mohnaat heer*
I've been learning German for two years.	Ich lerne seit zwei Jahren Deutsch.	*ish lerne ziyt tsviy yaaren doytsh*
It's early/late.	Es ist früh/spät.	*es ist frew/spayt*

✳ measurements

MEASUREMENTS

centimetres	Zentimeter	*tsenteemayter*
metres	Meter	*mayter*
kilometres	Kilometer	*keelomayter*
a litre	ein Liter	*iyn leeter*
gramme	Gramm	*gram*
100 grammes	100 Gramm	*iynhoondert gram*
200 grammes	200 Gramm	*tsviyhoondert gram*
kilo	Kilo(gramm)	*keelo(gram)*

CONVERSIONS

10cm = *4 inches*	1 inch = *2.45cm*
50cm = *19.6 inches*	1 foot = *30cm*
1 metre = *39.37 inches*	1 yard = *0.91m*
110 metres = *100 yards*	1 mile = *1.61 km*
1km = *0.62 miles*	1oz = *28g*
1 litre = *1.8 pints*	¼lb = *113g*
100g = *3.5oz*	½lb = *225g*
200g = *7oz*	1lb = *450g*
½ kilo = *1.1lb*	
1 kilo = *2.2 lb*	

To convert	*multiply by*	To convert	*multiply by*
centimetres to inches	*0.3937*	inches to centimetres	*2.54*
kilometres to miles	*0.6214*	miles to kilometres	*1.6090*
grammes to ounces	*0.0353*	ounces to grammes	*28.35*
kilogrammes to		pounds to	
pounds	*2.2050*	kilogrammes	*0.4536*

* clothes and shoe sizes

WOMEN'S CLOTHES

UK	8	10	12	14	16	18	20
Continent	34	36	38	40	42	44	46

MEN'S CLOTHES

UK	36	38	40	42	44	46	48
Continent	46	48	50	52	54	56	58

MEN'S SHIRTS

UK	14	14½	15	15½	16	16½	17
Continent	36	37	38	39	41	42	43

SHOES

UK	2	3	4	5	6	7
Continent	35	36	37	38	39	41

UK	8	9	10	11
Continent	42	43	44	45

* false friends

FALSE FRIEND...	NOT TO BE CONFUSED WITH...
Chef (boss)	chef (Küchenchef)
Chips (crisps)	chips (Pommes frites)
Fabrik (factory)	fabric (Stoff)
Gift (poison)	gift (Geschenk)
Handy (mobile phone)	handy (handlich)
Rente (pension)	rent (mieten)
sensibel (sensitive)	sensible (vernünftig)
sympatisch (nice, pleasant)	sympathetic (mitfühlend)
wenn (if)	when (wann)
wer (who)	where (wo)

the basics

21

✳ national holidays and festivals

Heiligabend	**Christmas Eve**	24 December
1. Weihnachts-feiertag	**Christmas Day**	25 December
2. Weihnachts-feiertag	**Boxing Day**	26 December
Neujahr	**New Year's Day**	1 January
Heilige drei Könige	**Epiphany**	6 January
Fastnachtsdienstag	**Shrove Tuesday**	
Karfreitag	**Good Friday**	
Ostermontag	**Easter Monday**	
1. Mai	**May Day**	1 May
Christi Himmelfahrt	**Ascension Day**	
Pfingstmontag	**Whit Monday**	
Nationalfeiertag Schweiz	**National holiday (Switzerland)**	1 August
Mariä Himmelfahrt	**Assumption**	15 August
Tag der deutschen Einheit	**Day of German Unification**	3 October
Nationalfeiertag Österreich	**National holiday (Austria)**	26 October
Allerheiligen	**All Saints' Day**	1 November

general conversation

● Guten Tag (good day) is a general greeting that can be used throughout the day. In southern Germany and Austria you are much more likely to be greeted with Grüß Gott (greetings to God). You'll also hear Servus in the south and in Austria, which means both 'hello' and 'goodbye'.

● Guten Morgen (good morning) and Guten Abend (good evening) are both used to greet people at the appropriate time of the day, while Gute Nacht is 'good night'.

● There are two ways of saying 'you' – the formal and the informal way. Sie (written with a capital letter) is formal and is used between people who are meeting for the first time or who don't know each other well, or between younger and older people. Du is informal and is used between family, friends, young people and to children. The form of the verb changes depending on whether you are addressing someone as Sie or du; where both forms are given in the phrases, the Sie form is given first. If in doubt which form to use, stick to Sie. In this book the form of address that is most suited to each context is used.

✳ greetings

● **Hello.**   Hallo.   *hallo*
(Germany, Austria, Switzerland)

● **Hello.**   Grüß Gott!   *grewss **gott***
(S. Germany, Austria)

general conversation

Hello. (N. Germany)	Hallo./Moin!	*hallo/moyn!*
Hello./Goodbye. (S. Germany, Austria and South Tyrol)	Servus!	*servooss!*
Good morning.	Guten Morgen.	***goohten** morgen*
Good afternoon.	Guten Tag.	***goohten** tag*
Good evening.	Guten Abend.	***goohten** aabent*
Good night.	Gute Nacht.	***goohte** nakt*
Goodbye.	Auf Wiedersehen.	*owf **vee**dersayen*
Bye.	Tschüss.	*tshewss*
See you later.	Bis später.	*bis **shpay**ter*
How are you? (informal)	Wie geht's dir?	*vee gayts deer*
Fine, thanks.	Gut, danke.	*gooht **dan**ke*
And you?	Und dir?	*oont deer*

✳ introductions

YOU MAY WANT TO SAY...

My name is...	Ich heiße...	*ish **hiy**sse...*
This is...	Das ist...	*das ist...*
David Brown	David Brown	David Brown
Jane Clark	Jane Clark	Jane Clark
my husband/ my partner	mein Mann/mein Lebensgefährte.	*miyn man/miyn **lay**bensgefayrte*

25

| my wife/my partner | meine Frau/meine Lebensgefährtin. | *miyne frow/miyne laybensgefayrtin* |
| Pleased to meet you. | Sehr angenehm. | *zayr angenaym* |

* talking about yourself

I'm...	Ich bin ...	*ish bin...*
English (m/f)	Engländer(in)	*englender(in)*
Irish (m/f)	Ire/Irin	*eere/eerin*
Scottish (m/f)	Schotte/Schottin	*shotte/shottin*
Welsh (m/f)	Waliser/Waliserin	*valeeser/valeeserin*

I'm from...	Ich komme aus...	*ish komme ows...*
England	England	*englant*
Ireland	Irland	*eerlant*
Scotland	Schottland	*shottlant*
Wales	Wales	*vales*

| We live in... | Wir leben in... | *veer layben in...* |
| Newcastle | Newcastle | *Newcastle* |

| I'm 25 years old. | Ich bin 25. | *ish bin fewnfoontswantsig* |

| He/She's five years old. | Er/sie ist fünf. | *er/zee ist fewnf* |

I'm a...	Ich bin...	*ish bin...*
web designer	Webdesigner	*webdesigner*
nurse (f)	Krankenschwester	*krankenshvester*
nurse (m)	Krankenpfleger	*krankenpflaiger*
student (m/f)	Student(in)	*shtoodent(in)*

I work in a/ for a...	Ich arbeite in einer/ für eine...	*ish arbiyte in iyner/ fewr iyne...*
bank	Bank	*bank*

I'm...	Ich bin...	*ish bin...*
unemployed	arbeitslos	*arbiytslohs*
self-employed	selbstständig	*zelbstshtendig*

I'm...	Ich bin...	*ish bin...*
married	verheiratet	*ferhiyraatet*
divorced	geschieden	*gesheeden*
separated	getrennt	*getrennt*
single	Single	*singel*

I have...	Ich habe...	*ish haabe...*
three children	drei Kinder	*driy kinder*
one sister	eine Schwester	*iyne shvester*

I don't have...	Ich habe...	*ish haabe...*
any children	keine Kinder	*kiyne kinder*
a partner (m)	keinen Partner	*kiynen partner*
a partner (f)	keine Partnerin	*kiyne partnerin*

I'm on holiday here.	Ich bin im Urlaub hier.	*ish bin im oohrlowp heer*

I'm here on business.	Ich bin auf Geschäftsreise hier.	*ish bin owf gesheftsriyze heer*

I'm here with...	Ich bin mit...	*ish bin mit...*
my family	meiner Familie	*miyner fameelye*
my colleague (m)	meinem Kollege	*miynem kollayge*
my colleague (f)	meiner Kollegin	*miyner kollaygin*

My husband is...	Mein Mann ist...	*Miyn man ist...*

My wife is...	Meine Frau ist...	*Miyne frow ist...*

✳ asking about other people

- Where are you from? — Woher kommen Sie? — *voher **kommen** zee*

- What's your name? — Wie heißen Sie? — *vee **hiyss**en zee*

- Are you married? — Sind Sie verheiratet? — *zint zee ferhiyraatet*

- Do you have... — Haben Sie... — ***haa**ben zee ...*
  - any children? — Kinder? — *kinder*
  - any brothers and sisters? — Geschwister? — *geshvister*
  - a girlfriend? — eine Freundin? — *iyne **froyn**din*
  - boyfriend? — einen Freund? — *iynen froynt*

- How old are you? — Wie alt sind Sie? — *vee alt zint zee*

- Is this your... — Ist das Ihr... — *ist das eer*
  - husband? — Mann? — *màn*
  - (boy)friend? — Freund? — *froynt*

- Is this your... — Ist das Ihre... — *ist das **eere**...*
  - wife? — Frau? — *frow*
  - (girl)friend? — Freundin? — *froyndin*

- Where are you going? — Wohin reisen Sie? — *vohin riyzren zee*

- Where are you staying? — Wo wohnen Sie? — *voh **vohnen** zee*

- Where do you live? — Wo sind Sie zu Hause? — *voh zint zee tsooh **how**ze*

✳ chatting

- Germany is very beautiful.
  Deutschland ist sehr schön.
  doytshlant ist zayr shern

- It's the first time I've been to Austria.
  Ich bin zum ersten Mal in Österreich.
  *ish bin tsoom **ersten** maal in **ersterriysh***

- I come to Germany often.
  Ich komme oft nach Deutschland.
  *ish komme oft naak **doytshlant***

- Do you live here?
  Wohnen Sie hier?
  vohnen zee heer

- Have you ever been to...
  Waren Sie schon einmal in...
  vaaren zee shohn iynmaal in...
    - London?
      London?
      London
    - Edinburgh?
      Edinburg?
      Edinburg

- Did you like it?
  Hat es Ihnen gefallen?
  *hat es **eenen** gefallen*

- Gefällt Ihnen Deutschland?
  *gefellt **eenen** **doytshlant***
  Do you like Germany?

- Waren Sie schon einmal in Deutschland?
  *vaaren zee shon iynmal in **doytshlant***
  Have you been to Germany before?

- Wie lange bleiben Sie hier?
  *vee lange **bliyben** zee heer*
  How long are you here for?

- Ihr Deutsch ist sehr gut.
  eer doytsh ist zayr gooht
  Your German is very good.

✳ the weather

- It's a beautiful day/morning! — Es ist ein schöner Tag/Morgen! — es ist iyn **sherner** taag/**morgen**

- What fantastic weather! — Was für ein herrliches Wetter! — vas fewr iyn **herr**likes **vett**er

- It's... — Es ist... — es ist...
    hot — warm — varm
    cold — kalt — kalt
    humid — schwül — shvewl

- What's the forecast? — Wie sieht die Wettervorhersage aus? — vee zeeht dee **vett**ervorhersaage ows

- It's raining. — Es ist regnerisch. — es ist **rayg**nerish

- It's pouring! — Es schüttet! — es **shew**ttet

✳ likes and dislikes

- I like... — Ich mag... — ish maag...
    strawberries — Erdbeeren — **ert**beeren

- I love... — Ich ... gern. — ish ... gern
    sailing — segle — **say**gle

- I don't like... — Ich mag... — ish maag...
    tomatoes — keine Tomaten — **kiy**ne to**maa**ten
    her — sie nicht — zee nisht

- I can't stand ... — Ich kann ... nicht ausstehen — ish kan ... nisht **ows**shtayen

| him | ihn | *een* |
| swimming | Schwimmen | *shvimmen* |

- Do you like... | Magst du... | *maagst dooh...* |
ice cream?	Eis?	*iys*
him?	ihn?	*een*
walking?	spazieren gehen?	*shpatseeren gayen*

- We quite like... | Wir mögen ... recht gerne. | *Veer **mer**gen ... resht **ger**ne* |

✶ feelings and opinions

YOU MAY WANT TO SAY...

- Are you all right? | Alles in Ordnung? | *alles in **ort**nung* |

- Are you happy/upset? | Bist du glücklich/verärgert? | *bist dooh **glewk**lish/fer**er**gert* |

- Are you (too) cold/hot? | Ist dir (zu) kalt/warm? | *ist deer (tsooh) kalt/varm* |

- I'm (just)... | Ich bin (nur)... | *ish bin (noohr)...* |
  | tired | müde | ***mew**de* |
  | sad | traurig | ***trow**rig* |

- I'm embarrassed. | Es ist mir (nur) peinlich. | *es ist meer (noohr) **piyn**lish* |

- I'm a bit annoyed. | Ich bin ein bisschen sauer. | *ish bin iyn **bis**shen **zow**er* |

- I'm very tired. | Ich bin sehr müde. | *ish bin zayr **mew**de* |

- What do you think of...? | Was hältst du von...? | *vas heltst du fon...* |

I think/We think it's...	Ich finde/Wir finden es...	*ish finde/veer finden es...*
great	großartig	***grohs**artig*
pathetic	zum Heulen	*tsoom **hoy**len*
Did you like it?	Hat es dir gefallen?	*hat es deer ge**fall**en?*
I thought/We thought it was...	Ich fand/Wir fanden es...	*ish fant/veer **fan**den es...*
beautiful	schön	*shern*
fantastic	fantastisch	*fan**tas**tish*
rubbish	Blödsinn	***blerd**zin*
Don't you like...	Magst du...	*maagst dooh...*
it?	es nicht?	*es nisht*
us?	uns nicht?	*uns nisht*
me?	mich nicht?	*mish nisht*
Do you fancy him/her?	Gefällt er/sie dir?	*ge**fellt** er/zee deer*
Do you fancy me?	Gefalle ich dir?	*ge**fall**e ich deer*
No way!	Auf keinen Fall!	*owf **kiy**nen fal*
What's your favourite film?	Was ist dein Lieblingsfilm?	*vas ist diyn **leeb**lingsfilm*
My favourite music is...	Meine Lieblingsmusik ist...	***miy**ne **leeb**lingsmoozik ist...*
How do people feel about...	Was denken die Leute über...	*vas **den**ken dee **loy**te **ew**ber...*
the government?	die Regierung?	*dee re**gee**rung*
the Brits?	die Briten?	*dee **bree**ten*
drugs?	Drogen?	***droh**gen*

32

* making arrangements

What are you doing tonight?	Was machst du heute Abend?	*vas makst dooh hoyte aabent*
Would you like... a drink? to go and eat?	Möchtest du... etwas trinken? etwas essen?	*mershtest dooh... etvas trinken etvas essen*
Do you fancy... meeting up later? going for a drink?	Hättest du Lust... später etwas gemeinsam zu machen? etwas trinken zu gehen?	*hettest dooh loost... spayter etvas gemiynzam tsooh maken etvas trinken tsoo gayen*
No, thank you.	Nein danke.	*niyn danke*
That'd be great.	Sehr gerne.	*zayr gerne*
What time shall we meet?	Um wie viel Uhr wollen wir uns treffen?	*oom vee feel oohr vollen veer oons treffen*
Where shall we meet?	Wo wollen wir uns treffen?	*voh vollen veer oons treffen*
See you later.	Bis später.	*bis spayter*
I can't wait.	Ich kann es kaum abwarten.	*ish kan es kowm apvarten*
Sorry, we're already doing something.	Tut mir Leid, wir haben schon etwas vor.	*tooht meer liyt veer haaben shohn etvas fohr*
I already have plans this evening.	Ich habe schon Pläne für heute Abend.	*ish haabe shohn playne fewr hoyte aabent*

general conversation

33

Please go away.	Geh bitte weg.	*gay bitte vek*
Leave us alone!	Lass uns in Ruhe!	*lass oons in roohe*
I'll email you.	Ich schicke dir eine E-Mail.	*ish shike deer iyne email*
What's your email address?	Wie lautet deine E-Mail-Adresse?	*vee lowtet diyne email adresse*

✳ useful expressions

Congratulations!	Herzlichen Glückwunsch!	*hertslishen glewkvoonsh*
Happy birthday!	Herzlichen Glückwunsch zum Geburtstag!	*hertslishen glewkvoonsh tsoom geboortstaag*
Happy Christmas!	Frohe Weihnachten!	*frohe viynakten*
Happy New Year!	Alles Gute im neuen Jahr!	*alles goohte im noyen yaar*
That's...	Das ist...	*das ist*
fantastic!	fantastisch!	*fantastish*
terrible!	schrecklich!	*shreklish*
Safe journey!	Gute Reise!	*goohte riyze!*
Enjoy your meal!	Guten Appetit!	*goohten appeteet*
Thank you, same to you.	Danke, gleichfalls.	*danke gliyshfalls*
Cheers!	Prost!/Zum Wohl!	*prohst/tsoom vohl*

travel&transport

✳ arriving in the country

● Whether you arrive by air, road or sea, formalities in Germany (passport control and customs) are quite straightforward. EU residents require a valid passport and they don't need a visa. If you plan to stay more than 90 days you need a residence permit, which can be obtained from the Ausländerbehörde of the town you're staying in. All other foreign nationals should contact the German embassy in their country of origin.

YOU MAY SEE...

Anmeldepflichtige Waren	Goods to declare
Ausgang	Exit/Way out
EU-Bürger	EU citizens
Gepäckausgabe	Baggage reclaim
Nicht-EU-Bürger	Non-EU citizens
Passkontrolle	Passport control
Zoll	Customs

YOU MAY WANT TO SAY...

● I am here...
   on holiday
   on business

Ich bin hier auf...
   Urlaub
   Geschäftsreise

ish bin heer owf...
   oohrlowp
   gesheftsriyze

● It's for my own
   personal use.

Es ist für meinen
persönlichen
Gebrauch bestimmt.

es ist fewr miynen
persernlishen
gebrowk beshtimmt

Ihren Pass, bitte.	*eeren pass bitte*	Your passport, please.
Was ist der Zweck Ihres Besuchs?	*was ist der tsvek eeres bezoohks*	What is the purpose of your visit?
Wie lange bleiben Sie hier?	*vee lange bliyben zee heer*	How long are you going to stay here?
Kommen Sie bitte mit mir/mit uns.	*kommen zee bitte mit meer/mit oons*	Come along with me/with us, please.

✳ directions

Bahnhof	Station
Burg	Castle/Fortress
Bushaltestelle	Bus stop
Dom	Cathedral
Fußgängerüberweg	Pedestrian crossing
Hauptbahnhof	Central railway station
Kirche	Church
Kunsthalle	Art gallery
Marktplatz	Market place
Platz	Square
Radweg	Cycle path
S-Bahn	Express underground or overground
Schloss	Castle/Palace
Stadtzentrum	Town centre
Straßenbahnhaltestelle	Tram stop

travel and transport

YOU MAY WANT TO SAY...

- Excuse me, please. — Entschuldigen Sie, bitte. — *entshool*digen zee *bit*te

- Where is... — Wo ist... — *voh* ist...
  - the tourist centre? — die Touristen-information? — dee tooristen-informats*yohn*
  - the town centre? — das Stadtzentrum? — das *shtatt*sentrum
  - the station? — der Bahnhof? — der *baan*hof

- Are there any toilets round here? — Gibt es hier Toiletten? — geept es heer toa*letten*

- How do we get to... — Wie kommen wir... — vee *kommen* veer...
  - the airport? — zum Flughafen? — tsoom *floogh*haafen
  - to Munich? — nach München? — naak *mewn*shen
  - the beach? — zum Strand? — tsoom shtrand

- I'm lost. — Ich habe mich verirrt. — ish *haa*be mish fer*irrt*

- Is this the right way to...? — Ist das die Straße nach...? — ist das dee *shtraasse* naak ...

- Can you show me on the map? — Könnten Sie mir das auf der Karte zeigen? — *kernn*ten zee meer das auf der *karte* tsiygen

- Is it far? — Ist es weit von hier? — ist es viyt fon heer

- Is there ... near here? — Gibt es ... hier in der Nähe? — geept es ... heer in der *nay*he
  - a bank — eine Bank — *iyne* bank
  - a supermarket — einen Supermarkt — *iynen* *zooh*permarkt

- Where is... — Wo ist... — *voh* ist...
  - the nearest restaurant? — das nächste Restaurant? — das *nek*ste restorang
  - the nearest letter box? — der nächste Briefkasten? — der *nek*ste *breef*kasten

YOU MAY HEAR...

Wir sind hier.	*veer zint heer*	We are here.
Es ist (nicht) weit.	*es ist nisht viyt*	It's (not) far away.
Fünf Minuten von hier.	*fewnf minoohten fon heer*	Five minutes from here.
Fahren Sie...	*faaren zee...*	Go...
über die Brücke	*ewber dee brewke*	over the bridge
die Straße entlang	*dee shtraasse entlang*	along the street
Nehmen Sie die dritte Ausfahrt.	*naymen zee dee dritte owsfaart*	Take the third exit.
Biegen Sie an der Ampel ab.	*beegen zee an der ampel ap*	Turn off at the traffic lights.
hier	*heer*	here
dort	*dort*	there
rechts	*reshts*	(to the) right
links	*links*	(to the) left
geradeaus	*geraadeows*	straight on
die erste...	*dee erste...*	the first...
Straße	*shtraasse*	street
Abzweigung	*abtsviygoong*	turning
an der Ecke	*an der eke*	on the corner
vor der Ampel	*for der ampel*	before the traffic lights
nach dem Dom	*naak daym dohm*	after/past the cathedral
richtung Stadtzentrum	*rishtoong shtattsentroom*	towards the town centre

travel and transport

39

* information and tickets
(see **telling the time**, page 17)

● Germany, Austria and Switzerland all have a good public transport system, and you'll find underground systems, trams and buses in all the larger towns and cities. In tourist areas you will find trains, buses and boats going to the major tourist attractions.

● Is there a train/ bus to Hanover (today)?

Gibt es (heute) einen Zug/Bus nach Hannover?

geept es (hoyte) iynen tsoohg/boos naak hannohver

● What time is...

Um wie viel Uhr fährt...

oom vee feel oohr fayrt...

the next train
the last train
the first train
... to Salzburg?

der nächste Zug
der letzte Zug
der erste Zug
... nach Salzburg?

*der nekste tsoohg
der letste tsoohg
der erste tsoohg
... naak zaltsboorg*

● Do the trains/ buses go often?

Fahren die Züge/ Busse häufig?

faaren dee tsewge/ busse hoyfig?

● What time does the train arrive in Bremen?

Um wie viel Uhr kommt der Zug in (Bremen) an?

oom vee feel oohr kommt der tsoohg in braymen an

● Must I change?

Muss ich umsteigen?

muss ish oomstiygen

● Can I get a ticket on the bus/train/ boat?

Kann ich die Fahrkarte im Bus/ Zug/Schiff kaufen?

kan ish dee faarkarte im boos/tsoohg/shiff kowfen

● Where can I buy ...

Wo kann ich ... kaufen?

voh kan ish ... kowfen

a ticket?	eine Fahrkarte	*iyne faarkarte*
a day pass?	eine Tageskarte	*iyne taageskarte*
Two tickets to Vienna, please.	Zwei Karten nach Wien, bitte.	*Tsviy karten naak veen bitte*
Single.	Einfache Fahrt.	*iynfake faart*
Return.	Hin und zurück.	*hin oont tsoorewk*
For...	Für...	*fewr...*
two adults	zwei Erwachsene	*tsviy ervaksene*
and two children	und zwei Kinder	*oont tsviy kinder*
and a car	und ein Auto	*oont iyn owto*
I want to reserve a seat.	Ich möchte einen Sitzplatz reservieren.	*ish mershte iynen zitsplats rezerveeren*
I want to reserve...	Ich möchte ... buchen.	*ish mershte ...boohken*
a cabin	eine Kabine	*iyne kabeene*
two couchettes	zwei Plätze im Liegewagen	*tsviy pletse im leegevaagen*
Is there a supplement?	Muss ich einen Zuschlag bezahlen?	*muss ish iynen tsoohshlaag betsaalen*
Is there a reduction for...	Gibt es eine Ermäßigung für...	*geept es iyne ermayssigung fewr...*
students?	Studenten?	*shtoodenten*
senior citizens?	Rentner?	*rentner*

YOU MAY HEAR...

Er fährt um zehn Uhr dreißig ab.	*er fayrt oom tsayn oohr driyssig ap*	It leaves at 10.30.
Er kommt um zehn nach vier an.	*er kommt oom tsayn naak feer an*	It arrives at ten past four.

travel and transport

41

• Sie müssen in (Kassel) umsteigen.	*zee mewssen in (kassel) oomshtiygen*	You have to change in (Kassel).
• Bahnsteig/ Anlegeplatz Nummer Vier.	*baanshtiyg/ anlaygeplatts nummer feer*	It's platform/pier number four.
• Sie können die Karten ... kaufen.	*zee kernnen dee karten ... kowfen*	You can buy a ticket...
im Bus/im Zug/ auf dem Schiff	*im boos/im tsoohg/ owf daym shiff*	on the bus/train/ boat
am Fahrkarten- automat/am Kiosk	*am faarkarten- owtomaat/am kiosk*	at the ticket machine/kiosk
• Sie können beim Fahrer bezahlen.	*zee kernnen biym faarer betsaalen*	You can pay the driver.
• Einfache Fahrt oder Rückfahrkarte?	*iynfake faart ohder rewkfaarkarte*	Single or return?
• Raucher oder nichtraucher?	*rowker ohder nishtrowker*	Smoking or non- smoking?

✳ trains

(see information and tickets, page 40)

● The German state railway is the Deutsche Bahn. You can check timetables and book tickets on the website, which has information in English (www.reiseauskunft.bahn.de).

YOU MAY SEE...	👁
Abfahrt	Departure
Ankunft	Arrival

Aufzug	Lift
Bahnsteig/Gleis	Platform
Eingang	Entrance
Ausgang	Exit
Fahrkarten	Tickets
Fahrkartenschalter/ Reisezentrum	Ticket office
Fahrplan	Train timetable
Fundbüro	Lost property office
Gepäckabfertigung/ Gepäckannahme	Luggage office
Gepäckaufbewahrung	Left luggage
Liegewagen	Couchette
Nicht hinauslehnen	Do not lean out
Reservierungen	Reservations
Schlafwagen	Sleeping-car
Schließfächer	Luggage lockers
Speisewagen	Dining car
täglich	daily
Warteraum	Waiting room
Zu den Gleisen	To the platforms

YOU MAY WANT TO SAY...

- **Is there a lift to the platform?** Gibt es einen Aufzug zu den Gleisen? *geept es iynen owftsoohg tsooh dayn gliyzen*

- **Does this train go to (Bern)?** Fährt dieser Zug nach (Bern)? *fayrt deezer tsoohg nach (bern)*

- **Excuse me, I've reserved...** Entschuldigung, ich habe ... reserviert. *entshooldigung ish haabe ... rezerveert*
  - **that seat** diesen Platz *deezen plats*

a couchette	einen Platz im Liegewagen	*iynen plats im leegevaagen*
Is this seat free?	Ist dieser Platz noch frei?	*ist deezer plats nok friy*
Do you mind if I... open the window? smoke?	Stört es Sie, wenn ich... das Fenster öffne? rauche?	*shtert es zee venn ish das fenster erffne rowke*
Where are we?	Wo sind wir?	*voh zint veer*
How long does the train stop here?	Wie lange hält der Zug hier?	*vee lange helt der tsoohg heer*
Can you tell me when we get to (Graz)?	Können Sie mir sagen, wann wir nach (Graz) kommen?	*kernnen zee meer zaagen van veer nak (graats) kommen*

* buses and coaches
(see **information and tickets**, page 40)

● In towns and cities you usually pay the driver as get you on the bus. There may be automatic ticket machines at bus stops. Tickets for some long-distance services can be bought at bus station ticket offices. If you intend to use the buses a lot in a town or city, you can buy eine Tageskarte (a day pass), which is valid on buses, trams and the underground.

YOU MAY SEE...

Bedarfshaltestelle	Request stop
Busbahnhof	Bus station
Bushaltestelle	Bus stop

Eingang	Entrance
Hinten einsteigen	Enter by the rear door
Kein Ausstieg	No exit
Kein Einstieg	No entry
Nächste Station	Next stop
(Not)ausgang	(Emergency) exit
Während der Fahrt nicht mit dem Fahrer sprechen	Do not talk to the driver while the bus is moving
In der Mitte aussteigen	Exit by the middle door
Bus hält	Bus stopping

YOU MAY WANT TO SAY...

- Where does the bus to the town centre leave from?
  Wo fährt der Bus zum Stadtzentrum ab?
  *voh fayrt der boos tsoom **shtatt**sentroom ap*

- Does the bus to the airport leave from here?
  Fährt hier der Bus zum Flughafen ab?
  *fayrt heer der boos tsoom **floohg**haafen ap?*

- Where is the bus stop?
  Wo ist die Bushaltestelle?
  *voh ist dee **boos**halteshtelle*

- Which number is the bus to the station?
  Welche Buslinie fährt zum Bahnhof?
  *velshe **boos**leenye fayrt tsoom **baan**hof*

- Does this bus go to the station?
  Fährt dieser Bus zum Bahnhof?
  *fayrt **dee**zer boos tsoom **baan**hof*

- Where can I buy tickets?
  Wo kann ich Fahrkarten kaufen?
  *voh kan ish **faar**karten **kow**fen*

travel and transport

45

- **Can you tell me where to get off, please?** / Können Sie mir sagen, wo ich aussteigen muss? / *kernnen zee meer zaagen voh ish owsshtiygen muss*

- **The next stop, please.** / Die nächste Haltestelle, bitte. / *dee nekste halteshtelle bitte*

- **Please open the door.** / Bitte die Tür öffnen! / *bitte dee tewr erffnen*

✳ underground
(see **information and tickets**, page 40)

● The underground is called U-Bahn, and there are systems in most of the larger German cities, and also in Vienna (Austria) and Zurich (Switzerland). The S-Bahn is an express underground, or overground, which goes further afield. You can buy tickets for your journey at automatic vending machines in the station. The systems usually operate a zone ticket – make sure you buy a ticket that covers all the zones you want to travel to.

YOU MAY SEE...

Ausgang	Exit
Eingang	Entrance
Hinweis	Information
S-Bahn	Express underground or overground
Rauchen verboten	No smoking
U-Bahn	Underground

travel and transport

46

YOU MAY WANT TO SAY...

Can I buy a weekly travelcard, please?	Eine Wochenkarte, bitte.	*iyne vokenkarte bitte*
An underground map, please.	Haben Sie einen U-Bahn-Plan?	*haaben zee iynen oohbaan-plaan*
Which line goes to...?	Welche Linie fährt nach...?	*velshe leenye fayrt naak...*
Which stop is it for...?	Wo muss ich für ... aussteigen?	*voh muss ish fewr ... owsshtiygen*
Is this the right stop for...?	Ist das hier die richtige Haltestelle für...?	*ist das heer dee rishtige halteshtelle fewr...*
Does this train go to the town hall?	Fährt dieser Zug zum Rathaus?	*fayrt deezer tsoohg tsoom raathows*

✳ boats and ferries
(see **information and tickets**, page 40)

● There are several tour operators who organise long- and short-distance cruises on the Rhine, Moselle, Elbe, Main, Oder and other rivers. There are also cruises and excursions on Lake Constance (der Bodensee), as well as a car ferry service.

● If you want to visit the German North Sea islands or the Baltic island of Fehmarn, one rail ticket will cover you for travel to the coast, the ferry across and transport on the other side. There are also motorail services to the islands.

YOU MAY SEE...

Anlegestelle	Pier, embarkation point
Autodeck	Car deck
Bootsfahrten	Cruises
Dampferfahrten	Steam cruises
Fähre	Ferry
Flussfahrten	River trips
Hafen	Port, harbour
Kabinen	Cabins
Luftkissenfahrzeug	Hovercraft
Rettungsring	Lifebelt
Schiffsrundfahrten	Round trips

YOU MAY WANT TO SAY...

- **A return ticket to ..., please.**
  Eine Rückfahrkarte nach ... bitte.
  iyne rewkfaarkarte naak ... bitte

- **Is there a car ferry to ... (today)?**
  Fährt (heute) ein Schiff nach ... ?
  fayrt (hoyte) iyn shiff naak ...

- **Are there any boat trips?**
  Gibt es Schiffsfahrten?
  geept es shiffsfaarten

- **How long is the cruise?**
  Wie lange dauert die Fahrt?
  vee lange dowert dee faart

- **Is there wheelchair access?**
  Gibt es einen Rollstuhlzugang?
  geept es iynen rollshtoohltsoohgang

- **What is the lake like today?**
  Wie ist der See heute?
  vee ist der zay hoyte

- **Can I/we go out on deck?**
  Kann man raus aufs Deck gehen?
  kan man rows owfs dek gayen

Schiffe fahren...	*shiffe faaren...*	Boats go on...
dienstags und freitags	*deenstaags oont friytaags*	Tuesdays and Fridays
jeden zweiten Tag	*yayden tsviyten taag*	every other day
Der See ist...	*der zay ist...*	The lake is...
ruhig	*roohig*	calm
unruhig	*oonroohig*	choppy

* air travel
(see information and tickets, page 40)

(see information and tickets, page 40)

YOU MAY SEE...

Abflughalle	Departure lounge
Abflug	Departures
Ankunft	Arrivals
Auslandsflüge	International departures
Autovermietung	Car hire
Bitte anschnallen	Fasten seatbelts
Filmsicher	Film safe
Flugsteig	Gate
Gepäck nicht unbeaufsichtigt lassen	Do not leave your luggage unattended
Gepäckausgabe	Luggage reclaim
Handgepäckkontrolle	Hand luggage control
Inlandsflüge	Domestic departures
Passkontrolle	Passport control
Sicherheitskontrolle	Security check

travel and transport

YOU MAY WANT TO SAY...

- **I want to ... my ticket.**
  Ich möchte mein Ticket...
  *ish **mershte** miyn tiket...*
  - change
    umbuchen
    oomboohken
  - cancel
    stornieren
    shtorneeren

- **What time do I/we have to check in?**
  Um wie viel Uhr muss ich/müssen wir einchecken?
  *oom vee feel oohr muss ish/**mew**ssen veer **iynt**sheken?*

- **Is the plane on time?**
  Ist der Flug pünktlich?
  *ist der floohg **pewnk**tlish*

- **Which gate is it?**
  Welcher Flugsteig ist es?
  *velsher **floohg**shtiyg ist es*

- **Have you got a wheelchair?**
  Haben Sie einen Rollstuhl?
  *haaben zee iynen **roll**shtoohl*

- **Where is the luggage from the London flight?**
  Wo ist das Gepäck vom Flug aus London?
  *voh ist das ge**pek** fom floohg ows **lon**don*

- **My luggage hasn't arrived.**
  Mein Gepäck ist nicht da.
  *miyn ge**pek** ist nisht daa*

- **Is there a bus/train to the centre of town?**
  Gibt es einen Bus/Zug zum Stadtzentrum?
  *geept es iynen boos/tsoohg tsoom **shtatt**sentrum*

YOU MAY HEAR...

Durchsage	**doorsh**zaage	call
Flug	*floohg*	flight
Flugsteig	**floohg**shtiyg	gate

letzter Aufruf	*letster owfroohf*	last call
verspätet	*fershpaytet*	delayed
gestrichen	*geshtrishen*	cancelled

* taxis
(see **information and tickets**, page 40)

● It's not usual in Germany to hail a taxi in the street. Go to a taxi rank or phone a Taxizentrale, taxi centre. Taxis are beige in most German cities.

● Swiss taxi drivers expect a tip – just round up at your discretion. In Austria taxis are metered in the larger cities. In smaller towns there may be fixed charges for certain destinations – tips are at your discretion.

YOU MAY WANT TO SAY...

Is there a taxi rank round here?	Gibt es einen Taxistand hier in der Nähe?	*geept es iynen taksishtant heer in der naye*
Can you order me a taxi...	Könnten Sie mir ein Taxi bestellen...	*kernnten zee meer iyn taksi beshtellen...*
immediately	für sofort	*fewr zofort*
for tomorrow at nine o'clock	für morgen um neun Uhr	*fewr morgen oom noyn oohr*
To this address, please.	Zu dieser Adresse bitte.	*tsooh deezer adresse bitte*
How much will it cost?	Wie viel wird es kosten?	*vee feel virt es kosten*

- **Can you put on the meter, please?** — Können Sie bitte den Gebührenzähler einschalten? — *kernnen zee bitte dayn gebewrentsayler iynshalten*

- **I'm in a hurry.** — Ich habe es eilig. — *ish haabe es iylig*

- **Stop here, please.** — Sie können hier anhalten. — *zee kernnen heer anhalten*

- **Can you wait for me, please?** — Könnten Sie bitte auf mich warten? — *kernnten zee bitte owf mish varten*

- **I think there's a mistake.** — Ich glaube, hier stimmt etwas nicht. — *ish glowbe heer shtimmt etvas nisht*

- **That's all right. (meaning: 'you can keep the change')** — Stimmt so. — *shtimmt so*

- **Can you give me a receipt?** — Könnte ich bitte eine Quittung haben? — *kernnte ish bitte iyne kvittoong haaben*

YOU MAY HEAR...

- Es wird ungefähr fünfzig Euro kosten. — *es virt oongefayr fewnftsig oyro kosten* — It'll cost about 50 euros.

- Das macht achtzehn Euro. — *das makt aktsayn oyro* — That's 18 euros.

- Dazu kommt ein Zuschlag... — *datsooh kommt iyn tsooshlaag...* — There's a supplement...
  - für das Gepäck — *fewr das gepek* — for the luggage
  - für jeden Koffer — *fewr yayden koffer* — for each suitcase
  - für die Fahrt zum Flughafen — *fewr dee faart tsoom floohghaafen* — to go to the airport

✳ hiring cars and bicycles

I'd like to hire...	Ich möchte ... mieten.	*ish **mershte** ... **mee**ten*
two bicycles	zwei Fahrräder	*tsviy **fa**rayder*
a small car	ein kleines Auto	*iyn **kli**ynes **ow**to*
an automatic car	einen Automatik- wagen	*iynen **ow**to**maa**tik- vaagen*
for...	für...	*fewr...*
the day	einen Tag	*iynen taag*
a week	eine Woche	*iyne **vo**ke*
two weeks	zwei Wochen	*tsviy **vo**ken*
until...	bis...	*bis...*
Friday	Freitag	*friytaag*
17th August	zum 17. August	*tsoom **zeeb**tsaynten ow**goost***
How much is it ...	Wie viel kostet das...	*vee feel kostet das...*
per day?	pro Tag?	*proh taag*
per week?	pro Woche?	*proh **vo**ke*
Is mileage included?	Ist die Kilometerzahl inbegriffen?	*ist dee keelo**may**ter- tsaal inbegriffen*
Is insurance included?	Ist die Versicherung inbegriffen?	*ist dee fer**zi**sheroong inbegriffen*
My partner (m/f) wants to drive too.	Mein Partner/meine Partnerin möchte den Wagen ebenfalls fahren.	*miyn **part**ner/**mi**yne **part**nerin **mer**shte den **vaa**gen **ay**benfalls **faa**ren*
Is there a deposit?	Muss ich Geld hinterlegen?	*muss ish gelt hinter**lay**gen*

YOU MAY HEAR...

Für wie lange?	*fewr vee lange*	For how long?
Ihren Führerschein, bitte.	*eeren fewrershiyn bitte*	Your driving licence, please.
Möchten Sie eine zusätzliche Versicherung abschließen?	*mershten zee iyne tsoohsetslishe fersisherung apshleessen*	Do you want extra insurance?
Sie müssen eine Anzahlung von 100 Euro leisten.	*zee mewssen iyne antsaalung fon hoondert oyro liysten*	You'll need to put down a deposit of 100 euros.
Haben Sie eine Kreditkarte?	*haaben zee iyne kredeetkarte*	Have you got a credit card?
Bringen Sie das Auto bitte mit vollem Tank zurück.	*bringen zee das owto bitte mit follem tank tsoorewk*	Please return the car with a full tank.

* driving
(see **directions**, page 37)

In Germany, Austria and Switzerland you drive on the right-hand side. If there are no traffic signs, traffic from the right has priority. Seatbelts are compulsory, both in the front and the back (if you have them). Crash helmets are compulsory for both drivers and passengers of motorbikes and scooters.

YOU MAY SEE...

Achtung	Caution
Ausfahrt	Exit
Autobahn	Motorway
Durchgangsverkehr	Through traffic
Einbahnstraße	One-way street
Fußgängerüberweg	Pedestrian crossing
Gefahr	Danger
Gefährliche Kurve	Dangerous bend
Glatteisgefahr	Black ice
Halten verboten	No stopping
Höchstgeschwindigkeit	Maximum speed
Langsam	Slow
Maut	Motorway toll
Mautstation	Toll station
Motor abschalten	Switch your engine off
Parken verboten	Parking prohibited
Reparaturwerkstatt	Car repairs/Garage
Schule	School
Stopp	Stop
Straße gesperrt	Road closed
Überholen verboten	No overtaking
Umleitung	Diversion
Vorfahrt achten	Give way
Zutritt verboten	No entry

YOU MAY WANT TO SAY...

- Where is the nearest petrol station?

Wo ist die nächste Tankstelle?

voh ist dee nekste tankshtelle

Fill it up with ... please.	Bitte einmal voll tanken mit...	*bitte iynmaal foll tanken mit...*
unleaded	Bleifrei Normalbenzin	*bliyfriy normaalbentseen*
diesel	Diesel	*deezel*
30 euros' worth of unleaded, please.	Für 30 Euro Normalbenzin, bitte.	*fewr driyssig oyro normaalbentseen bitte*
20 litres of super unleaded, please.	20 Liter Super, bitte.	*tsvantsig leeter zoohper bitte*
A can/A litre of oil, please.	Eine Dose/Einen Liter Öl, bitte.	*iyne dohze/iynen leeter erl bitte*
Can you...	Könnten Sie bitte...	*kernnten zee bitte...*
check the tyre pressure?	den Reifendruck prüfen?	*dayn riyfendrook prewfen*
change the tyre?	den Reifen wechseln?	*dayn riyfen vekseln*
Where is the air, please?	Wo ist die Luft, bitte?	*voh ist dee looft bitte*

* mechanical problems

My car has broken down.	Ich habe eine Panne.	*ish haabe iyne panne*
I've run out of petrol.	Der Tank ist leer.	*der tank ist layr*
I have a puncture.	Ich habe einen Platten.	*ish haabe iynen platten*

mechanical problems

Do you do repairs?	Nehmen Sie Reparaturen vor?	*naymen zee reparatoohren fohr*
I don't know what's wrong.	Ich weiß nicht, wo das Problem liegt.	*ish wiyss nisht, voh das problaym leegt*
I think it's the...	Ich glaube, es ist...	*ish glowbe es ist...*
I need...	Ich brauche ...	*ish browke ...*
Is it serious?	Ist es schlimm?	*ist es shlimm*
Can you repair it today?	Können Sie es heute reparieren?	*kernnen zee es hoyte repareeren*
When will it be ready?	Wann wird es fertig sein?	*van virt es fertig ziyn*
How much will it cost?	Wie viel wird es kosten?	*vee feel virt es kosten*

YOU MAY HEAR...

Was ist los damit?	*vas ist lohs damit*	What's wrong with it?
Ich muss die Ersatzteile bestellen.	*ish mooss dee erzatstiyle beshtellen*	I'll have to order the parts.
Es wird ... fertig sein.	*es virt ... fertig ziyn*	It'll be ready...
in einer Stunde	*in iyner shtoonde*	in an hour
am Montag	*am mohntaag*	on Monday
Es wird hundert Euro kosten.	*es virt hoondert oyro kosten*	It'll cost 100 euros.

✳ car parts

alternator	Drehstromgenerator	*drayshtrohm-generaator*
battery	Batterie	*batteree*
carburettor	Vergaser	*fergaazer*
distributor	Verteiler	*fertiyler*
engine	Motor	*mohtor*
fanbelt	Keilriemen	*kiylreemen*
fuelpump	Kraftstoffpumpe	*kraftshtoffpoompe*
points	Kontakte	*kontakte*
radiator	Kühler	*kewler*
spark plugs	Zündkerzen	*tsewntkertsen*
starter motor	Anlassermotor	*anlassermohtor*
accelerator	Gaspedal	*gaaspaydaal*
bonnet	Motorhaube	*mohtorhowbe*
boot	Kofferraum	*kofferrowm*
brakes	Bremsen	*bremzen*
exhaust pipe	Auspuff	*owspooff*
gears	Gangschaltung	*gangshaltung*
gearbox	Getriebe	*getreebe*
headlights	Scheinwerfer	*shiynverfer*
hazard lights	Warnblinkleuchte	*varnblink-loyshte*
ignition	Zündung	*tsewndung*
indicators	Blinker	*blinker*
rear lights	Heckleuchten	*hekloyshten*
side lights	Seitenleuchten	*ziytenloyshten*
reversing lights	Rückfahrlampen	*rewkfaarlampen*
spare wheel	Ersatzrad	*erzatsraat*
steering wheel	Steuerrad	*shtoyerraat*
front tyre	Vorderreifen	*forderriyfen*
back tyre	Hinterreifen	*hinterriyfen*
window	Fenster	*fenster*
windscreen	Windschutzscheibe	*vintshootsshiybe*
windscreen wipers	Scheibenwischer	*shiybenvisher*

travel and transport

accommodation

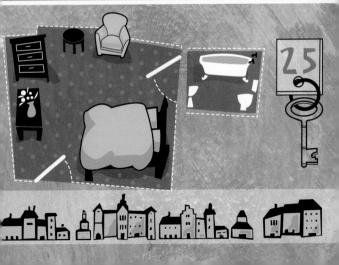

* general information

● Hotels in Germany are not officially graded but standards conform to the usual European star system. Prices are always displayed in the rooms. A Hotel garni offers bed and breakfast. A Pension is a guest house and a Gasthof is like a country inn and offers good food and a limited amount of accommodation. The sign Zimmer frei indicates rooms to let in a private house. Not all hotels and guest houses will accept credit cards, so it's best to ask about payment when you first check in.

REGISTRATION CARD INFORMATION

Vorname	first name
Familienname	surname
Wohnort/Straße/Hausnummer	home address/street/number
Postleitzahl	postcode
Nationalität	nationality
Beruf	occupation
Geburtsdatum	date of birth
Geburtsort	place of birth
Personalausweisnummer	passport number
Letzter Aufenthaltsort/ Reiseziel	coming from/going to
Ausgestellt in	issued at
Datum	date
Unterschrift	signature

accommodation

YOU MAY SEE...

Ausgang/Notausgang	Exit/Emergency Exit
Ausgebucht	Booked up
Bitte läuten	Please ring the bell
Campingplatz/Zeltplatz	Campsite
Duschen	Showers
Eingang	Entrance
Empfang/Rezeption	Reception
Erdgeschoss	Ground floor
Erster Stock	First floor
Esszimmer/Speisesaal	Dining room
Fahrstuhl/Aufzug	Lift
Frühstücksbüffet	Breakfast bar
Gasthof	Inn/Hotel
Gaststätte	Restaurant
Halbpension	Half board
Hotel garni	Bed and Breakfast
Jugendherberge	Youth hostel
Lagerfeuer verboten	Do not light fires
Müll, Abfälle	Rubbish
Müll abladen verboten	Do not dump rubbish
Parkplatz	Car park
Pension	Guest house
Strom	Electricity
Toiletten	Toilets
Trinkwasser	Drinking water
Vollpension	Full board
Wäscherei	Laundry
Zimmerservice	Room service
Zimmer frei	Rooms available

accommodation

61

✻ booking in advance

● Do you have a...	Haben Sie ein...	*haa*ben zee iyn...
single room?	Einzelzimmer?	*iyn*tseltsimmer
double room?	Doppelzimmer?	*do*ppeltsimmer
family room?	Familienzimmer?	*famee*lyentsimmer
twin-bedded room?	Zimmer mit zwei Einzelbetten?	*tsi*mmer mit tsviy *iyn*tselbetten
● Do you have space for...	Haben Sie Platz für...	*haa*ben zee plats fewr...
a tent?	ein Zelt?	iyn tselt
a caravan?	einen Wohnwagen?	*iynen* **vohn**vaagen
● I'd like to rent...	Ich möchte ... mieten.	ish *mer*shte ... *mee*ten
your cottage	Ihr Ferienhaus	eer *fayr*yenhows
an apartment	eine Ferienwohnung	*iyne* **fayr**yen- vohnung
● for...	für...	fewr...
one night	eine Nacht	*iyne* nakt
two nights	zwei Nächte	tsviy *nek*te
a week	eine Woche	*iyne* **vo**ke
● from ... to ...	von ... bis ...	fon ... bis ...
● with bath/shower	mit Bad/Dusche	mit baat/**doo**she
● How much is it...	Wie viel kostet es...	vee feel **kos**tet es...
per night?	pro Nacht?	proh nakt?
per week?	pro Woche?	proh **vo**ke?
● Is breakfast included?	Ist Frühstück inbegriffen?	ist **frew**shtewk **in**begriffen

Is there...	Gibt es...	*geept es...*
a reduction for children?	eine Ermäßigung für Kinder?	*iyne ermayssigung fewr kinder*
a single room supplement?	einen Einzelzimmer-zuschlag?	*iynen iyntsel-tsimmer-tsoohshlaag*
wheelchair access?	Zugang für Rollstuhlfahrer?	*tsoohgang fewr rollshtoohlfaarer*
Do you have...	Haben Sie...	*haaben zee...*
anything cheaper?	etwas Billigeres?	*etvas billigeres*
Can I pay by...	Kann ich mit...	*kann ish mit ...*
credit card?	Kreditkarte bezahlen?	*kredeetkarte betsaalen*
traveller's cheque?	Reisescheck bezahlen?	*riyzeshek betsaalen*
Can I book online?	Kann ich online buchen?	*kann ish onliyn boohken*
What's the address?	Wie lautet die Adresse?	*vee lowtet dee adresse*
What's your email address?	Wie lautet Ihre E-Mail-Adresse?	*vee lowtet eere eemail-adresse*
Can you recommend anywhere else?	Könnten Sie eine andere Unterkunft empfehlen?	*kernnten zee iyne andere oonterkoonft empfaylen*

YOU MAY HEAR...

Kann ich Ihnen helfen?	*kan ish eenen helfen*	Can I help you?

accommodation

63

checking in

Für wie viele Nächte?	fewr vee **fee**le **nek**te	For how many nights?
Für wie viele Personen?	fewr vee **fee**le per**zoh**nen	For how many people?
Einzel- oder Doppelzimmer?	**iynt**sel **oh**der **dopp**eltsimmer	Single or double room?
Mit... Badewanne? Dusche?	mit... **baa**devanne **doo**she	With... bath? shower?
Ihren Namen, bitte?	**ee**ren **naa**men **bitte**	What's your name, please?
Das macht 100 Euro pro Nacht.	das maakt **hoon**dert **oy**ro proh nakt.	It's 100 euros per night.
Tut mir Leid, wir sind voll belegt.	tooht meer liyt, veer sint foll be**laygt**	I'm sorry, we're full.

✳ checking in

YOU MAY WANT TO SAY...

I have a reservation for... tonight two nights a week	Ich habe eine Reservierung für... heute Nacht zwei Nächte eine Woche	ish **haabe** iyne rezer**vee**rung fewr... **hoy**te nakt tsviy **nek**te iyne **vo**ke
It's in the name of...	Gebucht auf den Namen...	ge**boohkt** owf dayn **naa**men...
Here's my passport.	Hier ist mein Ausweis.	heer ist miyn **ows**viys

YOU MAY HEAR...

Haben Sie ein Zimmer/einen Platz reserviert?	*haaben zee iyn tsimmer/iynen plats rezerveert*	**Have you reserved a room/space?**
Für wie viele Nächte?	*fewr vee feele nekte*	**For how many nights?**
Wie heißen Sie?	*vee hiyssen zee*	**What's your name?**
Dürfte ich bitte Ihren Ausweis sehen?	*dewrfte ish bitte eeren owsviys zayen*	**Can I see your passport, please?**

✳ hotels, B&Bs and hostels

YOU MAY WANT TO SAY...

Where can I park?	Wo kann ich parken?	*voh kan ish parken?*
Can I see the room, please?	Dürfte ich bitte das Zimmer sehen?	*dewrfte ish bitte das tsimmer zayen?*
Do you have...	Haben Sie ein...	*haaben zee iyn...*
a room with a view?	Zimmer mit Aussicht?	*tsimmer mit owssisht*
a bigger room?	ein größeres Zimmer?	*iyn grersseres tsimmer*
a cot for the baby?	ein Babybett?	*iyn baybeebett*
Is breakfast included?	Ist das Frühstück im Preis inbegriffen?	*ist das frewstewk im priys inbegriffen*

accommodation

65

hotels, B&Bs and hostels

- **What time...**
  - **is breakfast?**
  - **do you lock the front door?**

  Um wie viel Uhr...
  gibt es Frühstück?
  schließen Sie die Eingangstür ab?

  oom vee feel oohr...
  geept es frewstewk
  shleessen zee dee iyngangstewr ab?

- **Where is...**
  - **the dining room?**
  - **the bar?**

  Wo ist...
  das Speise-zimmer?
  die Bar?

  voh ist...
  das shpiyze-tsimmer
  dee bar

- **Is there...**
  - **24-hour room service?**
  - **an internet connection here?**
  - **a business centre here?**

  Haben Sie hier...
  Tag und Nacht Zimmerservice?
  Internet-Anschluss?
  Business-einrichtungen?

  haaben zee heer...
  taag oont nakt tsimmerservis
  internet anshlooss
  heer bizziness-iynrichtungen

YOU MAY HEAR...

Frühstück ist/ist nicht inbegriffen.	*frewstewk ist/ist nisht inbegriffen*	Breakfast is/isn't included.
Es gibt Frühstück von... bis...	*es geept frewstewk fon... bis...*	Breakfast is from... to...
Wir schließen die Eingangstür um ... Uhr ab.	*veer shleessen dee iyngangstewr um ... oohr ap*	We lock the front door at...
Zimmerdienst ist von ... bis ...	*tsimmerdeenst ist fon ... bis ...*	There's room service from ... to ...

accommodation

✳ camping and caravanning
(see **directions**, page 37)

There are plenty of campsites all over Germany, including special winter campsites. Further information and a list of sites is available from the German National Tourist Office. It is best to book in good time during the busy summer season.

YOU MAY WANT TO SAY...

● Is there a campsite/caravan site round here?

Gibt es hier einen Zeltplatz/ Wohnwagenplatz?

geept es heer iynen tseltplats/ vohnvaagenplats

● Can we camp here?

Dürfen wir hier zelten?

dewrfen veer heer tselten

● Can we park our caravan here?

Dürfen wir unseren Wohnwagen hier abstellen?

dewrfen veer oonzeren vohnvaagen heer apshtellen

● It's a two/four person tent.

Es ist ein Zwei-/ Vierpersonenzelt.

es ist iyn tsviy/feer-perzohnentselt

● Where are...
   the toilets?
   the showers?
   the dustbins?

Wo sind...
   die Toiletten?
   die Duschen?
   die Mülleimer?

voh zint...
   dee toaletten
   dee dooshen
   dee mewliymer

● Do we pay extra for the showers?

Müssen wir für die Dusche extra bezahlen?

mewssen veer fewr dee dooshe ekstra betsaalen

● Is it OK to drink the water?

Kann man das Wasser trinken?

kan man das vasser trinken

accommodation

67

Where's the electricity?	Wo gibt es einen Stromanschluss?	*voh geept es iynen shtrohm-anshlooss*

Der nächste Wohnwagenplatz ist...	*der nekste vohnvaagenplatts ist...*	The nearest caravan site is...
fünf Kilometer entfernt	*fewnf keelomayter entfernt*	five kilometres away
im nächsten Dorf	*im neksten dorf*	in the next village
Haben Sie eine Karte?	*haaben zee iyne karte*	Have you got a map?
Sie dürfen hier nicht zelten.	*zee dewrfen heer nisht tselten*	You can't camp here.
Die Duschen sind kostenlos.	*dee dooshen zint kostenlos*	The showers are free.
Einmal Duschen kostet ... Euro.	*iynmaal dooshen kostet ... oyro*	It's ... euros for a shower.
Der Stromanschluss ist dort drüben.	*Der shtrohm-anshlooss ist dort drewben*	The electricity is over there.

* requests and queries

Are there any messages for me?	Haben Sie irgend-welche Nachrichten für mich?	*haaben zee irgentvelshe naakrishten fewr mish*

- I'm expecting a phone call. | Ich erwarte einen Telefonanruf. | *ish ervarte iynen telefohnanroohf*

- Can you... | Können Sie es... | *kernnen zee es...*
  - charge it to my room? | auf die Zimmerrechnung setzen? | *owf dee tsimmerreshnoong zetsen*

- Can I leave this in the safe? | Kann ich dies im Safe lassen? | *kann ish dees im sayf lassen*

- Can I log on anywhere? | Gibt es hier irgendwo Internet-Anschluss? | *geept es heer irgentvoh internetanshlooss*

- Can you wake me up at eight o'clock? | Könnten Sie mich bitte um acht Uhr wecken? | *kernnten zee mish bitte oom akt oohr veken*

- Can you order me a taxi? | Könnten Sie mir bitte ein Taxi bestellen? | *kernnten zee meer bitte eyn taksee beshtellen*

- For right now. | Gleich. | *gliysh*

- For tomorrow morning at 8am. | Für morgen früh um acht Uhr. | *fewr morgen frew oom akt oohr*

- Do you have... | Haben Sie einen... | *haaben zee iynen...*
  - a babysitting service? | Babysitter-Service | *baybeesitter-servis*
  - a baby alarm? | Babyfon | *baybeefohn*

- I need... | Ich brauche... | *Ish browke...*
  - another pillow | noch ein Kopfkissen | *nok iyn kopfkissen*
  - a towel | ein Handtuch | *iyn hanttoohk*
  - an adaptor | einen Adapter | *iynen adapter*

● I've lost my key. Ich habe meinen Schlüssel verloren. *ish haabe miynen shlewssel ferlohren*

● I've left my key in the room. Ich habe meinen Schlüssel im Zimmer vergessen. *ish haabe miynen schlewssel im tsimmer fergessen*

* problems and complaints

YOU MAY WANT TO SAY...

● Excuse me... Entschuldigen Sie bitte... *entshooldigen zee bitte...*

● The room is... Das Zimmer ist... *das tsimmer ist...*
  too hot zu warm *tsooh varm*
  too cold zu kalt *tsooh kalt*
  too small zu klein *tsooh kliyn*

● There's no... Es ist kein ... da. *es ist kiyn daa*
  toilet paper Toilettenpapier *toaletten-papeer*
  power Strom *shtrohm*

● There's no hot water. Ich habe kein warmes Wasser. *ish haabe kiyn varmes vasser*

● There aren't any... Es sind keine ... da. *es zint kiyne ... daa*
  towels Handtücher *hanttewsher*

● I can't... Ich kann... *ish kann...*
  open the window das Fenster nicht öffnen *das fenster nisht erffnen*
  turn the tap off den Wasserhahn nicht abdrehen *den vasserhaan nisht apdrayen*
  work the TV den Fernseher nicht bedienen *dayn fernsayher nisht bedeenen*

The bed is uncomfortable.	Das Bett ist unbequem.	*das bett ist* ***oon****bequaym*
The bathroom is dirty.	Das Badezimmer ist schmutzig.	*das* ***baa****detsimmer ist* ***shmoot****sig*
The toilet doesn't flush.	Die Klospülung geht nicht.	*dee* ***kloh****shpewlung gayt nisht*
It's very noisy.	Es ist sehr laut.	*es ist zayr lowt*
The light doesn't work.	Das Licht funktioniert nicht.	*das lisht foonktsyo****neert*** *nisht*
The ... is broken	Die ... ist kaputt.	*dee ... ist ka****poot***
shower	Dusche	***doo****she*
remote control	Fernbedienung	***fern****bedeenung*
There's a smell of gas.	Es riecht nach Gas.	*es reesht naak gaas*
I want to speak to the manager!	Ich möchte mit dem Geschäftsführer sprechen!	*ish* ***mersh****te mit daym ge****shefts****fewrer* ***shpre****shen*

* checking out

checking out

YOU MAY WANT TO SAY...

The bill, please.	Die Rechnung, bitte.	*dee* ***resh****noong bitte*
I'd like to...	Ich möchte...	*ish* ***mersh****te...*
check out	abreisen	***ap****riyzen*
stay another night	noch eine Nacht bleiben	*nok* ***iyne*** *nakt* ***bliy****ben*
What time is checkout?	Um wie viel Uhr muss ich das Zimmer räumen?	*oom vee feel oohr muss ish das* ***tsi****mmer* ***roy****men*

self-catering

- **Can I leave my bags here?** — Kann ich meine Taschen hier lassen? — *kan ish miyne tashen heer lassen*

- **There's a mistake in the bill.** — In der Rechung ist ein Fehler. — *in der reshnoong ist iyn fayler*

- **I/We've had a great time here.** — Es hat mir/uns sehr gut gefallen hier. — *es hat meer/oons zayr gooht gefallen heer*

YOU MAY HEAR...

- Sie müssen bis ... abreisen. — *zee mewssen bis... apriyzen* — Checkout is at...

- Sie können das Zimmer bis ... haben. — *zee kernnen das tsimmer bis ... haaben* — You can have the room till...

- Wie viele Taschen? — *vee feele tashen?* — How many bags?

- Lassen Sie sie hier. — *lassen zee zee heer* — Leave them here.

- Darf ich es einmal sehen? — *darf ish es iynmaal zayen* — Let me check it.

- Besuchen Sie uns bald wieder! — *bezoohken zee oons balt veeder* — Come again!

* self-catering
(see **problems and complaints**, page 70)

YOU MAY WANT TO SAY...

- **My name is...** — Ich heiße... — *ish hiysse...*

I've rented...	Ich habe ... gemietet.	*ish **haabe** ... **gemeetet***
a chalet	ein Chalet	*iyn sha**lay***
an apartment	eine Wohnung	*iyne **voh**nung*
We're in number...	Wir sind in Nummer...	*veer zint in **noo**mmer...*
Can you give me the key, please?	Könnten Sie mir bitte den Schlüssel geben?	*kernn**ten** zee meer **bitte** dayn **shlew**ssel **gay**ben*
Where is the...	Wo ist der...	*voh ist der...*
fusebox?	Sicherungskasten?	*zishe**roongs**kasten*
stopcock?	Haupthahn?	***howpt**haan*
How does the ... work?	Wie funktioniert...	*vee **foonk**tsyoneert...*
cooker	der Herd?	*der hert*
hot water	das Warmwasser?	*das **varm**vasser*
Is there...	Gibt es eine...	*geept es iyne ...*
air-conditioning?	Klimaanlage?	***klee**ma-an**laage***
another gas bottle?	zweite Gasflasche?	*tsviyte **gas**flashe*
Are there...	Gibt es...	*geept es...*
any more blankets?	noch mehr Bettdecken?	*nok mayr **bett**decken*
any shops round here?	hier in der Nähe Geschäfte?	*heer in der **naye** ge**shef**te*
Where do I put the rubbish?	Wo stelle ich den Müll hin?	*voh **shtelle** ish dayn mewl hin*
When does the cleaner come?	Wann kommt die Putzfrau?	*vann kommt dee **poots**frow*

accommodation

- **Can I borrow a corkscrew?** Könnten Sie mir einen Korkenzieher leihen? *kernten zee meer iynen korkentseeher liyhen*

- **What shall we do with the key when we leave?** Was soll ich bei der Abreise mit dem Schlüssel machen? *vas zoll ish biy der apriyze mit dem shlewssel maken*

YOU MAY HEAR...

- Es funktioniert so. *es foonktsyoneert zoh* It works like this.

- Drücken Sie diesen Knopf/Schalter. *drewken zee deezen knopf/shalter* Press this button/switch.

- Tun Sie Ihre Abfälle... *toohn zee eere abfelle...* Put the rubbish...

    in den Mülleimer. *in den mewliymer* in the dustbin

- Der Müll wird am (Donnerstag) abgeholt. *der mewl virt am (donnerstaag) apgehohlt* The rubbish is collected on (Thursday).

- Die Putzfrau kommt am... *dee poottsfrow kommt am...* The cleaner comes on...

- Meine Handynummer ist... *miyne hendy-noommer ist...* My (mobile) number is...

food&drink

● Meal times in Germany, Austria and Switzerland are roughly the same as in Britain. Lunch, Mittagessen, is the largest meal of the day. Many Germans only have light supper, Abendbrot, in the evening, unless they are eating out.

● Schnellimbiss, Imbissstube, Würstchenbude: all offer a cheap but filling hot meal, which might mean a plate of chips with mayonnaise or ketchup, a sausage such as a Bratwurst or Currywurst, soup, omelette or potato salad. You can often get similar snacks in a Kneipe or Wirtschaft, including Bratkartoffeln, fried potatoes. In Switzerland these are known as Rösti. A Weinstube usually serves more upmarket food.

YOU MAY SEE...

Beisel	Pub (Austria)
Biergarten	Beer garden
Bierkeller	Beer cellar
Chinarestaurant	Chinese restaurant
Döner Kebap	Doner Kebab
Eisdiele	Ice-cream parlour
Fischrestaurant	Fish restaurant
Garderobe	Cloakroom
Gasthof	Inn
Gaststätte	Restaurant/Pub
Gastwirtschaft	Inn, guest house
Grillstube	Steak house
Hähnchen-Grill	Roast chicken takeaway
Heurigenlokal	Wine bar, garden (Austria)

making bookings

Imbissstube	Snack bar
Kneipe/Lokal	Pub
Autobahnraststätte	Motorway rest area
Ratskeller	Restaurant (often in basement of local town hall)
Rastplatz	Picnic area
Schnellimbiss	Snack bar
Selbstbedienungsrestaurant	Self-service
Toiletten	Toilets
Weinbar	Wine bar
Bratwurststand	Hot dog stand

✳ making bookings

YOU MAY WANT TO SAY...

● I'd like to reserve a table for...

Ich möchte einen Tisch reservieren für...

ish mershte iynen tish rezerveeren fewr...

two people

zwei Personen

tsviy perzohnen

two adults and three children

zwei Erwachsene und drei Kinder

tsviy ervaksene oont driy kinder

tomorrow evening

morgen Abend

morgen aabent

this evening at seven o'clock

heute Abend um sieben Uhr

hoyte aabent oom zeeben oor

● My name is...

Mein Name ist...

miyn naame ist...

● My telephone number is....

Meine Telefonnummer ist....

miyne telefohnnoommer ist...

● Could you squeeze us in earlier/later?

Hätten Sie ein bisschen früher/später für uns Platz?

hetten zee iyn bisshen frewer/shpayter fewr oons platts

food and drink

77

YOU MAY HEAR...

- Für wann möchten Sie den Tisch? — *fewr van **mersh**ten zee dayn tish* — When would you like the table for?

- Für wie viele Personen? — *fewr vee **fee**le per**zohn**en* — For how many people?

- Auf welchen Namen? — *owf **vel**shen **naa**men* — What name is it?

- Tut mir Leid, wir haben keine Tische frei. — *toot mir liyt veer **haa**ben **kiy**ne tishe friy* — I'm sorry, we're fully booked.

- Raucher oder Nichtraucher? — *rowker ohder nisht**row**ker* — Smoking or non-smoking?

✳ at the restaurant

YOU MAY WANT TO SAY...

- I've booked a table. — Ich habe einen Tisch bestellt. — *ish **haa**be iynen tish be**shtellt***

- My name is... — Mein Name ist... — *miyn **naa**me ist...*

- We haven't booked. — Wir haben keinen Tisch bestellt. — *veer **haa**ben kiynen tish be**shtellt***

- Have you got a table for four, please? — Hätten Sie einen Tisch für vier Personen? — *hetten zee iynen tish fewr feer per**zohn**en*

- Outside/on the terrace, if possible. — Draußen/auf der Terrasse, wenn's möglich ist. — *drowssen/owf der terasse venns **merg**lish ist*

- **Have you got a high chair?** | Haben Sie einen Babystuhl? | *haaben zee iynen baybeeshtool*
- **How long's the wait?** | Wie lange müssen wir warten? | *vee lange mewssen veer varten*
- **Can we wait at the bar?** | Können wir an der Bar warten? | *kernnen veer an der bar varten*
- **Do you take credit cards?** | Nehmen Sie Kreditkarten? | *naymen zee kredeetkarten*

YOU MAY HEAR...

- Haben Sie reserviert? | *haaben zee rezerveert* | Have you got a reservation?
- Wo möchten Sie sitzen? | *voh mershten zee zitsen* | Where would you like to sit?
- Raucher oder Nichtraucher? | *Rowker ohder nishtrowker* | Smoking or non-smoking?
- Einen Moment, bitte. | *iynen moment bitte* | Just a moment.
- Möchten Sie warten? | *mershten zee varten* | Would you like to wait?
- Tut mir Leid,... | *toot mir liyt...* | I'm sorry...
  - wir haben keinen Tisch frei | *veer haaben kiynen tish friy* | we're full
  - die Küche ist geschlossen | *dee kewshe ist geshlossen* | the kitchen's closed
- Wir nehmen (keine) Kreditkarten. | *wir naymen (kiyne) kredeetkarten* | We (don't) accept credit cards.

food and drink

79

✳ ordering your food

● Excuse me!	Hallo, Bedienung!	*hallo bedeenoong*
● The menu, please.	Die Speisekarte, bitte.	*die shpiyzekarte, bitte*
● Do you have...	Haben Sie...	*haaben zee...*
a kids' menu?	ein Kindermenü?	*iyn kindermenew*
vegetarian food?	vegetarische Gerichte?	*vegetaarishe gerishte*
a tourist menu?	ein Touristenmenü?	*iyn turistenmenew*
an à la carte menu?	Gerichte à la carte?	*gerishte a la kart*
● Is it self-service?	Ist hier Selbstbedienung?	*ist heer zelbstbedeenoong*
● We're ready to order.	Wir möchten bestellen.	*veer mershten beshtellen*
● Can I have...?	Könnte ich ... häben?	*kernnte ish... haaben*
● I'd like ...	Ich hätte gerne ...	*ish hette gerne ...*
for starters	als Vorspeise	*als fohrshpiyze*
for main course	als Hauptgericht	*als howptgerisht*
for dessert	zum Nachtisch	*tsoom naaktish*
● I'd like ... followed by ...	Ich nehme zuerst ..., dann ...	*ish nayme tsooerst ... dann ...*
● Does that come with vegetables?	Gibt es dazu Gemüse?	*geept es datsoo gemewze*
● What are your specials today?	Was ist Ihre Spezialität des Tages?	*vas ist eere shpetsyalitayt des taages*

food and drink

What's this, please?	Was ist dies, bitte?	*vas ist dees bitte*
What's the local speciality?	Was wäre eine einheimische Spezialität?	*vas vayre iyne iynhiymishe shpetsyalitayt*
I'll have the same as him/her/them.	Ich nehme das Gleiche wie er/sie/sie.	*ish nayme das gliyshe vee er/zee/zee*
I'd like it ..., please.	Ich hätte es gerne ... durchgebraten.	*ish hette es gerne ... durshgebraaten.*
rare	nicht	*nikt*
medium	halb	*halp*
well done	ganz	*gantz*
Excuse me, I've changed my mind.	Entschuldigung, ich habe mich anders entschlossen.	*entshooldigoong, ish haabe mish anders entshlossen*

YOU MAY HEAR...

Haben Sie ausgesucht?	*haaben zee owsgesookt*	Have you decided?
Was möchten Sie als...	*vas mershten zee als...*	What would you like for...
Vorspeise?	*fohrshpiyze*	starters?
Hauptgericht?	*howptgerisht*	main course?
Nachtisch?	*naaktish*	dessert?
Wir empfehlen...	*veer empfaylen*	We recommend...
Sonst noch etwas?	*zonst nok etvas*	Anything else?

* ordering your drinks

● In bars and cafés you often pay for all your drinks and so on when you leave, though in the larger, busy bars you will probably have to pay for each round.

● Can I see the wine list, please?	Könnte ich bitte die Weinkarte sehen?	*kernnte ish bitte dee viynkarte zayen*
● A bottle of this, please.	Eine Flasche von diesem, bitte.	*iyne flashe fon deezem bitte*
● Half a litre of this, please.	Einen halben Liter von diesem, bitte.	*iynen halben leeter fon deezem bitte*
● A glass of the ..., please.	Ein Glas von dem ..., bitte.	*iyn glas fon daym... bitte*
● We'll have the house red/white, please.	Wir nehmen den roten/weißen Hauswein, bitte	*veer naymen den rohten/viyssen howsviyn bitte*
● What beers do you have, please?	Welche Biersorten haben Sie?	*velshe beerzorten haaben zee*
● Can I have a...	Könnte ich einen ... haben?	*kernnte ich iynen ... haaben*
gin and tonic?	Gin Tonic	*jin tonik*
whisky?	Whisky	*whisky*
vodka and coke?	Wodka-Cola	*vodka kohla*
● A bottle of mineral water, please.	Eine Flasche Mineralwasser, bitte.	*iyne flashe mineraalvasser bitte*
● What soft drinks do you have, please?	Was haben Sie an alkoholfreien Erfrischungsgetränken?	*vas haaben zee an alkohohlfriyen erfrishoongs-getrenken*

Stilles Wasser oder mit Kohlensäure?	*shtilles vasser ohder mit kohlenzoyre*	**Still water or fizzy?**
Eine große oder eine kleine Flasche?	*iyne grohsse ohder iyne kliyne flashe*	**A large or a small bottle?**

* bars, cafés and snack bars

● Bars and cafés serve all kinds of drinks – alcohol, soft drinks, coffee and tea, etc. Cafés usually serve cakes or flans and perhaps omelettes. Sandwiches and rolls are often sold to take away at a Metzgerei, a Feinkostgeschäft or a Bäckerei.

I'll have...	Ich nehme...	*ish nayme...*
A (black) coffee, please.	Einen (schwarzen) Kaffee, bitte.	*iynen (shvartsen) kaffay bitte*
A cup of tea.	Eine Tasse Tee, bitte.	*iyne tasse tay bitte*
with milk/lemon	mit Milch/Zitrone	*mit milsh/tsitrohne*
A glass of ... please.	Ein Glas ... bitte.	*iyn glas ... bitte*
tap water	Leitungswasser	*liytoongsvasser*
wine	Wein	*viyn*
No ice, thanks.	Ohne Eis, bitte.	*ohne iys bitte*
A bottle of water.	Eine Flasche Wasser.	*iyne flashe vasser*

- **A piece of ... please.** Ein Stück ... bitte. *iyn stewk ... bitte*
  cheesecake Käsekuchen *kaysekooken*
  black forest Schwarzwälder *shvartsvelder*
  gateau Kirschtorte *kirshtorte*

- **What kind of ...** Was für ... haben Sie? *vas fewr ... haaben zee*
  do you have?

- **Is there any...** Haben Sie... *haaben zee...*
  tomato ketchup? Tomatenketchup? *tomaatenketshap*
  pepper and salt? Pfeffer und Salz? *pfeffer oont zalts*

- **Same again, please.** Das Gleiche noch *das gliyshe nok*
  einmal, bitte. *iynmaal bitte*

- **How much is that?** Wie viel kostet das? *vee feel kostet das*

YOU MAY HEAR...

- Was hätten Sie *vas hetten zee gern* What would you
  gern? like?

- Groß oder klein? *grohss ohder kliyn* Large or small?

- Mit oder ohne *mit ohder ohne* Fizzy or still?
  Kohlensäure? *kohlenzoyre*

- Mit Eis? *mit iys* With ice?

✳ comments and requests

YOU MAY WANT TO SAY...

- **This is delicious.** Das ist ausgezeichnet. *das ist owsgetsiyshnet*

Can I have more ... please?	Könnte ich bitte noch etwas... haben?	*kernnte ich bitte nok etvas ... haaben*
bread	Brot	*broht*
water	Wasser	*vasser*
Another bottle of wine, please.	Noch eine Flasche Wein, bitte?	*nok iyne flashe viyn bitte*
I can't eat another thing.	Ich bin rundum satt.	*ish bin runtum zatt*

YOU MAY HEAR...

Ist alles in Ordnung?	*ist alles in ortnoong*	**Is everything all right?**
Schmeckt es Ihnen?	*shmekt es eenen*	**Are you enjoying your meal?**

* special requirements

YOU MAY WANT TO SAY...

I'm diabetic.	Ich bin Diabetiker.	*ish bin deeahbaytiker*
I'm allergic to...	Ich bin allergisch auf...	*ish bin allergish owf...*
nuts	Nüsse	*nüsse*
cow's milk	Kuhmilch	*koomilsh*
MSG	Monosodium- glutamat	*mohnozohdium- gloohtamaat*
shellfish	Schalentiere	*shaalenteere*

food and drink

85

● I'm/We're... | Ich bin/Wir sind | *ish bin/veer sint*
   vegetarian | Vegetarier | *vegetaarier*
   vegan | Veganer | *vegaaner*

● I can't eat... | Ich darf keine | *ish darf kiyne*
    | ... essen. | *... essen*

   dairy products | Milchprodukte | *milshprodookte*
   wheat products | Weizenprodukte | *wiytsenprodookte*

● Is there anything | Haben Sie etwas | *haaben zee etvas*
without (meat)? | ohne (Fleisch)? | *ohne (fliysh)*

● Do you have... | Haben Sie... | *haaben zee...*
   halal food? | Halal-Gerichte? | *halal-gerishte*
   kosher food? | koschere | *kohshere gerishte*
    | Gerichte? |

● Does that have | Sind da (Nüsse) drin? | *zint da (newsse) drin*
(nuts) in? | |

YOU MAY HEAR...

● Ich werde den Koch fragen. | *ish verde dayn kok fraagen* | I'll check with the kitchen.

● Es ist überall (Butter) drin. | *es ist ewberall bootter drin* | It's all got (butter) in.

* problems and complaints

YOU MAY WANT TO SAY...

● Excuse me. | Entschuldigen Sie, bitte. | *entshooldigen zee bitte*

- This is... | Dies ist... | *deez ist...*
  - cold | kalt | *kalt*
  - underdone | nicht gar | *nisht gar*
  - burnt | angebrannt | *angaybrannt*

- I didn't order this. | Das habe ich nicht bestellt. | *das **haabe** ish nisht be**shtellt***

- I ordered the... | Ich habe ... bestellt. | *ish **haabe** ... be**shtellt***

- Is our food coming soon? | Müssen wir noch lange auf das Essen warten? | ***mew**ssen veer nok **lange** owf das **essen var**ten*

✳ paying the bill

YOU MAY WANT TO SAY...

- The bill, please. | Die Rechnung, bitte. | *dee **resh**noong **bitte***

- Is service included? | Ist die Bedienung im Preis inbegriffen? | *ist dee be**dee**noong im priys **in**begriffen*

- There's a mistake here. | Hier ist ein Fehler in der Rechnung. | *heer ist iyn **fay**ler in der **resh**noong*

- That was fantastic, thank you. | Das war hervorragend. Vielen Dank. | *das var her**fohr**raagent **fee**len dank*

Bedienung ist nicht im Preis inbegriffen.	bedeenoong ist nisht im prys inbegriffen	Service isn't included.
Tut mir Leid, wir nehmen nur Bargeld.	toot meer liyt veer naymen noor baargelt	Sorry, we only accept cash.

✳ buying food

● When you go shopping in a supermarket you will have to pay for carrier bags, so it's best to take your own with you.

● I'd like ... , please.	Ich möchte bitte...	ish mershte bitte...
some of those/ that...	etwas von dem...	etvas fon daym...
a kilo (of...)	ein Kilo...	iyn keelo....
half a kilo (of...)	ein halbes Kilo...	iyn halbes keelo...
200 grammes (of...)	zweihundert Gramm...	tsviyhoondert gramm...
a piece of...	ein Stück...	iyn shtewk...
two slices (of...)	zwei Scheiben...	tsviy shiyben...
● How much is...	Wie viel kostet...	vee feel kostet...
that?	das?	das
a kilo of cheese?	ein Kilo Käse?	iyn keelo kayze
● What's that?	Was ist das?	vas ist das
● Have you got...	Haben Sie...	haaben zee...
any bread?	Brot?	broht
any more?	ein wenig mehr?	iyn vaynig mayr

A bit more, please.	Ein bisschen mehr, bitte.	*iyn bissshen mayr bitte*
A bit less, please.	Ein bisschen weniger, bitte.	*iyn bissshen vayniger bitte*
That's all thank you.	Das ist alles, danke schön.	*das ist alles danke shern*
I'm looking for...	Ich suche...	*ish zooke*
frozen food	das Tiefkühlfach	*das teefkewlfaak*
dairy products	die Milchprodukte	*dee milshprodookte*
Can I have a bag, please?	Könnte ich bitte eine Tüte haben?	*kernnte ish bitte iyne tewte haaben*

menu reader

DRINKS

Apfelkorn **distilled apple spirit**
Apfelsaft **apple juice**
Apfelschorle **apple juice with fizzy water**
Bier **beer**
  Alsterwasser **shandy (north Germany)**
  Altbier **bitter with high hop content**
  Altbierbowle **bitter punch with bits of pineapple**
  Berliner Weiße **light Berlin ale with raspberry juice**
  Bockbier **strong, malt beer**
  Doppelbock **strong, malt Munich beer**
  Dunkles Bier **dark, malt beer**
  Malzbier **dark, sweet malt beer**

  Pilsener **strong, hoppy lager**
  Radler(maß) **(a litre of) shandy**
  Weißbier **yeasty beer brewed with wheat**
  Weizenbier **light beer brewed with wheat**
Fruchtsaft **fruit juice**
Eierlikör **egg nog**
Gespritzter Wein (süß oder sauer) **white wine with lemonade or mineral water**
Glühwein **mulled wine**
Heiße Schokolade **hot chocolate**
Johannisbeersaft **blackcurrant juice**
Kaffee **coffee**
  Einspänner **black with whipped cream**
  Espresso **strong, black espresso**

Großer Brauner **large black coffee with a dash of milk**
Großer Schwarzer **large black coffee**
Kleiner Brauner **small black coffee with a dash of milk**
koffeinfrei **decaffeinated**
Melange **half coffee, half warm milk**
mit Sahne **with cream**
Mokka **strong black coffee**
Kirschwasser **cherry brandy**
Korn **distilled grain spirit**
Limonade **lemonade**
Milchshake **milk shake**
Mineralwasser **mineral water**
mit Kohlensäure **sparkling**
ohne Kohlensäure **still**
Orangeade **orangeade**
Orangensaft **orange juice**
Pflümliwasser **plum brandy**
Sekt **German equivalent to champagne**
Schorle **white wine with mineral water**
Schnaps **brandy**
Steinhäger **juniper berry brandy (like gin)**
Tee **tea**
Eistee **iced tea**

Hagebuttentee **rose-hip tea**
Kamillentee **camomile tea**
Pfefferminztee **peppermint tea**
Kräutertee **herbal tea**
mit Milch **with milk (usually UHT milk)**
mit Zitrone **with lemon**
Tomatensaft **tomato juice**
Wein **wine**
Auslese **medium dry wine made with late grapes**
Beerenauslese **medium sweet wine made with overripe grapes**
herb **dry**
lieblich **sweet**
Rotwein **red wine**
Spätlese **dry wine made with late grapes**
süß **sweet**
trocken **dry**
Trockenbeerenauslese **sweet dessert wine made with dried grapes**
vollmundig **full-bodied**
Weißwein **white wine**
Schaumwein **sparkling wine**
Weinbrand **brandy**
Weizenkorn **distilled wheat spirit**

FOOD

Aal **eel**
Aalsuppe **eel soup**
Altenburger **mild goat's cheese**
Ananas **pineapple**
Apfel **apple**
Apfelmus **apple sauce**
Apfelstrudel **apple, nuts and raisins in layers of flaky pastry**
Apfelsine **orange**
Appenzeller **mild, firm Swiss cheese**

Aprikose **apricot**
Artischocke **artichoke**
Aubergine **aubergine**
Auflauf **souffle**
Aufschnitt **sliced cold meat and sausage**
Austern **oysters**
Backpflaumen **prunes**
Backsteinkäse **strong, Bavarian cheese**
Bananen **bananas**

Barsch freshwater perch

Basilikum basil

Basler Mehlsuppe thick soup with grated cheese (Switzerland)

Bauernfrühstück egg, bacon and potatoes (lit. farmer's breakfast)

Bauernomelett bacon and onion omelette

Bauernschmaus sauerkraut with bacon, sausages, pork, dumpling and potatoes

Belegtes Brot open sandwich

Bemme open sandwich

Berliner jam doughnut

Berner Platte sauerkraut (or green beans) with various cooked meats (pork, beef, sausages, bacon)

Bienenstich honey and almond cake

Bierwurst smoked pork and beef sausage

Birne pear

Blumenkohl cauliflower

Blutwurst black pudding

Bockwurst Frankfurter

Bohnen beans

Bohnensuppe bean soup

Bouillon broth, consommé

Braten roast meat

Bratkartoffeln fried potatoes

Bratwurst spicy, fried sausage

Brombeeren blackberries

Brot bread

Brötchen bread roll

Brühe broth

Cervelatwurst salami

Champignons button mushrooms

Currywurst curry sausage

Datteln dates

Dorsch cod

Eier eggs

Eintopf stew

Eis ice cream

Eisbecher ice cream sundae

Eisbombe ice cream bomb

Eisbein pig's knuckle

Emmentaler mild, Swiss cheese

Ente duck

Erbsen peas

Erdäpfel potatoes (Austria)

Erdbeeren strawberries

Erdnuss peanut

Fasan pheasant

Feigen figs

Fischbeuschelsuppe fish roe and vegetable soup

Fisolen french beans (Austria)

Forelle trout

Frikadellen meatballs

Froschschenkel frogs' legs

Früchte fruit

Früchte der Saison seasonal fruit

Frühlingssuppe spring vegetable soup

Gans goose

Gedämpft steamed

Gedünstet steamed

Gefüllt stuffed

Gekochtes Ei boiled egg

Gemischter Salat mixed salad

Geräuchert smoked

Gewürzt spicy

Götterspeise jelly (lit. food of the Gods)

Granatrührei scrambled egg with prawns

Grießnockerl semolina dumpling

grüne Bohnen green (French) beans

Grüner Salat green salad

Hackbraten meatloaf

Hackfleisch mince

Hähnchen chicken

Hase hare, rabbit

Haselnuss hazelnut

Hausfrauenart served with apple, sour cream and onions

Hausgemacht homemade

Heilbutt halibut

Hendl chicken (Austria)
Hering herring
Himbeeren raspberries
Himmel und Erde bacon and meat casserole with apple sauce
Hoppel-Poppel scrambled egg with diced bacon and sausage
Hühnchen chicken
Hummer lobster
Hummerkrabben king prawns
Ingwer ginger
Jagdwurst smoked sausage with garlic and mustard
Jägerart served in red wine sauce with mushrooms (lit. hunter's style)
Jägerschnitzel escalope of veal in a mushroom sauce
Jakobsmuscheln scallops
Johannisbeeren redcurrants
Jungfernbraten roast pork with bacon
Kabeljau cod
Kalbfleisch veal
    Kalbsrolle braised stuffed veal roll
Kaninchen rabbit
Karfiol cauliflower
Karotten carrots
Karpfen carp
Kartoffeln potatoes
    Kartoffelbrei mashed potatoes
    Kartoffelkroketten croquettes
Käse cheese
    Käsesahnekuchen/Käsekuchen fresh creamy curd cheese gateau
    Käseschnitte open, melted cheese sandwich
    Käseteller plate of assorted cheeses
    Käsewähe hot cheese tart (Switzerland)
Kasseler Rippen roast smoked loin of pork
Kastanien chestnuts
Kirschen cherries

Klopse chop
Klöße dumplings
Knoblauch garlic
Knödel dumplings
Kohl cabbage
    Kohlroulade cabbage leaves stuffed with minced meat
    Kohlrabi kohlrabi (cross between cabbage and turnip)
Kompott stewed fruit
Königinpastete puff pastry filled with chopped meat and mushrooms
Königinsuppe soup with beef, sour cream and almonds
Königsberger Klopse meatballs in white caper sauce
Kopfsalat lettuce salad
Kotelett chop, cutlet
Krabben prawns
Kraftbrühe beef consommé
Kräuter herbs
    Kräuterbutter garlic butter
Krebs crab, crayfish
Kren horseradish (Austria)
Kuchen cake
Kümmelkäse mild cheese with caraway seeds
Kürbis pumpkin
Labkaus thick stew of minced meat with mashed potatoes
Lachs salmon
Lammfleisch lamb
    Lammkeule leg of lamb
Lauch leek
Leberknödelsuppe soup with liver dumplings
Lebkuchen gingerbread
Leipziger Allerlei vegetable and meat stew
Lende loin
Linsensuppe lentil soup
Linzertorte almond flan with a

raspberry topping

Mais **sweetcorn**

Makrele **mackerel**

Mandeln **almonds**

Marillen **apricots (Austria)**

Mark **bone marrow**

Matjeshering **young, salted herring**

Meeresfrüchte **sea food**

Merrettich **horseradish**

mit Einlage **with a garnish**

Möhren/Mohrrüben **carrots**

Mus **puréed stewed fruit**

Muskatnuss **nutmeg**

Nelken **cloves**

Nieren **kidneys**

Nockerl **dumpling**

Nudeln **pasta**

Nürnberger Bratwurst **Nuremberg sausage cooked on a charcoal grill**

Nuss **nut**

   Nussstrudel **flaky pastry with nuts and honey**

Obst **fruit**

   Obstsalat **fruit salad**

Ochsenschwanzsuppe **oxtail soup**

Oliven **olives**

Palatschinken **pancakes (Austria)**

Pampelmuse **grapefruit**

Paniert **cooked in egg and breadcrumbs**

Paradeiser **tomatoes (Austria)**

Pellkartoffeln **potatoes boiled in their skins**

Petersilie **parsley**

   Petersilienkartoffeln **boiled potatoes with parsley and butter**

Pfannkuchen **pancakes**

Pfeffersteak **steak covered with half peppercorns**

Pfirsich **peach**

Pflaumen **plums**

Pichelsteiner Eintopf **mixed meat and vegetable stew**

Pilze **mushrooms**

Pommes frites **chips**

Porree **leeks**

Powidl **thick plum jam**

   Powidltatschkerln **pancake with a filling of thick plum jam**

Preiselbeeren **cranberries**

Pudding **blancmange**

Pute **turkey**

Quark **curd cheese (fromage frais)**

   Quarkkeulchen **sweet dessert made with potatoes and quark**

   Quarkspeise **dessert made with quark and (usually) fruit**

Rahm **cream**

   Rahmschnitzel **escalope of veal in cream sauce**

Räucheraal **smoked eel**

Rauchwurst **smoked sausage**

Rebhuhn **partridge**

Reh **venison**

   Rehrücken **saddle of venison**

Reis **rice**

Rhabarber **rhubarb**

Rindfleisch **beef**

Roggenbrot **rye bread**

Rohschinken **cured ham**

Rollmops **pickled herring wrapped round slices of onion**

Rosenkohl **brussels sprout**

Rosinen **raisins**

Rosmarin **rosemary**

Rösti **fried potatoes (Switzerland)**

Rote Beete **beetroot**

Rote Grütze **red fruit jelly**

Rotkohl **red cabbage**

Rouladen **slices of rolled beef or veal in gravy**

Rührei **scrambled egg**

Rumpsteak **rump steak**

Russische Eier **hard-boiled eggs with mayonnaise**

Sachertorte **rich chocolate cake** (from Sacher's café in Vienna)

Sahne **cream**

Salat **salad**

Salbei **sage**

Salzburgernockerl **sweet egg soufflé flavoured with vanilla**

Salzkartoffeln **boiled potatoes with salt**

Sardellen **anchovies**

Sauerbraten **braised beef marinated in vinegar**

Sauerkraut **pickled white cabbage**

Schildkrötensuppe **turtle soup**

Schinken **ham**

Schlachtplatte **assorted cold meat and sausages**

Schlagobers **whipped cream (Austria)**

Schlagsahne **whipped cream**

Schmelzkäse **soft cheese, used in cooking**

Schnittlauch **chives**

Schnitzel **escalope (usually veal)**

Schokolade **chocolate**

Scholle **plaice**

Schwarzbrot **black bread, pumpernickel**

Schwarzwälder Kirschtorte **black forest gateau**

Schweinefleisch **pork**

Seebarsch **sea bass**

Sellerie **celery**

Semmel **bread roll (Austria, S. Germany)**

Serbische Bohnensuppe **spicy Serbian bean soup**

Soße **sauce**

Spargel **asparagus**

Spätzle **tiny dumplings**

Speck **smoked bacon**

Spiegelei **fried egg**

Spinat **spinach**

Stachelbeeren **gooseberries**

Steinbutt **turbot**

Stelze **pig's knuckle (Austria)**

Stollen **cake with almonds, nuts and candied and dried fruits (often eaten at Christmas)**

Strammer Max **raw ham and fried eggs served on rye bread**

Streuselkuchen **cake with a butter, sugar, flour and cinnamon topping**

Sülzkotelett **pork chop in aspic**

Suppe **soup**

Teig **dough**

Teigwaren **pasta**

Thunfisch **tuna fish**

Tomaten **tomatoes**

Tomatensuppe **tomato soup**

Topfen **curd cheese (Austria)**

Topfenstrudel **thin layers of pastry filled with curd cheese**

Torte **gateau, flan**

Truthahn **turkey**

Überbacken **baked**

Vollkornbrot **wholemeal bread**

Walnuss **walnut**

Weintrauben **grapes**

Weißbrot **white bread**

Weißwurst **veal, bacon, parsley and onion sausage**

Wienerli **Vienna-style Frankfurter**

Wienerschnitzel **escalope of veal cooked in egg and breadcrumbs**

Wildschwein **wild boar**

Wurst **sausage**

Zimt **cinnamon**

Zitrone **lemon**

Zucchini **courgettes**

Zwetschgen **plums**

Zwiebel **onion**

sightseeing
&activities

● Most towns and cities have their own tourist office – look for the sign Touristeninformation or ask for the Fremdenverkehrsamt or Fremdenverkehrsbüro.

✳ at the tourist office

● **Do you speak English?** — Sprechen Sie Englisch? — *shpreshen zee english*

● **Do you have...** — Haben Sie... — *haaben zee...*

  a map of the town? — einen Stadtplan? — *iynen shtattplaan*

  a list of hotels? — eine Hotelliste? — *iyne hotelliste*

● **Can you recommend...** — Können Sie... empfehlen? — *kernnen zee... empfaylen*

  a cheap hotel? — ein preiswertes Hotel — *iyn priyswertes hotel*

  a good campsite? — einen guten Campingplatz? — *iynen goohten campingplats*

  a traditional restaurant? — ein typisches Restaurant? — *iyn tewpishes restorang*

● **Do you have information...** — Haben Sie Informationen... — *haaben zee informatsyohnen...*

  in English? — auf Englisch? — *owf english*

  about opening times? — zu Öffnungszeiten? — *tsooh erffnoongstsiyten*

Can you book...	Könnten Sie bitte...	**Kernn**ten zee **bitte**...
a hotel room for me?	ein Hotelzimmer für mich buchen?	iyn ho**telt**simmer fewr mish **booh**ken
this day trip for me?	diesen Tagesausflug für mich buchen?	**dee**zen **taa**gesowsfloohg fewr mish **booh**ken

Where is...	Wo ist...	voh ist...
the old town?	die Altstadt?	dee **alt**shtatt
the art gallery?	die Kunsthalle?	dee **koonst**halle
the ... museum?	das ... Museum?	das ... moo**zay**oom

Is there...	Gibt es...	geept es...
a swimming pool?	ein Schwimmbad?	iyn **shvimm**baat
a bank?	eine Bank?	**iyne** bank

| Is there a post office near here? | Gibt es eine Post hier in der Nähe? | geebt es **iyne** post heer in der **nay**he |

| Can you show me on the map? | Können Sie mir das auf dem Stadtplan zeigen? | **kern**nen zee meer das owf daym **shtatt**plaan **tsiy**gen |

sightseeing and activities

YOU MAY HEAR...

| Kann ich Ihnen helfen? | kann ish **eenen hel**fen | Can I help you? |
| Welche Art von Unterkunft möchten Sie? | velshe art fon **oon**terkoonft **mersh**ten zee | What kind of accommodation do you want? |

97

Es ist in...	*es ist in...*	It's in...
der Altstadt	*der **alt**shtatt*	the old town
im Stadtzentrum	*im **shtattt**sentrum*	the centre of town

✳ opening times
(see **telling the time**, page 17)

YOU MAY WANT TO SAY...

- **What time does the (castle)...** Um wie viel Uhr ... (das Schloss)? *oom vee feel oohr ... (das shloss)*
  - **open?** öffnet *erffnet*
  - **close?** schließt *shleesst*

- **When does the exhibition open?** Wann wird die Ausstellung eröffnet? *vann vird dee **ows**shtelloong erer**ff**net*

- **Is it open** ist es ... geöffnet? *ist es ... ge**erff**net*
  - **on Mondays?** montags *mohntaags*
  - **at the weekend?** am Wochenende *am **vo**kenende*

- **Is it open to the public?** Ist es für die Öffentlichkeit zugänglich? *ist es fewr dee **erff**entlishkiyt tsooh**geng**lish*

YOU MAY HEAR...

- Es ist jeden Tag außer (Montag) geöffnet. *es ist **yay**den taag **ow**sser (**moh**ntaag) ge**erff**net* It's open every day except (Monday).

Es ist von (neun) bis (achtzehn Uhr) geöffnet.	es ist fon (noyn) bis (aktsayhn oohr) geerffnet	It's open from (9am) to (6pm).
Es ist (sonntags) geschlossen.	es ist (zonntaags) geshlossen	It's closed on (Sundays).
Es ist ... geschlossen. im Winter	es ist ... geshlossen im vinter	It's closed in... the winter

✳ visiting places

YOU MAY SEE...

Bitte nicht berühren.	Do not touch.
Fotografieren mit Blitzlicht verboten	No flash photography
Führungen	Guided tours
Geöffnet	Open
Kein Zutritt	No entry
Öffnungszeiten	Opening hours
Privat	Private
Wegen Renovierung geschlossen	Closed for restoration

YOU MAY WANT TO SAY...

How much does it cost to get in?	Wie viel kostet der Eintritt?	vee feel kostet der iyntritt
One adult, please.	Ein Erwachsener, bitte.	iyn ervaksener bitte

Two adults, please.	Zwei Erwachsene, bitte.	*tsviy ervaksene bitte*
One adult and two children, please.	Ein Erwachsener und zwei Kinder, bitte.	*iyn ervaksener und tsviy kinder bitte*
A family ticket, please.	Eine Familienkarte, bitte.	*iyne fameelyenkarte bitte*
Is there a reduction for...	Gibt es eine Ermäßigung für...	*geebt es iyne ermayssigoong fewr...*
students?	Studenten?	*shtoodenten*
pensioners?	Rentner?	*rentner*
children?	Kinder?	*kinder*
people with disabilities?	Behinderte?	*behinderte*
Is there...	Gibt es...	*geebt es...*
an audio tour?	eine Audio-führung?	*iyne owdio-fewroong*
a picnic area?	einen Picknick-platz?	*iynen pikniknlats*
wheelchair access?	einen Zugang für Rollstuhlfahrer?	*iynen tsoohgang fewr rollshtoohl-faarer*
Are there guided tours (in English)?	Gibt es Führungen (auf Englisch)?	*geept es fewroongen (owf english)*
Is it OK to take photos?	Kann man fotografieren?	*kan man fotografeeren*
When was this built?	Wann wurde das erbaut?	*vann voorde das erbowt*
Who painted that?	Wer hat das gemalt?	*ver hat das gemaalt*
How old is it?	Wie alt ist es?	*vee alt ist es*

YOU MAY HEAR...

Es kostet ... Euro pro Person.	*es kostet ... **oyro** pro per**zohn***	It costs ... euros per person.
Es gibt Ermäßigung für Studenten/ Rentner.	*es geebt er**mayss**igoong fewr shtoo**den**ten/**rent**ner*	There's a reduction for students/senior citizens.
Wie alt sind Ihre Kinder?	*vee alt sind **eere kin**der*	How old are your children?
Kinder unter (zehn Jahren) sind kostenlos.	***kin**der unter (tsayn **yaa**ren) zint **kos**tenlohs*	Children under (ten) go free.
Es gibt Rollstuhlrampen.	*es geebt **roll**shtoohlrampen*	There are wheelchair ramps.

✱ going on tours and trips

YOU MAY WANT TO SAY...

We'd like to join the tour to...	Wir möchten gerne den Ausflug nach ... mitmachen.	*Veer **mersh**ten **ger**ne dayn **ows**floohg naak ... **mit**maken*
What time... does it leave? does it get back?	Um wie viel Uhr... geht es los? kommen wir zurück?	*oom vee feel oohr... gayt es lohs **kom**men veer tsoo**rewk***
How long is it?	Wie lange dauert es?	*vee **lan**ge **dow**ert es*
Where does it leave from?	Wo fahren wir ab?	*voh **faa**ren veer ap*

Does the guide speak English?	Spricht der Führer Englisch?	shprisht der fewrer english
How much is it?	Wie viel kostet es?	vee feel kostet es
Is lunch/ accommodation included?	Ist Mittagessen/ Übernachtung inbegriffen?	ist mittaagessen/ ewbernaktoong inbegriffen
When's the next day trip?	Wann ist der nächste Tagesausflug?	van ist der naykste taagesowsflug
Can we hire an (English-speaking) guide?	Können wir einen (englischsprachigen) Führer mieten?	kernnen veer iynen (english-shpraakigen) fewrer meeten
I'd like to see....	Ich möchte ... besichtigen.	ish mershte ... besishtigen
I'm with a group.	Ich gehöre zu einer Reisegruppe.	ish geherre tsooh iyner riyzegrooppe
I've lost my group.	Ich habe meine Reisegruppe verloren.	ish haabe miyne riyzegrooppe ferlohren

sightseeing and activities

YOU MAY HEAR...

Es geht um ... los.	es gayt oom ... lohs	It leaves at...
Rückkehr ist...	rewkkayr ist...	It gets back at...
Der Treffpunkt ist...	der treffpoonkt ist...	It leaves from....
Er/sie nimmt ... pro Tag.	er/zee nimmt ... proh taag	He/she charges ... per day.

Wie heißt Ihre Reisegruppe?	*vee hiysst eere riyzegrooppe*	**What's the name of your group?**

✳ entertainment

● The main cities for opera, classical music and theatre in Germany are Hamburg, Berlin, Munich, Dresden and Leipzig. Bayreuth is famous for its annual Wagner Festival. Berlin and Munich in particular have a strong cabaret tradition.

● Austria has a famous music tradition. The Salzburg festival takes place every July and August. Vienna's musical attractions include a famous opera house, the Vienna Philharmonic Orchestra and the Vienna Boys' Choir, der Wiener Knabenchor.

YOU MAY SEE...

Abendvorstellung	evening performance
Ausverkauft	sold out
Diskothek	disco
Einlass ab 18 Jahren	No admittance to under-18s
Erster Rang	dress circle.
Kein Einlass während der Vorstellung.	No entry once the performance has begun.
Keine Pausen	no intervals
Kino	cinema
Konzertsaal	concert hall
Logen	boxes

sightseeing and activities

103

entertainment

Matinée	matinee
Opernhaus	opera house
Orchestersitze	orchestra stalls
Parkett	stalls
Reihe	row, tier
Rennbahn	racecourse
Tageskasse	tickets for today's performance
Theater	theatre
Tribüne, Haupttribüne	stand, grandstand
Vorverkauf	advance booking
Zirkus	circus
Zutritt	entry

YOU MAY WANT TO SAY...

● What's on in the evenings here?	Was kann man hier abends unternehmen?	vas kan man heer aabents unternaymen
● Is there anything for children?	Gibt es etwas für Kinder?	geept es etvas fewr kinder
● Is there ... round here?	Gibt es ... hier in der Nähe?	geebt es ... heer in der nayhe
a cinema	ein Kino	iyn keeno
a good club	einen guten Club	iynen goohten cloob
● What's on...	Was wird ... gespielt?	vas virt ... geshpeelt
tonight?	heute Abend	hoyte aabent
tomorrow?	morgen	morgen
● at the theatre	im Theater	im tayaater
● at the cinema	im Kino	im keeno

Is there a match on this weekend?	Gibt es dieses Wochenende ein Spiel?	*geebt es deezes vokenende iyn shpeel*
How long is it?	Wie lange dauert es?	*vee lange dowert es*
Do we need to book?	Müssen wir Karten reservieren?	*mewssen veer karten rezerveeren*
Where can I/we get tickets?	Wo kann man Karten kaufen?	*voh kan man karten kowfen*
Is it suitable for children?	Ist es für Kinder geeignet?	*ist es fewr kinder geiygnet*
Has the film got subtitles?	Ist der Film mit Untertiteln?	*ist der film mit oontertiteln*
Who's playing?	Wer spielt?	*ver shpeelt*
Who's in that?	Wer spielt darin mit?	*ver shpeelt darin mit*

YOU MAY HEAR...

Es fängt um (sieben) an.	*es fengt oom (zeeben) an*	It starts at (seven).
Es ist um (halb elf) zu Ende.	*es ist oom (halp elf) tsooh ende*	It finishes at (ten thirty).
Er ist synchronisiert.	*er ist sewnkronizeert*	It's dubbed.
Er hat (englische) Untertitel.	*er hat (englishe) oontertitel*	It's got (English) subtitles.

105

* booking tickets

- **Can you get me tickets for...** — Können Sie mir Karten für ... besorgen? — *kernnen zee meer karten fewr ... bezorgen*

    the ballet? — das Ballett — *das ballett*
    the theatre? — das Theater — *das tayaater*

- **Are there any seats left for Saturday?** — Haben Sie noch Karten für Samstag? — *haaben zee nok karten fewr zamstaag*

- **I'd like to book...** — Ich möchte ... reservieren — *ich mershte ... rezerveeren*

    a box — eine Loge — *eine lohshe*
    two seats — zwei Plätze — *tsviy pletse*

- **in the stalls** — im Parkett — *im parket*
  in the dress circle — im ersten Rang — *im ersten rang*

- **Do you have anything cheaper?** — Haben Sie etwas Billigeres? — *haaben zee etvas billigeres*

- **Is there wheelchair access?** — Gibt es einen Rollstuhlzugang? — *geept es iynen rollshtoohltsoohgang*

- Wie viele? — *vee feele* — How many?
- Für wann? — *fewr vann* — When for?
- Haben Sie eine Kreditkarte? — *haaben zee iyne kredeetkarte* — Do you have a credit card?

✱ at the show

Two for tonight's performance.	Zwei Karten für heute Abend, bitte.	tsviy fewr **hoyte aabent bitte**
One adult and two children, please.	Ein Erwachsener und zwei Kinder, bitte.	iyn er**vak**sener und tsviy **kin**der **bitte**
How much is that?	Wie viel kostet das?	vee feel **kostet** das
We'd like to sit...	Wir möchten ... sitzen.	veer **mersh**ten ... **zit**sen
at the front	vorne	**for**ne
at the back	hinten	**hin**ten
in the middle	in der Mitte	in der **mitte**
We've reserved seats.	Wir haben Karten zurücklegen lassen.	veer **haa**ben **karten** tsoo**rewk**laygen **lassen**
My name is...	Mein Name ist...	miyn **naa**me ist...
Is there an interval?	Gibt es eine Pause?	geept es **iyne powze**
Where's...	Wo ist...	voh ist...
the dress circle?	der erste Rang?	der **erste rang**
Where are the toilets?	Wo sind die Toiletten?	voh sint dee to**aletten**
Can you stop talking, please?	Könnten Sie bitte leise sein!	**kernn**ten zee **bitte liy**ze ziyn

YOU MAY HEAR...

- Tut mir Leid, wir sind heute Abend ausverkauft. — *tooht mir liyt, veer sint **hoyte aa**bent **ows**ferkowft* — **Sorry, we're full tonight.**

- Wo möchten Sie sitzen? — *voh **mersh**ten zee **zit**sen* — **Where do you want to sit?**

* sports and activities

YOU MAY SEE...

Angeln verboten	no fishing
Erste Hilfe	first aid
Freibad	outdoor swimming pool
Fußballplatz	football pitch
Gefahr	danger
Hallenbad	indoor swimming pool
Schwimmbad	swimming pool
Schwimmen verboten	no swimming
Skiverleih	ski hire
Strand	beach
Tennisplatz	tennis court

YOU MAY WANT TO SAY...

- Can I... — Kann ich... — *kann ish...*
  - go fishing? — angeln gehen? — *angeln **gay**en*
  - go skiing? — Ski laufen? — *shee **low**fen*
  - go swimming? — schwimmen gehen? — *sh**vim**men **gay**en*

Where can I/we...	Wo kann man...	*voh kann man...*
play tennis?	Tennis spielen?	**tenn**is **shpeel**en
play golf?	Golf spielen?	golf **shpeel**en
I'm...	Ich bin...	*ish bin...*
a beginner	Anfänger	**an**fenger
quite experienced	ziemlich erfahren	**tseem**lish er**faar**en
How much does it cost...	Wie viel kostet es...	*vee feel **kost**et es...*
per hour?	pro Stunde?	proh **shtoond**e
per day?	pro Tag?	proh taag
per week?	pro Woche?	proh **vok**e
Can I hire...	Kann ich ... mieten?	*kann ish ... **meet**en*
equipment?	die Ausrüstung	dee **ows**rewstoong
clubs?	Golfschläger	**golf**shlayger
Is it possible to have lessons?	Kann man Stunden nehmen?	*kann man **shtoond**en **naym**en*
Do you have to be a member?	Muss man Mitglied sein?	*mooss man **mit**gleet ziyn*
Can children do it too?	Können auch Kinder mitmachen?	*kernnen owk **kin**der **mit**maken*
What's...	Wie ist...	*vee ist...*
the water like?	das Wasser?	das **vass**er

* at the beach, river or pool

Is it OK to swim...	Kann man ... schwimmen?	*kann man ... **shvimm**en*
here?	hier	heer

at the beach, river or pool

in the river?	im Fluss	*im flooss*
● **Is it dangerous?**	Ist es gefährlich?	*ist es **gefayr**lish*
● **Is it safe for children?**	Ist es sicher für Kinder?	*ist es **sisher** fewr **kinder***
● **Is the water clean?**	Ist das Wasser sauber?	*ist das **vasser** zowber*

YOU MAY HEAR...

● Seien Sie vorsichtig, es ist gefährlich.	*ziyen zee **fohr**zishtig, es ist **gefayr**lish*	Be careful, it's dangerous.
● Die Strömung ist sehr stark.	*dee **shtrer**moong ist zayr shtark*	The current is very strong.
● Es ist sehr windig.	*es ist zayr **vin**dig*	It's very windy.

shops&services

* shopping

Andenkenladen	souvenirs
Bäckerei	baker's
Bitte nicht berühren	please do not touch
Buchhandlung	bookshop
Delikatessen	delicatessen
Drogerie	chemist
Durchgehend geöffnet	open all day
Eingang	entrance
Elektrogeschäft	electrical goods
Feinkostgeschäft	delicatessen
Fischladen	fishmonger's
Fleisch- und Wurstwaren	butcher's
Friseursalon	hairdresser's
Geöffnet	open
Geschenkartikel	gift shop/souvenirs
Geschlossen	closed
Juwelier	jeweller's
Sonderangebot	on offer
Kasse	cashier
Kiosk	newsagent's
Konditorei	cake shop
Lebensmittel	groceries
Metzgerei	butcher's
Modegeschäft	clothes/fashions
Nachtdienst/Sonntagsdienst	duty chemist (or doctor)
Obst- und Gemüsehandlung	fruit and veg shop
Optiker	optician's
Öffnungszeiten	opening hours

Postamt	post office
Reduziert	sale
Reformhaus	health foods
Reinigung	dry cleaner's
Schallplatten	records
Ausverkauf	closing down sale
Schuhgeschäft	shoe shop
Spielwarengeschäft	toy shop
Süßwaren	sweet shop
Umkleidekabine	fitting rooms
Warenhaus	department store
Weinhandlung	off licence (wine shop)

YOU MAY WANT TO SAY...

● Where is...	Wo ist...	*voh ist...*
the main shopping street?	die Haupteinkaufsstraße?	*dee howptiynkowfsstraasse*
the post office?	das Postamt?	*das postamt*
● Where can I buy...	Wo kann ich ... kaufen?	*voh kann ish ... kowfen*
mobile phone cards?	Handykarten	*hendeekarten*
walking boots?	Wanderschuhe	*vandershoohe*
● I'd like ..., please.	Ich hätte gerne ... bitte.	*ish hette gerne ... bitte*
that one there	dieses dort	*deezes dort*
two of those	zwei von diesen	*tsviy fon deezen*

shopping

- **Have you got...?** — Haben Sie...? — *haaben zee...*

- **How much does it/they cost?** — Was kostet es/sie? — *vas kostet es/zee*

- **Can you write it down, please?** — Könnten Sie das bitte aufschreiben? — *kernnten zee das bitte owfshriyben*

- **I'm just looking.** — Ich möchte mich nur umschauen. — *ish mershte mish noohr oomshowen*

- **You've got one in the window.** — Sie haben eins im Schaufenster. — *zee haaben iyns im showfenster*

- **I'll take it.** — Ich nehme es. — *ish nayme es*

- **Is there a guarantee?** — Gibt es eine Garantie darauf? — *geept es iyne garantee darowf*

- **I need to think about it.** — Ich muss es mir noch einmal überlegen. — *ish moss es meer nok iynmaal ewberlaygen*

YOU MAY HEAR...

- Was darf's sein? — *vas darfs ziyn* — Can I help you?

- Es kostet ... Euro. — *es kostet ... oyro* — It costs ... euros.

- Tut mir Leid, ausverkauft. — *tooht meer liyt, owsferkowft* — I'm sorry, we've sold out.

- Wir können es Ihnen bestellen. — *veer kernnen es eenen beshtellen* — We can order it for you.

* paying

- **Where do I pay?** Wo muss ich bezahlen? *voh mooss ish betsaalen*

- **Do you take credit cards?** Nehmen Sie Kreditkarten? *naymen zee kredeetkarten*

- **Can you wrap it, please?** Könnten Sie es bitte einpacken? *kernnten zee es bitte iynpaken*

- **Can I have...** Dürfte ich ... haben? *dewrfte ish ... haaben*

  the receipt? den Kassenzettel *dayn kassentsettel*
  a bag, please? eine Tüte *iyne tewte*

- **Sorry, I haven't got any change.** Tut mir Leid, ich habe kein Kleingeld. *tooht mir liyt ish haabe kiyn kliyngelt*

- Ist es ein Geschenk? *ist es iyn geshenk* Is it a gift?

- Möchten Sie eine Tüte? *mershten zee iyne tewte* Do you want a bag?

- Wie möchten Sie bezahlen? *vee mershten zee betsaalen* How do you want to pay?

- Dürfte ich bitte Ihren Ausweis sehen? *dewrfte ish bitte eeren owsviys zayen* Can I see your passport, please?

- Haben Sie es kleiner? *haaben zee es kliyner* Have you got anything smaller?

shops and services

115

✳ buying clothes and shoes
(see **clothes and shoe sizes**, page 21)

(see **clothes and shoe sizes**, page 21)

YOU MAY WANT TO SAY...

- Have you got...
  the next size
  up/down?
  another colour?

  Haben Sie es ...
  eine Nummer
  größer/kleiner?
  in einer anderen
  Farbe?

  haaben zee es...
  *iyne noommer
  grersser/kliyner*
  *in iyner anderen
  farbe*

- Do you know
  what size this is in
  British sizes?

  Wissen Sie, welcher
  britischen Größe das
  entspricht?

  *vissen zee, velsher
  breetishen grersse das
  entshprisht*

- I'm size...

  Ich habe Größe...

  ish haabe grersse...

- I'm looking for...
  a shirt
  a jumper

  Ich suche...
  ein Hemd
  einen Pullover

  *ish soohke...
  iyn hemt
  iynen pullohver*

- a pair of...
  trainers
  shoes

  ein Paar...
  Turnschuhe
  Schuhe

  *iyn paar...
  toornshoohe
  shoohe*

- Where are the
  changing rooms?

  Wo sind die
  Umkleidekabinen?

  *voh zint dee
  oomkliydekabeenen*

✳ changing rooms

YOU MAY WANT TO SAY...

- Can I try this on,
  please?

  Dürfte ich es
  anprobieren?

  *dewrfte ish es
  anprobeeren*

- It doesn't fit.

  Es passt nicht.

  es passt nisht

shops and services

It's too big.	Es ist zu groß.	*es ist tsooh grohss*
It's too small.	Es ist zu klein.	*es ist tsooh kliyn*
It doesn't suit me.	Es steht mir nicht.	*es shtayt meer nisht*

✳ exchanges and refunds

YOU MAY WANT TO SAY...

Excuse me, this is faulty.	Entschuldigung, dies hat einen Fehler.	*ent**shool**digoong dees hat **iy**nen **fay**ler*
Excuse me, this doesn't fit.	Entschuldigung, es passt nicht.	*ent**shool**digoong es passt nisht*
Can I have a refund, please?	Könnte ich mein Geld zurückhaben?	***kernn**te ish miyn gelt tsoo**rewk**haaben*
Can I exchange this, please?	Kann ich es umtauschen?	*kann ish es **oom**towshen*
I'd like...	Ich möchte dies...	*ish **mersh**te dees...*
to return this	zurückbringen	*tsoo**rewk**bringen*
to change this	umtauschen	***oom**towshen*

YOU MAY HEAR...

Haben Sie den Kassenzettel?	*haaben zee dayn kassentsettel*	Have you got the receipt?
Sie können es umtauschen.	*zee kernnen es oomtowshen*	You can exchange it.

shops and services

117

✳ bargaining

- Is this your best price? — Können Sie mir keinen besseren Preis machen? — *kernnen zee meer kiynen besseren priys maken*

- It's too expensive. — Es ist zu teuer. — *es ist tsooh toyer*

- Is there a reduction for cash? — Gibt es Barzahlerrabatt? — *geebt es baartsaalerrabatt*

- That's my final offer. — Dies ist mein letztes Angebot. — *dees ist miyn letstes angeboht*

✳ at the drugstore
(see **at the chemist's**, page 130)

● Although you may find some toiletries and cosmetics at the chemist's (Apotheke), these are usually medicated or for special conditions such as delicate skins or allergies. For toiletries, cosmetics, perfumes, creams, etc. you need a drugstore (Drogerie).

- I need... — Ich brauche... — *ish browke...*
  - shampoo — Shampoo — *shampoo*
  - shower gel — Duschgel — *dooshgayl*
  - toothpaste — Zahnpasta — *tsaanpasta*
  - tampons — Tampons — *tampongs*
  - sanitary towels — Damenbinden — *daamenbinden*
  - suntan lotion — ein Sonnen-schutzmittel — *iyn zonnen-shootsmittel*

shops and services

118

aftersun	Aftersun-Lotion	*aftersun-lohtyohn*
I am looking for...	Ich suche nach einem...	*ish zoohke naak iynem...*
a perfume	Parfüm	*parfewm*
a pink nail varnish	rosafarbenen Nagellack	*rohzafarbenen naagellak*

* photography

Can you develop this film for me?	Können Sie diesen Film für mich entwickeln?	*kernnen zee deezen film fewr mish entvikeln*
I have a digital camera.	Ich habe eine Digitalkamera.	*ish haabe iyne digitaalkamera*
Can you print from (this memory card)?	Können Sie Abzüge von (dieser Speicherkarte) machen?	*kernnen zee aptsewge von (deezer shpiysherkarte) maken*
When will it be ready?	Wann wird es fertig sein?	*van virt es fertig ziyn*
Do you have an express service?	Haben Sie einen Schnelldienst?	*haaben zee iynen shnelldeenst*
How much does it cost...	Wie viel kostet ...	*vee feel kostet...*
per film?	ein Film?	*iyn film*
per print?	ein Abzug?	*iyn aptsoohg*

at the off-licence

- **I need...** — Ich brauche... — *ish browke*
  - **a colour film** — einen Farbfilm — *iynen farpfilm*
  - **a black and white film** — einen Schwarzweißfilm — *iynen shwartswyssfilm*
  - **a memory card** — eine Speicherkarte — *iyne shpiysherkarte*

- **I'd like ... please.** — Ich hätte gerne... — *ish hette gerne...*
  - **a 24-exposure film** — einen 24er-Film — *iynen feeroontsvantsiger film*
  - **a disposable camera** — eine Wegwerf-kamera — *iyne vegverfkamera*

YOU MAY HEAR...

In welcher Größe möchten Sie Ihre Abzüge?	*in velsher grersse mershten zee eere aptsewge*	What size do you want your prints?
Möchten Sie matt oder Hochglanz?	*mershten zee matt ohder hokglants*	Do you want them matt or glossy?
Welche Filmgeschwindigkeit möchten Sie?	*velshe filmgeshvindigkiyt mershten zee*	What speed film do you want?

✳ at the off-licence

YOU MAY WANT TO SAY...

- **Have you got any...** — Haben Sie... — *haaben zee...*
  - **local beers?** — einheimisches Bier? — *iynhiymishes beer*
  - **special offers?** — irgendwelche Sonderangebote? — *irgentvelshe zonderangebohte*

shops and services

120

- A case of this wine, please.
  Eine Kiste von diesem Wein, bitte.
  iyne kiste fon deezem viyn bitte

- A crate of this beer, please.
  Einen Kasten von diesem Bier, bitte.
  iynen kasten fon deezem beer bitte

- Can you recommend...
  Können Sie ... empfehlen?
  kernnen zee ... empfaylen

  a local wine?
  einen einheimischen Wein
  iynen iynhiymishen viyn

  a light beer?
  ein leichtes Bier
  iyn liyshtes beer

- Is this sweet or dry?
  Ist der lieblich oder trocken?
  ist der leeplish ohder troken

✳ at the post office

- Post offices (Postamt) in Germany, Austria and Switzerland are generally open from 8am–12pm and 2pm–6 or 7pm Monday–Friday, and Saturday mornings. Letterboxes (Briefkasten) are painted yellow.

- If you only want stamps, you can get them at Kiosks or from any shop that sells postcards.

YOU MAY WANT TO SAY...

- A stamp/Five stamps for...
  Eine Briefmarke/Fünf Briefmarken nach...
  iyne breefmarke/ fewnf breefmarken nak...

  Great Britain
  Großbritannien
  grohssbreetannyen

  America
  Amerika
  amayreeka

- **Can I send this...**   Kann ich dies per ...   *kan ish dees per ...*
                                  schicken?   *shiken*

  registered?   Einschreiben   *iynshriyben*
  airmail?   Luftpost   *looftpost*

- **It contains...**   Es ist/sind ... drin.   *es ist/zint ... drin*

- **Do you change**   Kann ich hier Geld   *kan ish heer **gelt***
  money here?   wechseln?   *vekseln*

- **Can I have a**   Dürfte ich eine   *dewrfte ich iyne*
  receipt, please?   Quittung haben?   *kvittoong haaben*

YOU MAY HEAR...

- Postkarten oder   ***post**karten **ohder***   **For postcards or**
  Briefe?   ***bree**fe*   **letters?**

- Legen Sie es bitte   *layqen zee es **bitte***   **Put it on the scales,**
  auf die Waage.   *owf dee **vaage***   **please.**

- Was ist darin?   *vas ist da**rin***   **What's in it?**

- Füllen Sie   *fewllen zee*   **Please fill in this**
  bitte dieses   ***bitte dee**zes*   **customs declaration**
  Paketformular aus.   *pa**kayt**formoolaar   **form.**
                           ows*

✳ at the bank

- Outside the large city centres, banks in Germany, Austria and Switzerland are usually open Mondays to Fridays. Most of them close for lunch for two hours.

shops and services

YOU MAY WANT TO SAY...

Excuse me, where's the foreign exchange counter?	Entschuldigung, wo kann ich Devisen wechseln?	*entshooldigoong voh kan ish dayveezen vekseln*
Is there a cash machine here?	Gibt es hier einen Geldautomaten?	*geept es heer iynen geltowtomaaten*
The cash machine has retained my card.	Der Geldautomat hat meine Karte eingezogen.	*der geltowtomaat hat miyne karte iyngetsohgen*
I've forgotten my PIN.	Ich habe meine PIN-Nummer vergessen.	*ish haabe miyne pin-noommer fergessen*
Can I check my account, please?	Dürfte ich bitte mein Konto überprüfen?	*dewrfte ish bitte miyn konto ewberprewfen*
My account number is...	Meine Kontonummer ist...	*miyne kontonoommer ist...*
My name is...	Mein Name ist...	*miyn naame ist...*
Has my money arrived yet?	Ist das Geld schon angekommen?	*ist das gelt shohn angekommen*

YOU MAY HEAR...

Ihren Ausweis bitte.	*eeren owsviys bitte*	ID/Passport, please.
Wie heißen Sie?	*vee hiyssen zee*	What's your name?

Es sind ... auf Ihrem Konto.	*es zint... owf eerem konto*	Your balance is...
Sie haben Ihr Konto um ... überzogen.	*zee haaben eer konto oom... ewbertsohgen*	You're overdrawn by...

✳ changing money

● You can change money, traveller's cheques or Eurocheques into euros at banks, and other places (hotels, travel agencies, airports, etc.) where you see the sign Wechselstube or Wechselbüro.

YOU MAY WANT TO SAY...

● I'd like to change...	Ich möchte gerne...	*ish mershte gerne...*
these traveller's cheques	diese Reiseschecks einlösen	*deeze riyzesheks iynlerzen*
one hundred pounds	einhundert Pfund wechseln	*iynhoondert pfoont vekseln*
● Can I have...	Könnte ich ... haben?	*kernnte ish ... haaben*
small/new notes?	kleinere/neue Banknoten	*kliynere/noye banknohten*
some change?	etwas Kleingeld	*etvas kliyngelt*
● Can I get money out on my credit card?	Kann ich mit meiner Kreditkarte Geld abheben?	*kann ish mit miyner kredeetkarte gelt aphayben*
● What's the rate today for...	Wie ist der heutige Wechselkurs für...	*vee ist der hoytige vekselkoors fewr...*
the pound?	englische Pfund?	*englishe pfoont*
the dollar?	den Dollar?	*dayn dollar*
the euro?	den Euro?	*dayn oyro*

YOU MAY HEAR...

Wie viel?	*vee feel*	How much?
Ihren Pass, bitte.	*eeren pass bitte*	Passport, please.
Bitte hier unterschreiben.	*bitte heer oontershriyben*	Sign here, please.
Ein Pfund sind ... Euro.	*iyn pfoont zint... oyro*	It's at ... euros to the pound.

✴ telephones

To call abroad, first dial 00, then the code for the country you are dialling – for the UK it's 44 from Germany, Austria and Switzerland. Follow this with the town code minus the first zero, and then the number you want. For example, to call a London number, dial 00 44 20, then the usual 8-digit number.

YOU MAY WANT TO SAY...

Where's the (nearest) phone?	Wo ist das (nächste) Telefon?	*voh ist das nekste telefohn*
Is there a public phone?	Gibt es hier eine Telefonzelle?	*geept es heer iyne telefohntselle*
Do you have change for the phone?	Haben Sie Kleingeld fürs Telefon?	*haaben zee kliyngelt fewrs telefohn*

I'd like to...	Ich möchte...	ish *mershte*...
buy a phone card	eine Telefonkarte	*iyne* telefohnkarte
make a call to England	einen Anruf nach England machen	*iynen* anroohf nak englant maken
make a reverse charge call	ein R-Gespräch führen	iyn *err*-geshprayk *fewren*
The number is...	Die Nummer ist...	dee *noommer* ist...
How much does it cost per minute?	Wie viel kostet die Minute?	vee feel kostet dee minoohte
What's the area code for...?	Wie ist die Vorwahl für...?	vee ist dee fohrvaal fewr...
What's the country code for...?	Wie ist die Landesvorwahl für...?	vee ist dee landesforvaal fewr...
How do I get an outside line?	Wie bekomme ich eine externe Leitung?	vee bekomme ish iyne eksterne liytoong
Hello.	Hallo.	hallo
It's ... speaking.	... am Apparat.	... am apparaat
Can I speak to...?	Dürfte ich bitte mit ... sprechen?	dewrfte ish bitte mit ... shpreshen
When will he/she be back?	Wann ist er/sie zurück?	vann ist er/zee tsoorewk
I'll ring back later.	Ich rufe später noch einmal an.	ish roohfe shpayter nok iynmaal an
Can I leave a message?	Kann ich eine Nachricht hinterlassen?	kann ish iyne naakrisht hinterlassen
Can you say ... called?	Könnten Sie bitte ausrichten, dass ... angerufen hat?	kernnten zee bitte owsrikten dass ... angeroohfen hat

My number is...	Meine Telefonnummer ist...	*miyne telefohnnoomer ist*
Sorry, I've got the wrong number.	Entschuldigung, ich habe mich verwählt.	*entshooldigoong ish haabe mish fervaylt*
More slowly, please.	Langsamer, bitte.	*langzamer bitte*

YOU MAY HEAR...

Hallo.	*hallo*	Hello.
Am Apparat.	*am apparaat*	Speaking.
Wer ist am Apparat?	*ver ist am apparaat*	Who's calling?
Einen Moment, bitte.	*iynen moment bitte*	Just a moment.
Es ist besetzt.	*es ist bayzetst*	It's engaged.
Möchten Sie dranbleiben?	*mershten zee dranbliyben*	Do you want to hold?

* mobiles

● You can buy prepaid cards for your mobile (Handy) from phone shops (which often carry the same logo as in the UK), from petrol stations and at Kiosken.

YOU MAY WANT TO SAY...

Have you got...	Haben Sie...	*haaben zee...*
a charger for this phone?	ein Ladegerät für dieses Handy?	*iyn laadgerayt fewr deezes hendy*
a SIM card?	eine SIM-Karte?	*iyne zimkarte*

- **Can I hire a mobile?** / Kann ich ein Handy mieten? / *kann ish iyn **hend**y **meet**en*
- **What's the tariff?** / Wie hoch ist der Tarif? / *vee hok ist der ta**reef***
- **Are text messages included?** / Sind SMS inbegriffen? / *zint es-em-es **in**begriffen*
- **Do I have to dial a code?** / Muss ich eine Vorwahlnummer wählen? / *mooss ish **iyne** **fohr**vaalnoommer **vay**len*

✳ the internet

YOU MAY WANT TO SAY...

- **I'd like to...** / Ich möchte gerne... / *ish **mersh**te gerne...*
  - **log on** / ins Internet / *ins **internet***
  - **check my emails** / meine E-Mail lesen / *miyne eemail **lay**zen*
- **Can you...** / Könnten Sie dies... / *kernnten zee dees...*
  - **print this?** / ausdrucken? / *owsdrooken*
  - **scan this?** / einscannen? / *iynskennen*
- **Do you have...** / Haben Sie... / *haaben zee...*
  - **a CD rom?** / eine CD-ROM? / *iyne tsay-day-**rom***
  - **a USB lead?** / ein USB-Kabel? / *iyn ooh-es-**bay**-kaabel*

✳ faxes

YOU MAY WANT TO SAY...

- **What's your fax number?** / Wie ist Ihre Faxnummer? / *vee ist **eere** **faks**noommer*
- **Can you send this fax for me, please?** / Könnten Sie bitte dieses Fax für mich schicken? / *kernnten zee bitte deezes faks fewr mish **shik**en*

health&safety

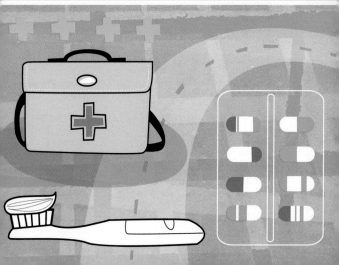

* at the chemist's
(see **at the drugstore**, page 118)

● Chemists (Apotheken) have the same opening hours as shops. They sell both prescription medicines (rezeptpflichtige Medikamente) and pharmacy-bound medicines (apothekenpflichtige Medikamente). Apotheken also sell high-quality and medicated cosmetics and skin care products. For cosmetics, toiletries, perfumes and health foods, go to a Drogerie.

● Have you got something for...	Haben Sie etwas gegen...	*haaben zee etvas gaygen...*
sunburn?	Sonnenbrand?	*zonnenbrant*
diarrhoea?	Durchfall?	*doorshfall*
period pains?	Monatsschmerzen?	*mohnaats-shmertsen*
headaches?	Kopfschmerzen?	*kopfshmertsen*
stomach ache?	Magenschmerzen?	*maagenshmertsen*
a sore throat?	Halsweh?	*halsvay*
● I need some ... please.	Ich hätte gerne...	*Ich hette gerne...*
aspirin	Aspirin	*aspeereen*
plasters	Pflaster	*pflaster*
painkillers	Schmerztabletten	*shmertstabletten*
insect repellent	ein Insekten-schutzmittel	*iyn inzekten-shootsmittel*
travel sickness pills	ein Mittel gegen Reisekrankheit	*iyn mittel gaygen riyzekrankhiyt*

Can you make up this prescription, please?	Dieses Rezept, bitte.	*deezes retsept bitte*

✳ at the doctor's
(see **medical complaints and conditions**, page 133)

(see **medical complaints and conditions**, page 133)

YOU MAY WANT TO SAY...

I need a doctor (who speaks English).	Ich brauche einen Arzt (der Englisch spricht).	*ish browke iynen artst (der english sprisht)*
Can I have an appointment for today/tomorrow?	Könnte ich für heute/ morgen einen Termin haben?	*kernnte ich fewr hoyte/morgen iynen termeen haaben?*
I've run out of my medication.	Mir sind die Medikamente ausgegangen.	*meer zint dee medeekamente owsgegangen*
I'm on medication for...	Ich nehme Medikamente gegen...	*ish nayme medeekamente gaygen...*
I've had a ... jab.	Ich bin gegen ... geimpft.	*ish bin gaygen ... gayimpft*
tetanus	Tetanus	*tetanoos*
typhoid	Typhus	*tewfoos*
rabies	Tollwut	*tollvooht*
He/She has had a ... vaccination.	Er/Sie ist gegen ... geimpft.	*er/zee ist gaygen ... gayimpft*
polio	Kinderlähmung	*kinderlaymoong*
measles	Masern	*maazern*
mumps	Mumps	*moomps*

health and safety

He/She has had the triple MMR vaccination.	Er/Sie ist gegen Masern, Mumps und Röteln geimpft worden.	er/zee ist gaygen maazern moomps oont rerteln gayimpft vorden
Can I have a receipt for my health insurance?	Könnte ich ein Quittung für meine Krankenkasse haben?	kernnte ish iyne kvittoong fewr miyne krankenkasse haaben

✳ describing your symptoms

● To indicate where the pain is you can simply point and say 'It hurts here' (Es tut hier weh).

YOU MAY WANT TO SAY...

I don't feel well.	Ich fühle mich nicht wohl.	ish fewle mish nisht vohl
It's my...	Es ist mein...	es ist miyn
It hurts here.	Es tut hier weh.	es tooht heer vay
My ... hurts. stomach head face	Mein ... tut weh. Bauch Kopf Gesicht	miyn ... tooht vay bowk kopf gezisht
His ears hurt.	Seine Ohren tun weh.	ziyne ohren toohn vay
Her feet hurt.	Ihre Füße tun weh.	eere fewsse toohn vay
I've got... a sore throat diarrhoea	Ich habe... Halsschmerzen Durchfall	ish haabe... halsshmertsen doorshfall

● I feel...	Mir ist...	*meer ist...*
sick	schlecht	*shlesht*
dizzy	schwindlig	***shvindlig***
● I can't...	Ich kann nicht...	*ish kann nisht...*
breathe	atmen	***aatmen***
sleep	schlafen	***shlaafen***
● I've cut myself.	Ich habe mich geschnitten.	*ish **haabe** mish ge**shnitten***
● I've burnt myself.	Ich habe mich verbrannt.	*ish **haabe** mish fer**brannt***
● I've been sick.	Ich habe mich übergeben.	*ich **haabe** mish ewber**gayben***

✻ medical complaints and conditions

YOU MAY WANT TO SAY...

● I am...	Ich habe...	*ish **haabe**...*
asthmatic	Asthma	***astma***
diabetic	Diabetes	*dee**abaytes***
arthritic	Arthritis	*aar**treetis***
● I am...	Ich bin...	*ish bin...*
blind	blind	*blint*
deaf	schwerhörig	*shvayr**herrig***
a wheelchair user	im Rollstuhl	*im **rollshtoohl***
● I have difficulty walking.	Ich kann schlecht laufen.	*ish kann shlesht **lowfen***
● She is pregnant.	Sie ist schwanger.	*zee ist **shvanger***

health and safety

133

medical complaints

- **I have high/low blood pressure.**
  Ich habe zu hohen/ niedrigen Blutdruck.
  ish haabe tsooh hohen/needrigen bloohtdrook

- **I have a heart condition.**
  Ich bin herzkrank.
  ish bin hayrtskrank

- **I am allergic to...**
  Ich habe eine Allergie gegen...
  ish haabe iyne allergee gaygen...
    - **antibiotics**
      Antibiotika
      antibeeyohtika
    - **cortisone**
      Cortison
      kortizohn

- **I suffer from...**
  Ich leide an...
  ish liyde an...
    - **hayfever**
      Heuschnupfen
      hoyshnoopfen
    - **angina**
      Angina
      angeena

YOU MAY HEAR...

Wo tut es weh?	*voh tooht es vay*	Where does it hurt?
Nehmen Sie Medikamente ein?	*naymen zee medeekamente iyn*	Are you on medication?
Haben Sie irgendwelche Allergien?	*haaben zee irgentvelshe allergee-en*	Are you allergic to anything?
Machen Sie sich bitte frei.	*maken zee zish bitte friy*	Get undressed, please.
Machen Sie bitte den Oberkörper frei.	*maken zee bitte dayn ohberkerper friy*	Take your top off.
Sie haben eine Infektion.	*zee haaben iyne infektion*	You've got an infection.

health and safety

134

Ich brauche...	ish *browke*...	I need...
eine Blutprobe	*iyne blooht*prohbe	a blood sample
eine Urinprobe	*iyne ooreen*prohbe	a urine sample

| Das muss geröntgt werden. | das mooss ger*erntkt verden* | You need an X-ray. |

| Ich gebe Ihnen eine Spritze. | ish *gaybe eenen iyne shpritse* | I'm going to give you an injection. |

| Sind Sie allergisch gegen Penizillin? | zint zee *allergish gaygen peneetsilleen* | Are you allergic to pencillin? |

| Sie brauchen Ruhe. | zee *browken roohe* | You must rest. |

| Sie dürfen nichts trinken. | zee *dewrfen nishts trinken* | You mustn't drink. |

| Sie müssen ins Krankenhaus. | zee *mewssen ins kranken*hows | You need to go to hospital. |

| Sie haben Ihren Knöchel verstaucht. | zee *haaben eeren knershel fershtowkt* | You've sprained your ankle. |

| Sie haben Ihren Arm gebrochen. | zee *haaben eeren arm gebroken* | You've broken your arm. |

Sie haben...	zee *haaben*...	You've got ...
eine Grippe	*iyne grippe*	flu
Bronchitis	*bronsheetis*	bronchitis

✳ parts of the body

YOU MAY WANT TO SAY...

ankle	der Knöchel	*knershel*
appendix	der Blinddarm	*blintdarm*
arm	der Arm	*arm*

back	der Rücken	*rewken*
bladder	die Blase	*blaaze*
blood	das Blut	*blooht*
bone	der Knochen	*knoken*
bottom	das Gesäß	*gesayss*
breast	die Brust	*broost*
cartilage	der Knorpel	*knorpel*
chest	der Brustkorb	*broostkorp*
chin	das Kinn	*kin*
collar bone	das Schlüsselbein	*shlewsselbiyn*
ear	das Ohr	*ohr*
eye	das Auge	*owge*
face	das Gesicht	*gezisht*
finger	der Finger	*finger*
foot	der Fuß	*foohss*
genitals	die Genitalien	*genitaalyen*
gland	die Drüse	*drewze*
hand	die Hand	*hant*
head	der Kopf	*kopf*
heart	das Herz	*hayrts*
hip	die Hüfte	*hewfte*
joint	das Gelenk	*gelenk*
kidney	die Niere	*neere*
knee	das Knie	*knee*
leg	das Bein	*biyn*
ligament	das Band	*bant*
lip	die Lippe	*lippe*
liver	die Leber	*layber*
lung	die Lunge	*loonge*

mouth	der Mund	*moont*
muscle	der Muskel	*mooskel*
neck	der Hals	*hals*
nerve	der Nerv	*nerf*
nose	die Nase	*naaze*
penis	der Penis	*pehnis*
rib	die Rippe	*rippe*
shoulder	die Schulter	*shoolter*
skin	die Haut	*howt*
spine	das Rückgrat	*rewkgraat*
stomach	der Magen	*maagen*
testicles	die Hoden	*hohden*
thigh	der Oberschenkel	*ohbershenkel*
throat	die Kehle	*kayle*
toe	der Zeh	*tsay*
tongue	die Zunge	*tsoonge*
tonsils	die Mandeln	*mandeln*
tooth	der Zahn	*tsaan*
vagina	die Vagina	*vageena*
vein	die Ader	*aader*
wrist	das Handgelenk	*hantgelenk*

✻ at the dentist's

YOU MAY WANT TO SAY...

● I've got toothache. | Ich habe Zahnschmerzen. | *ish haabe tsaanshmertsen*

● It's my wisdom teeth. | Es sind meine Weisheitszähne. | *es zint miyne viyshiytstsayne*

at the dentist's

- I've lost...
  - a filling
  - a crown/cap

  Ich habe ... verloren.
  eine Füllung
  eine Krone

  ish haabe ... ferlohren
  iyne fewlloong
  iyne krohne

- He/She's lost...
  - a filling
  - a crown/cap

  Er/Sie hat ... verloren.
  eine Füllung
  eine Krone

  er/zee hat ... ferlohren
  iyne fewlloong
  iyne krohne

- I've broken a tooth.

  Mir ist ein Stück
  Zahn abgebrochen.

  meer ist iyn stewk
  tsaan apgebroken

- Can you fix it
  temporarily?

  Können Sie es
  provisorisch
  reparieren?

  kernnen zee es
  provizohrish
  repareeren

- How much will it
  cost?

  Wie viel wird es
  kosten?

  vee feel virt es kosten

YOU MAY HEAR...

- Bitte den Mund
  weit aufmachen.

  bitte dayn moont viyt
  owfmaken

  Open wide.

- Sie brauchen eine
  Füllung.

  zee browken iyne
  fewlloong

  You need a filling.

- Der Zahn muss
  raus.

  der tsaan moos rows

  I'll have to take it
  out.

- Ich werde Ihnen
  eine Spritze geben

  ish verde eenen iyne
  shpritse gayben

  I'm going to give
  you an injection.

health and safety

✳ emergencies

EMERGENCY TELEPHONE NUMBERS

Country	Police	Fire	Ambulance
Germany	110	112	110
Austria	133	122	144
Switzerland	117	118	144

YOU MAY WANT TO SAY...

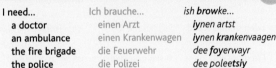

- I need...
  a doctor
  an ambulance
  the fire brigade
  the police

  Ich brauche...
  einen Arzt
  einen Krankenwagen
  die Feuerwehr
  die Polizei

  ish browke...
  iynen artst
  iynen kran{kenvaagen
  dee foyerwayr
  dee poleetsiy

- Immediately!

  Sofort!

  zofort

- Help!

  Hilfe!

  hilfe

- There's a fire.

  Es brennt.

  es brennt

- There's been an accident.

  Es hat einen Unfall gegeben.

  es hat iynen oonfall gegayben

- I've been...
  attacked
  mugged

  Ich bin ... worden.
  angegriffen
  überfallen

  ish bin ... vorden
  angegriffen
  ewberfallen

- I have to use the phone.

  Ich müsste mal telefonieren.

  ish mewsste maal telefoneeren

- I'm lost.

  Ich habe mich verirrt.

  ish haabe mish ferirrt

- Stop!

  Halt!

  halt

* police

- Sorry, I didn't realise it was against the law.

  Entschuldigung, ich habe nicht gewusst, dass das verboten ist.

  entshooldigoong ish haabe nisht gewoosst dass das ferbohten ist

- Here are my documents.

  Hier sind meine Papiere.

  heer zint miyne papeere

- I haven't got my passport on me.

  Ich habe meinen Ausweis nicht bei mir.

  ish haabe miynen owsviys nisht biy meer

- I don't understand.

  Ich verstehe Sie nicht.

  ish vershtaye zee nisht

- I'm innocent.

  Ich bin unschuldig.

  ish bin oonshooldig

- I need a lawyer (who speaks English).

  Ich brauche einen Anwalt (der Englisch spricht).

  ish browke iynen anvalt (der english sprisht)

- I want to contact my embassy/consulate.

  Ich möchte mit meiner Botschaft sprechen.

  Ish mershte mit miyner bohtshaft shpreshen

- Sie müssen ein Bußgeld bezahlen.

  zee mewssen iyn boohssgelt betsaalen

  You have to pay a fine.

- Ihre Papiere bitte.

  eere papeere bitte

  Your documents, please.

- Sie sind verhaftet.

  zee zint ferhaftet

  You're under arrest.

✶ reporting crime

- I want to report a theft.

  Ich möchte einen Diebstahl melden.

  *ish **mershte** iynen **deepshtaal** **melden***

- My ... has been stolen.

  Mein ... ist gestohlen worden.

  *miyn ... ist **geshtohlen** vorden*

    purse

  Portemonnaie

  portmonnay

    passport

  Ausweis

  owsviys

- Our car has been stolen.

  Unser Auto ist gestohlen worden.

  *oonzer owto ist **geshtohlen** vorden*

- Our car has been broken into.

  Unser Auto ist aufgebrochen worden.

  *oonzer owto ist **owfgebroken** vorden*

- I've lost my credit cards.

  Ich habe meine Kreditkarten verloren.

  *ish **haabe** miyne kre**deet**karten fer**lohren***

- I've lost my luggage.

  Ich habe mein Gepäck verloren.

  *ish **haabe** miyn gepek fer**lohren***

- I've been...

  Ich bin ... worden.

  ish bin ... vorden

    mugged

  überfallen

  *ewber**fallen***

    attacked

  angegriffen

  *an**gegriffen***

- Wann ist es passiert?

  *vann ist es pas**seert***

  When did it happen?

- Wo?

  voh

  Where?

- Was ist passiert?

  *vas ist pas**seert***

  What happened?

health and safety

141

Füllen Sie bitte dieses Formular aus.	*fewllen zee bitte deezes formoolaar ows*	Fill in this form, please.
Können Sie ihn/sie beschreiben?	*kernnen zee een/zee beshriyben*	What did he/she look like?
Wie sahen sie aus?	*vee zaahen zee ows*	What did they look like?

YOU MAY WANT TO SAY...

It happened ...	Es ist... passiert.	*es ist... passeert*
just now	gerade erst	*geraade erst*
(ten) minutes ago	vor (zehn) Minuten	*fohr (tsayn) minoohten*
this morning	heute Morgen	*hoyte morgen*
on the beach	am Strand	*am shtrand*
in the market square	am Marktplatz	*am marktplatts*

He/She had...	Er/Sie hatte...	*er/zee hatte*
dark/blonde hair	dunkle/blonde Haare	*doonkle/blonde haare*
a knife	ein Messer	*iyn messer*

He/She was...	Er/Sie war...	*er/zee var...*
tall	groß	*grohss*
young	jung	*yoong*
short	klein	*kliyn*

He/She was wearing...	Er/Sie trug...	*er/zee troohg*
jeans	Jeans	*jeens*
a denim jacket	eine Jeansjacke	*iyne jeensyake*
a (red) shirt	ein (rotes) Hemd	*iyn (rohtes) hemt*

basic grammar

✱ nouns

Nouns in German have one of three genders: masculine, feminine or neuter. Some word endings give a clue as to what gender a noun is. For example, -heit, -keit and -ung are always feminine, while the suffix -chen is always neuter: das Mädchen (the girl). On the whole, though, genders have to be learnt through hearing and reading the language.

Nouns in German are always written with a capital letter.

plurals

Plurals are formed by adding an ending and/or an umlaut to the noun. Endings vary and although feminine words ending in -keit, -heit und -ung usually add -en to make the plural, most plural endings have to be learnt. Dictionaries give the plural endings of words in the German-English section. Some words don't change in the plural, e.g. der Knochen (bone).

✱ articles (a, an, the)

The definite article changes according to whether a noun is masculine (der), feminine (die), neuter (das) or plural (die):

masculine: der Mann (the man) die Männer (the men)
feminine: die Frau (the woman) die Frauen (the women)
neuter: das Haus (the house) die Häuser (the houses)

The indefinite articles are ein (masculine), eine (feminine) and ein (neuter).

✳ cases

German has four cases: nominative, accusative, genitive and dative. The nominative is used for the subject of a sentence, the accusative for the direct object. The genitive is the possessive case and the dative goes with the indirect object. There are also certain prepositions (see p. 146), which either take the accusative or the dative, and verbs that take the dative.

The definite and indefinite articles may change according to what case the noun is in:

	MASC.	FEM.	NEUTER	PLURAL
definite article				
nom	der Mann	die Frau	das Haus	die Männer
acc	den Mann	die Frau	das Haus	die Männer
gen	des Mannes	der Frau	des Hauses	der Männer
dat	dem Mann	der Frau	dem Haus	den Männern
indefinite article				
nom	ein Mann	eine Frau	ein Haus	
acc	einen Mann	eine Frau	ein Haus	
gen	eines Mannes	einer Frau	eines Hauses	
dat	einem Mann	einer Frau	einem Haus	

✳ possessive adjectives

These take the same endings as the indefinite article:

mein: (my)	mein Vater (my father)	meine Mutter (my mother)
dein/Ihr: (your*)	deine Schwester (your sister)	deine Kinder (your children)

sein (his, its) ihr (her/their)
unser (our) euer (your*)

*See 'you' on page 147.

basic grammar

✱ adjectives

Adjectives come before the noun. The ending changes according to the gender of the noun, whether it is singular or plural, and whether it is with a definite or an indefinite article or with no article at all.

	MASC.	FEM.	NEUTER	PLURAL
with a definite article				
nom	der arme Mann	die arme Frau	das arme Mädchen	die armen Männer
acc	den armen Mann	die arme Frau	das arme Mädchen	die armen Männer
gen	des armen Mannes	der armen Frau	des armen Mädchens	der armen Männer
dat	dem armen Mann	der armen Frau	dem armen Mädchen	den armen Männern

	MASC.	FEM.	NEUTER
with an indefinite article			
nom	ein armer Mann	eine arme Frau	ein armes Mädchen
acc	einen armen Mann	eine arme Frau	ein armes Mädchen
gen	eines armen Mannes	einer armen Frau	eines armen Mädchens
dat	einem armen Mann	einer armen Frau	einem armen Mädchen

	MASC.	FEM.	NEUTER	PLURAL
without an article				
nom	guter Wein	gute Milch	gutes Bier	gute Leute
acc	guten Wein	gute Milch	gutes Bier	gute Leute
gen	guten Weins	guter Milch	guten Bier	guter Leute
dat	gutem Wein	guter Milch	gutem Bier	guten Leuten

✳ comparatives and superlatives

To make an adjective comparative, add -er to the stem and then add the endings on page 145. To make an adjective superlative, add -st on the stem and then the endings.

der reiche Mann (the rich man)
der reichere Mann (the richer man)
der reichste Mann (the richest man)

ein schnelles Auto (a fast car)
ein schnelleres Auto (a faster car)
das schnellste Auto (the fastest car)

Some common adjectives, e.g. groß (big), lang (long) alt (old), add an umlaut as well to make the comparative and superlative. e.g. meine ältere Schwester (my older sister)

✳ prepositions

Aus, bei, mit, seit, nach, von and zu always take the dative. Bis, entlang, durch, ohne, gegen, wider, um and für always take the accusative.

Other prepositions can take either the accusative or the dative. The accusative usually indicates movement, e.g. in den Garten (into the garden), while the dative indicates position, e.g. im (in + dem) Garten (in the garden).

✳ subject pronouns (I, you, he, she, etc.)

SINGULAR		PLURAL	
ich	I	wir	we
du	you *(informal)*	ihr	you *(informal)*
er	he	sie	they
sie	she	Sie	you *(formal)*
es	it		
Sie	you *(formal)*		

'you'

There are three words for 'you' in German:

Du is informal and is used when you are talking either to someone you know well, or to a child or someone much younger than yourself. Young people tend to address each other as du as well.

Ihr is informal and is used in the same situations as du when you are addressing more than one person.

Sie is always written with a capital letter and is the formal word for 'you.' It can be used to address one person or a group of people. Always use it when you don't know the person you are talking to, or if they are much older than you.

If in doubt, stick to Sie.

The possessive adjective 'your' (dein, euer or Ihr in German), follows the same guidelines.

✱ word order

Normally the main verb in a sentence comes second. However, certain words send the verb to the end of the sentence or clause. The most common ones are: dass (that), weil (because) and wenn (when, if).

e.g. Sie kommt nicht, **weil** sie krank **ist**.
     She's not coming because she is ill.

The present perfect tense ('I have been...', 'We have been...', etc.) is made up of two parts in German: the auxiliary verb (haben or sein), and the past participle, which always goes to the end of the sentence or clause.

e.g. Ich **habe** ihn im Theater **gesehen**.
     I've seen him in the theatre.
     Wir **haben** sie für nächsten Dienstag **eingeladen**.
     We've invited them/her next Tuesday.

basic grammar

✳ verbs

Verb endings change according to (a) the subject of the verb and (b) the tense of the verb. Regular verbs are known as weak verbs. Their present-tense endings are:

SAGEN (to say)			
ich	sage	wir	sagen
du	sagst	ihr	sagt
er/sie/es	sagt	Sie/sie	sagen

The endings are added to the stem of the verb. To find the stem, knock -en off the infinitive, which is the form of the verb given in a dictionary.

Irregular verbs are known as 'strong' verbs. Sein (to be) and haben (to have), are both strong verbs:

SEIN (to be)		HABEN (to have)	
ich	bin	ich	habe
du	bist	du	hast
er/sie/es	ist	er/sie/es	hat
wir	sind	wir	haben
Ihr	seid	ihr	habt
Sie/sie	sind	Sie/sie	haben

Some strong verbs change the vowel in the second person singular (du) and the third person singular (er, sie, es). For example:

FAHREN (to drive, to go)		GEBEN (to give)	
ich	fahre	ich	gebe
du	fährst	du	gibst
er/sie/es	fährt	er/sie/es	gibt
wir	fahren	wir	geben
ihr	fahrt	ihr	gebt
Sie/sie	fahren	Sie/sie	geben

Another useful irregular verb is wissen (to know):

WISSEN (to know)			
ich	weiß	wir	wissen
du	weißt	ihr	wisst
er/sie/es	weiß	Sie/sie	wissen

negatives

To make a verb negative, add nicht. For example:

Ich kann nicht.	I can't.
Wir verstehen nicht.	We don't understand.

separable verbs

Many verbs change or add to their meaning by adding a prefix.
For example:

fahren (to go, drive)	abfahren (to leave)
kommen (to come)	ankommen (to arrive)

In a sentence the prefix usually splits from the rest of the verb and
goes to the end of the sentence. For example:

Er kommt um neun Uhr an.   He's arriving at nine o'clock.

✳ modal verbs

Modals are a group of verbs that are very useful if you want to
express attitudes or intentions. Modal verbs include:

dürfen:	darf ich?	may I?
	Sie dürfen	you may, you are allowed to
können:	ich kann	I can
	Sie können	you can
mögen:	ich mag	I like
	Sie mögen	you like
müssen:	ich muss	I must, have to
	Sie müssen	you must, have to
wollen:	ich will	I want
	Sie wollen	you want

They are often used in the 'conditional' form or in the simple past rather than in the present. For example:

ich könnte	I could
ich möchte	I'd like
Was möchten Sie?	What would you like?
ich sollte	I should, I ought to
ich musste	I had to

Some verbs in other tenses you may find useful:

sein:	ich war	I was, I used to be
	ich bin gewesen	I have been
haben:	ich hatte	I had, I used to have
	wir hatten	we had, we used to have
gehen:	ich ging	I went, I used to go
	wir gingen	we went, we used to go

The future tense is used relatively little in German and the verb tends to stay in the present tense, especially when time is mentioned. For example:

You'll pick me up tomorrow morning then?	Du holst mich also morgen früh ab?
We're going there tomorrow.	Wir gehen morgen dahin.

✳ questions

To ask a question, use a question word and invert the subject and verb. For example:

Was machst du?	What are you doing?
Was wollen Sie?	What do you want?
Wer bist du?	Who are you?

If there is no question word simply invert the subject and verb:

Kommen Sie?	Are you coming?
Verstehst du?	Do you understand?

English – German dictionary

German nouns are given with their gender in brackets:
(m) for masculine, (f) for feminine and (n) for neuter.
Other abbreviations: (m/pl) – masculine plural; (f/pl)
– feminine plural; (n/pl) – neuter plural; (adj.) – adjective.

Where nouns have different endings or forms for masculine
and feminine, the masculine is given first,
e.g. Künstler/in (m/f) *kewnst*ler/in.

For English terms that are also used in German, no
pronunciation is given.

There's a list of **car parts** on page 58 and **parts of the
body** on page 135. See also the **menu reader** on page 89,
and **numbers** on page 14.

A

a, an ein, eine *iyn*, *iyne*
abbey Klosterkirche (f) *kloh*sterkirshe
about *(relating to)* über +acc. *ewber*
approximately ungefähr *oon*gefayr
abroad im Ausland *im ows*lant
abscess Abszess (m) *aps*tsess
to **accept** *(take)* nehmen *nay*men
accident Unfall (m) *oon*fall
accommodation Unterkunft (f)
   *oon*terkoonft
account *(bank)* Konto (n) *kon*to
ache Schmerz (m) *shmerts*
acid *(adj.)* sauer *zower*
across über + acc. *ewber*, *(opposite)*
   gegenüber + dat. *gaygenewber*
to **act** handeln, spielen *handeln*, *shpeelen*
   » **actor** Schauspieler (m) *showshpeeler*
   » **actress** Schauspielerin (f)
      showshpeelerin

adaptor Adapter (m) *adapter*
addicted süchtig *sewshtig*
address Adresse (f) *adresse*
admission Eintritt (m) *iyntritt*
   » **admission charge** Eintrittsgeld (n)
      iyntrittsgelt
adopted adoptiert *adopteert*
adult Erwachsener (m), Erwachsene (f)
   ervaksener, *ervaksene*
advance Vorschuss (m) *fohrshooss*
   » **in advance** im Voraus *im fohrows*
advanced *(level)* fortgeschritten
   fortgeshritten
advertisement, advertising Werbung (f)
   verboong
aerial Antenne (f) *antenne*
aeroplane Flugzeug (n) *floohgtsoyg*
after nach + dat. *naak*
   » **afterwards** nachher *naakher*
afternoon Nachmittag (m) *nakmittag*

aftershave Aftershave (n) *aaftershave*

again wieder *veeder*

against gegen + acc. *gaygen*

age Alter (n) *alter*

agency Agentur (f) *agentoohr*

ago vor + dat. *fohr*

to **agree** vereinbaren *feriynbaaren*

AIDS Aids (n) *aids*

air Luft (f) *looft*

» **by air** mit dem Flugzeug *mit daym floohgtsoyg*

» **(by) air mail** (per) Luftpost *(per) looftpost*

air conditioning Klimaanlage (f) *kleemaanlaage*

air force Luftwaffe (f) *looftvaffe*

airport Flughafen (m) *floohghaafen*

aisle Gang (m) *gang*

alarm Alarm (m) *alarm*

» **alarm clock** Wecker (m) *veker*

alcohol Alkohol (m) *alkohohl*

» **alcoholic** *(content)* alkoholisch *alkohohlish*

alive lebendig *lebendig*

all alle *alle*

allergic to allergisch auf + acc. *allergish owf*

alley Gasse (f) *gasse*

to **allow** erlauben *erlowben*

» **allowed** erlaubt *erlowpt*

all right *(OK)* in Ordnung *in ortnoong*

almond Mandel (f) *mandel*

along entlang + acc. *entlang*

already schon *shohn*

also auch *owk*

always immer *immer*

ambassador Botschafter (m) *bohtshafter*

ambitious ehrgeizig *ayrgiytsig*

ambulance Krankenwagen (m) *krankenvaagen*

amount *(money)* Betrag (m) *betraag*

anaesthetic *(local)* örtliche Betäubung (f) *errtlishe betoyboong*
(general) Vollnarkose (f) *follnarkohse*

and und *oont*

angry zornig *tsornig*

animal Tier (n) *teer*

ankle Knöchel (m) *knershel*

anniversary Jahrestag (m) *jaarestaag*

annoyed verärgert *ferergert*

anorak Anorak (m) *anorak*

another (one) noch ein *nok iyn*

to **answer** antworten *antvorten*

antibiotic Antibiotikum (n) *antibyohtikoom*

antifreeze Frostschutzmittel (n) *frostshootsmittel*

antique Antiquität (f) *antikveetayt*

antiseptic antiseptisch *antizeptish*

anxious ängstlich *engstlish*

any irgendein/e *irgentiyn/e*

anyone jemand *yaymant*

anything (irgend)etwas *irgentetvas*

» **anything else** noch etwas *nok etvas*

anywhere irgendwo *irgentvoh*

apartment Appartement (n) *appartmang*

appendicitis Blinddarmentzündung (f) *blintdarmentsewndoong*

apple Apfel (m) *apfel*

appointment Termin (m) *termeen*

approximate(ly) ungefähr *oongefayr*

apricot Aprikose (f) / Marille (f) *(Austria) apreekohze/marille*

arch Bogen (m) *bohgen*

architect Architekt (m) *arshitekt*

area Gegend (f) *gaygent*

argument Auseinandersetzung (f) *owsiynandersetzoong*

arm Arm (m) *arm*

armbands *(swimming)* Schwimmflügel (m/pl) *shvimmflewgel*

army Armee (f) *armay*

to **arrange** *(fix)* vereinbaren *veriynbaaren*

arrest: under arrest verhaftet *ferhaftet*

arrival Ankunft (f) *ankoonft*

to **arrive** ankommen *ankommen*

» **he's arriving at 5pm** er kommt um fünf

Uhr an *er* **kommt** *oom fewnf oohr an*

art Kunst (f) *koonst*

» **art gallery** Kunsthalle (f) *koonsthalle*

» **fine arts** schöne Künste (f/pl) *sherne kewnste*

arthritis Arthritis (f) *artreetis*

article Artikel (m) *artikel*

artificial künstlich *kewnstlish*

artist Künstler/in (m/f) *kewnstler/in*

as *(like)* wie *vee*

as far as I know soviel ich weiß *zofeel ish viyss*

ash Asche (f) *ashe*

ashtray Aschenbecher (m) *ashenbesher*

to **ask** fragen *fraagen*

asparagus Spargel (m) *shpargel*

aspirin Aspirin (n) *aspireen*

assistant Assistent/in (m/f) *assistent/in*

asthma Asthma (n) *astma*

at an + dat. or acc. *an*

athletics Leichtathletik (f) *liyshtatlaytik*

atmosphere Atmosphäre (f) *atmosfayre*

to **attack** angreifen *angriyfen*

(mug) überfallen *ewberfallen*

attendant *(bathing)* Bademeister/in (m/f) *baademiyster/in*

attractive attraktiv *attrakteef*

aubergine Aubergine (f) *obersheene*

aunt Tante (f) *tante*

author Schriftsteller/in (m/f) *shriftshteller/in*

automatic automatisch *owtomaatish*

autumn Herbst (m) *herpst*

avenue Allee (f) *allay*

avocado Avocado (f) *avokaado*

to **avoid** vermeiden *fermiyden*

awful schrecklich *shreklish*

B

baby Baby (n) *baybee*

» **baby food** Babynahrung (f) *baybeenaaroong*

» **baby wipes** Babytücher (n/pl) *baybeetewsher*

baby's bottle Babyflasche (f) *baybeeflashe*

babysitter Babysitter/in (m/f)

back *(reverse side)* Rückseite (f) *rewkziyte*

backwards rückwärts *rewkverts*

bacon Speck (m) *shpek*

bad schlecht *shlesht*

bag Tüte (f), Tasche (f) *tewte, tashe*

baggage Gepäck (n) *gepek*

baker's Bäckerei (f) *bekeriy*

balcony *(theatre etc.)* Empore (f) *empohre*

bald kahl *kaal*

ball *(tennis, football etc.)* Ball (m) *bal*

ballet Ballet (n) *ballett*

ballpoint pen Kugelschreiber (m) *koohgelshriyber*

banana Banane (f) *banaane*

band *(music)* Band (f) Musikgruppe (f) *bent, moohzeekgrooppe*

bandage Verband (m) *ferbant*

bank *(money)* Bank (f) *bank*

banker Bankfachmann (m), Bankfachfrau (f) *bankfakmann, bankfakfrow*

bar Bar (f) *bar*

barber's Friseur (m) *frizerr*

bargain Sonderangebot (n) *zonderangeboht*

baseball Baseball (m)

basement Untergeschoss (n) *oontergeshoss*

basin *(bowl)* Schüssel (f) *(sink)* Waschbecken (n) *shewssel, vashbeken*

basket Korb (m) *korb*

basketball Basketball (m)

bath Bad (n) *baat*

» **to have a bath** ein Bad nehmen *iyn baat naymen*

» **to bathe** baden *baaden*

bathroom Badezimmer (n) *baadetsimmer*

battery Batterie (f) *batteree*

bay Bucht (f) *bookt*

to be sein *ziyn*

beach Strand (m) *shtrant*

beans Bohnen (f/pl) *bohnen*

» **French/green beans** grüne Bohnen (f) *grewne bohnen*

» **kidney/haricot** getrocknete Bohnen (f) *getrocknete bohnen*

beard Bart (m) *bart*

beautiful schön *shern*

because weil, da *viyl, daa*

bed Bett (n) *bett*

bedroom Schlafzimmer (n) *shlaaftsimmer*

bee Biene (f) *beene*

beef Rindfleisch (n) *rintfliysh*

beer Bier (n) *beer*

before bevor, vor + dat. *befohr, fohr*

to begin anfangen, beginnen *anfangen, beginnen*

» **it begins at 8pm** es fängt um acht Uhr abends an *es fengt oom akt oohr aabents an*

beginner Anfänger (m) *anfenger*

beginning Anfang (m) *anfang*

behind hinter + dat. or acc. *hinter*

beige beige *baysh*

to believe glauben *gl...*

bell Glocke (f) *gloke*

below unten *oonten*

belt Gürtel (m) *gewrtel*

bend Kurve (f) *koorve*

bent gebogen *gebohgen*

berry Beere (f) *bayre*

berth (on ship) Bett (n) *bett*

best beste/r/s *beste/r/s*

better besser *besser*

between zwischen + dat. *tsvishen*

bib Lätzchen (n) *letsshen*

Bible Bibel (f) *beebel*

bicycle Fahrrad (n) *faaraat*

big groß *grohss*

bigger größer *grersser*

bill Rechnung (f) *reshnoong*

bin (rubbish) Mülleimer (m) *mewliymer*

» **bin liner** Müllbeutel (m) *mewlboytel*

binding (ski) Skibindung (f) *sheebindoong*

binoculars Fernglas (n) *fernglaas*

biochemistry Biochemie (f) *beeoshaymee*

biology Biologie (f) *beeologee*

bird Vogel (m) *fohgel*

birthday Geburtstag (m) *geboortstaag*

biscuit Keks (m) *kayks*

bishop Bischof (m) *bishoff*

a bit ein bisschen *iyn biss-shen*

to bite beißen *biyssen*

bitter bitter *bitter*

black schwarz *shvarts*

» **black and white** (film) schwarzweiß *shvartsviyss*

» **black coffee** schwarzer Kaffee *shvartser kaffay*

blackberry Brombeere (f) *brombayre*

blackcurrant schwarze Johannisbeere (f) *shvartse yohannisbayre*

blanket Bettdecke (f) *betdeke*

to bleed bluten *bloohten*

blind blind *blint*

blister Blase (f) *blaaze*

to block (road) blockieren, sperren *blokeeren, shperren*

blocked verstopft *fershtopft*

» **(road)** gesperrt *geshperrt*

blonde blond *blont*

blood Blut (n) *blooht*

blouse Bluse (f) *bloohze*

to blow blasen *blaazen*

to blow-dry fönen *fernen*

blue blau *blow*

blusher Rouge (n) *roosh*

to board an Bord gehen *an bort gayen*

boarding card Bordkarte (f) *bortkarte*

boat Schiff (n) *shiff*

» **boat trip** Schiffsfahrt (f) *shiffsfaart*

body Körper (m) *kerrper*

to boil kochen *koken*

boiled egg gekochtes Ei (n) *gekoktes iy*

boiler Boiler (m) *boyler*

bomb Bombe (f) *bombe*

bone Knochen (m) *knoken*

book Buch (n) *boohk*

to book buchen, reservieren *boohken, rezerveeren*

booking Buchung (f), Reservierung (f) *boohkoong, rezerveeroong*

booking office (rail) Fahrkartenschalter (m) *faarkartenshalter* (theatre) Vorverkaufsstelle (f) *fohrferkowfsshtelle*

booklet (bus tickets) Fahrscheinheft (n) *faarshiynheft*

bookshop Buchhandlung (f) *boohkhandloong*

boot (shoe) Stiefel (m) *shteefel*

border (frontier) Grenze (f) *grentse*

boring langweilig *langviylig*

both beide *biyde*

bottle Flasche (f) *flashe*

bottle opener Flaschenöffner (m) *flashenerffner*

bottom Boden (m), Grund (m) *bohden, groont*; (body) Gesäß (n) *gezayss*

bow (ship) Bug (m) *boohg*

bow (knot) Schleife (f) *shliyfe*

bowl Schüssel (f) *shewssel*

box Karton (n) *kartong* (theatre) Loge (f) *lohshe*

box office Kasse (f) *kasse*

boy Junge (m) *yoonge*

boyfriend Freund (m) *froynt*

bra Büstenhalter, BH (m) *bewstenhalter, bay-haa*

bracelet Armband (n) *armbant*

braces Hosenträger (m/pl) *hohzentrayger*

brain Gehirn (n) *gehirn*

branch (bank etc.) Zweigstelle (f) *tsviygshtelle*

brand Marke (f) *marke*

brandy Weinbrand (m) *viynbrant*

brass Messing (n) *messing*

brave mutig *moohtig*

bread Brot (n) *broht*

» **bread roll** Brötchen (n), Semmel (f) (Austria) *brertshen, zemmel*

» **wholemeal bread** Vollkornbrot (n) *follkornbroht*

to break (incl. limb) brechen *breshen*

to break down eine Panne haben *iyne panne haaben*

breakdown truck Abschleppwagen (m) *apshleppvaagen*

breakfast Frühstück (n) *frewstewk*

breast Brust (f) *broost*

to breathe atmen *aatmen*

bride Braut (f) *browt*

bridegroom Bräutigam (m) *broyteegam*

bridge Brücke (f) *brewke*

briefcase Aktentasche (f) *aktentashe*

bright (colour) leuchtend *loyshtend* (light) hell, strahlend *hell, shtraalend*

to bring bringen *bringen*

British britisch *breetish*

broad breit *briyt*

brochure Broschüre (f), Prospekt (m) *broshewre, prospekt*

broken kaputt *kapoott*

bronchitis Bronchitis (f) *bronsheetis*

bronze Bronze (f) *brongse*

broom Besen (m) *bayzen*

brother Bruder (m) *brooder*

brother-in-law Schwager (m) *shvaager*

brown braun *brown*

» **brown sugar** brauner Zucker (m) *browner tsooker*

bruise blauer Fleck (m) *blower flek*

brush Bürste (f) *bewrste*

buffet Büffet (n) *bewffay*

to build bauen *bowen*

builder Bauarbeiter/in (m/f) *bowarbiyter/in*

building Gebäude (n) *geboyde*

building site Baustelle (f) *bowshtelle*

bulb (light) Glühbirne (f) *glewbirne*

bumper (car) Stoßstange (f) *shtossshtange*

burn (on skin) Verbrennung (f) *ferbren-noong*

to burn brennen *brennen*

burnt (food) angebrannt *angebrannt*

bus Bus (m) *boos*

» **by bus** mit dem Bus *mit daym boos*

bus-driver Busfahrer (m) *boosfaarer*

bush Busch (m) *boosh*

business Geschäft (n) *gesheft*

» **business trip** Geschäftsreise (f) *geshefts*riyze

» **on business** geschäftlich *gesheftlish*

businessman/woman Geschäftsmann/frau (m/f) *geshefts*man/frow

business studies Wirtschaftslehre (f) *virtshaftslayre*

bus station Busbahnhof (m) *boosbaanhof*

bus stop Bushaltestelle (f) *booshalteshtelle*

busy beschäftigt *besheftigt*

but aber *aaber*

butane gas Butangas (n) *bootaangaas*

butcher's Metzgererei (f), Fleischerei (f) *metsgeriy, fliysheriy*

butter Butter (f) *bootter*

button Knopf (m) *knopf*

to buy kaufen *kowfen*

by (author etc.) von + dat. *fon*

C

cabbage Kohl (m) *kohl*

cabin Kabine (f) *kabeene*

cable car Drahtseilbahn (f) *draatziylbaan*

café Café (n) *kaffay*

cake Kuchen (m) *koohken*

cake shop Konditorei (f) *konditoriy*

calculator Taschenrechner (m) *tashenreshner*

call (phone) Telefonanruf (m) *telefohnanroof*

to call anrufen *anroohfen*

to be called heißen *hiyssen*

calm ruhig *roohig*

camera Kamera (f), Fotoapparat (m) *kameraa, foto-apparaat*

camomile tea Kamillentee (m) *kamillentay*

to camp zelten, campen *tselten, kempen*

» **camp bed** Campingliege (f) *kempingleege*

» **camping gas** Campinggas (n) *kempingaas*

campsite Campingplatz (m) *kempingplats*

can (to be able) können *kernnen*

can (tin) Dose (f) (petrol) Kanister (m) *dohze, kanister*

can opener Dosenöffner (m) *dohzenerffner*

to cancel rückgängig machen, abbrechen, *rewkgengig maken, apbreshen* (an appointment) absagen *apzaagen*

cancer Krebs (m) *krebs*

candle Kerze (f) *kertse*

canoe Kanu (n) *kaanooh*

capital (city) Hauptstadt (f) *howptshtatt*

captain (boat) Kapitän (m) *kapitayn*

car Auto (n) *owto*

» **by car** mit dem Auto *mit daym owto*

» **car hire** Autoverleih (m) *owtoferliy*

car park Parkplatz (m) *parkplats*

caravan Wohnwagen (m) *vohnvaagen*

caravan site Wohnwagenplatz (m) *vohnvaagenplats*

career Karriere (f) *karriayre*

careful vorsichtig *fohrzishtig*

careless sorglos (driver) unvorsichtig *sorglohz, oonfohrzishtig*

carpenter Schreiner (m), Tischler (m) *shriyner, tishler*

carpet Teppich (m) *teppish*

carriage (rail) Waggon (m) *vaggong*

carrier bag Tragetasche (f) *traagetashe*

carrot Möhre (f), Karotte (f) *merre, karotte*

to carry tragen *traagen*

to carry on (walking/driving) weiterfahren,

weitergehen **viy**terfaaren, **viy**tergayen

car wash Autowäsche (f) **ow**toveshe

case: in case Fall: für den Fall, falls *fall: fewr dayn fall, falls*

cash Bargeld (n) **baar**gelt

» **to pay cash** bar bezahlen *baar betsaalen*

to cash einlösen **iyn**lerzen

» **cash desk** Kasse (f) **kasse**

cassette Kassette (f) kas**sette**

castle *(palace)* Schloss (n) *shloss* *(fortress)* Burg (f) *boorg*

cat Katze (f) **katse**

catalogue Katalog (m) kata**lohg**

to catch *(train/bus)* nehmen **nay**men

cathedral Kathedrale (f), Dom (m) kate**draa**le, dohm

Catholic katholisch ka**toh**lish

cauliflower Blumenkohl (m), Karfiol (m) *(Austria)* **bloom**enkohl, karfi**ohl**

to cause verursachen fer**ooh**rzaken

caution Vorsicht (f) **fohr**zisht

cave Höhle (f) **her**le

CD CD (f) tsay-**day**

» **CD-Rom** CD-ROM (f) tsay-day-**rom**

ceiling Decke (f) **deke**

cellar Keller (m) **keller**

cemetery Friedhof (m) **freed**hohf

centimetre Zentimeter (m) **tsenti**mayter

central zentral tsen**traal**

central heating Zentralheizung (f) tsen**traal**hiytsoong

centre Zentrum (n) **tsen**troom

century Jahrhundert (n) **yaar**hoondert

CEO (chief exectuive officer) Geschäftsführer/in (m/f) ge**shefts**fewrer/in

cereal (food) Getreideflocken (f/pl), Cerealien (f/pl) ge**triy**defloken, tsere**aa**lyen

certain sicher **sisher**

certainly sicherlich **sisher**lish

certificate Zertifikat (n), Bescheinigung (f) tsertifi**kaat**, be**shiy**nigoong

chain Kette (f) **kette**

chair Stuhl (m) **shtool**

» **chair lift** Sessellift (m) **zessel**lift

chalet Chalet (n) **shalay**

champagne Champagner (m), Sekt (m) sham**pan**ya, zekt

change *(small coins)* Kleingeld (n) **kliyn**gelt

to change *(clothes)* umziehen **oom**tseehen *(money)* wechseln **vek**seln *(trains)* umsteigen **oom**shtiygen

changing room Umkleidekabine (f) **oom**kliydekabeene

chapel Kapelle (f) ka**pelle**

charcoal Holzkohle (f) **holts**kohle

charge *(money)* Gebühr (f) ge**bewr**

charter flight Charterflug (m) **tsharter**floohg

cheap billig **billig**

to check prüfen, kontrollieren **prew**fen, kontrol**leeren**

checked *(pattern)* kariert ka**reert**

check-in *(desk)* Abfertigungsschalter (m) **ap**fertigoongsshalter

to check in einchecken **iyn**tsheken

cheek Wange (f) **vange**

cheeky frech **fresh**

cheers! Prost! **prohst**

cheese Käse (m) **kayze**

cheesecake Käsekuchen (m) **kayze**koohken

chef Chefkoch (m) **shef**kok

chemist Chemiker/in (m/f) **shay**miker/in

chemistry Chemie (f) she**mee**

cheque Scheck (m) shek

cherry Kirsche (f) **kirshe**

chess Schach (n), Schachspiel (n) shak, **shak**shpeel

chewing gum Kaugummi (m) **kow**goommi

chicken Hähnchen (n) **hayn**shen

chickenpox Windpocken (f/pl) **vint**poken

child Kind (n) kint

children Kinder (f) **kinder**

chin Kinn (n) *kin*

china Porzellan (n) *portsellaan*

chips Pommes frites (pl) *pomm fritt*

chocolate Schokolade (f) *shokolaade*

chocolates Pralinen (f/pl) *praleenen*

to **choose** wählen, aussuchen *vaylen, owszooken*

chop (lamb/pork) Kotelett (n) *kotlett*

Christian christlich *kristlish*

» **Christian name** Vorname (m) *fohrnaame*

Christmas Weihnachten (n) *viynakten*

» **Christmas Day** der erste Weihnachtstag (m) *der erste viynaktstaag*

» **Christmas Eve** Heiligabend (m) *hiylishaabent*

church Kirche (f) *kirshe*

cigar Zigarre (f) *tsigarre*

cigarette Zigarette (f) *tsigarette*

cinema Kino (n) *keeno*

circle Kreis (m) *kriys*

(theatre) erster Rang (m) *erster rang*

city Großstadt (f) *grohsshtatt*

civil servant Beamter (m), Beamtin (f) *beamter, beamtin*

class Klasse (f) *klasse*

classical music klassische Musik (f) *klassishe moohzeek*

claustrophobia Klaustrophobie (f) *klowstrofohbee*

to **clean** sauber machen *zowber maken*

clean sauber *zowber*

cleaner Putzfrau (f) *pootsfrow*

cleansing lotion Reinigungslotion (f) *riynigoongs-lotsyohn*

clear klar *klaar*

clerk Büroangestellte (m/f) *bewrohangeshtellte*

clever klug, schlau *kloog, shlow*

cliff Felsen (m), *felzen*

climate Klima (n) *kleema*

to **climb** klettern *klettern*

climber Bergsteiger/in (m/f) *bergshtiygerfin*

clinic Klinik (f), Sprechstunde (f) *kleenik, shpreshshtoonde*

cloakroom Garderobe (f) *garderohbe*

clock Uhr (f) *oohr*

close (by) in der Nähe, nahe *in der naye, naahe*

to **close** schließen *shleessen*

closed geschlossen *geshlossen*

cloth Tuch (n) *toohk*

clothes Kleider (n/pl) *kliyder*

cloudy wolkig *volkig*

club Klub (m), Verein (m) *kloob, feriyn*

coach Bus (m) *boos*

(railway) Wagen (m) *vaagen*

coal Kohle (f) *kohle*

coarse grob *grohb*

coast Küste (f) *kewste*

coat Mantel (m) *mantel*

coat-hanger Kleiderbügel (m) *klyiderbewgel*

cocktail Cocktail (m) *koktayl*

coffee Kaffee (m) *kaffay*

coin Münze (f) *mewntse*

cold kalt *kalt*

to **have a cold** erkältet sein *erkeltet ziyn*

collar Kragen (m) *kraagen*

colleague Kollege (m), Kollegin (f) *kollayge, kollaygin*

to **collect** (ein)sammeln *(iyn)zammeln*

collection (e.g. stamps) Sammlung (f) *zammloong*

(postal/rubbish) Abholung (f) *aphohloong*

college Institut (n) *institooht*

colour Farbe (f) *farbe*

colour-blind farbenblind *farbenblint*

comb Kamm (m) *kamm*

to **come** kommen *kommen*

» to **come back** zurückkommen *tsoorewkkommen*

» to **come in** hereinkommen *heriynkommen*

come in! herein! *heriyn*

to **come off** (e.g. button) abgehen, sich

lösen *apgayen, zish lerzen*

comedy Komödie (f) *komerdye*

comfortable komfortabel, bequem
komfortaabel, beqvaym

comic *(magazine)* Comic-Heft (n)
komikheft

commercial kommerziell *kommertsyell*

common *(usual)* gewöhnlich *gevernlish*
(shared) gemeinsam *gemiynzam*

communion Abendmahl (n) *aabentmaal*

communism Kommunismus (m)
kommoonismus

company Firma (f) *firma*

compared with verglichen mit + dat.
ferglishen mit

compartment Abteil (n) *aptiyl*

compass Kompass (m) *kompass*

to complain klagen, sich beschweren
klaagen, zish beshvayren

» complaint Klage (f), Beschwerde (f)
klaage, beshvayrde

complete *(finished)* fertig *fertig*
(whole) komplett *komplett*

complicated kompliziert *komplitseert*

compulsory obligatorisch *obligatohrish*

composer Komponist/in (m/f)
komponist, komponistin

computer Computer (m) *compyooter*

computer operator EDV-Arbeiter
(m), EDV-Arbeiterin (f) *ay-day-fow-
arbiyter, ay-day-fow-arbiyterin*

computer programmer Programmierer/
in (m/f) *prohgrammeerer/in*

» computer science Informatik (f)
informaatik

concert Konzert (n) *kontsert*

concert hall Konzerthalle (f), Konzertsaal
(m) *kontserthalle, kontsertzaal*

concussion Gehirnerschütterung (f)
gehirnershewtteroong

condition *(state)* Zustand (m)
tsooshtant

conditioner Pflegespülung (f)
pflaygeshpewloong

condom Kondom (n), Präservativ (n)
kondohm, prayzervateef

conference Konferenz (f) *konferents*

confirm bestätigen *beshtaytigen*

conjunctivitis Bindehautentzündung (f)
bindehowtentsewndoong

connection *(travel, computer)*
Verbindung (f) *ferbindoong*

conscious bei Bewusstsein *biy
bewoosstziyn*

conservation Naturschutz (m)
natoohrshoots

conservative konservativ *konzervateef*

constipation Verstopfung (f)
fershtopfoong

consulate Konsulat (n) *konzoolaat*

consultant Berater/in (m/f) *beraater/in*

contact lens Kontaktlinse (f)
kontaktlinze

contact lens cleaner
Kontaktlinsenreiniger (m)
kontaktlinzenriyniger

continent Kontinent (m) *kontinent*

contraceptive Verhütungsmittel (n)
ferhewtoongsmittel

contract Vertrag (m) *fertraag*

control *(passport)* Kontrolle (f) *kontrolle*

convent Frauenkloster (n)
frowenklohster

convenient günstig *gewnstig*

cook Koch (m) *kok*

to cook kochen *koken*

» cooked gekocht, gar *gekokt, gaar*

cooker Herd (m) *hert*

cool kühl *kewl*

cool box Kühlbox (f) *kewlboks*

copper Kupfer (n) *koopfer*

copy Kopie (f) *kopee*

cork Korken (m) *korken*

corkscrew Korkenzieher (m)
korkentseeher

corner *(outside)* Ecke (f) *eke*

correct korrekt, richtig *korrekt, rishtig*

corridor Gang (m), Korridor (m) *gang,
korridor*

cosmetics Kosmetik (f), *kos**may**tik*

to **cost** kosten *kos**ten***

cot Kinderbett (n) *kinderbett*

cottage kleines Haus (n) *klyines hows*

cotton *(material)* Baumwolle (f) ***bowm**volle*

(thread) Nähgarn (n) ***nay**garn*

cotton wool Watte (f) *vatte*

couchette Liegewagen (m) ***lee**gevaagen*

cough Husten (m) *hoosten*

to **cough** husten *hoosten*

(I, he, she, it) could *(see 'can')* könnte *kernnte*

to **count** zählen *tsaylen*

counter *(post office)* Schalter (m) ***shal**ter*

country *(nation)* Land (n) *lant*

country(side) Landschaft (f) *lantshaft*

  » **in the country** auf dem Land *owf daym lant*

couple *(pair)* Paar (n) *paar*

courgettes Zucchini (f) *tsookeenee*

course *(lessons)* Kurs (m) *koors*

court *(law)* Gericht (m) *gerisht*

(tennis) Platz (m) *plats*

cousin Cousin (m), Kusine (f) *koozeng, koozeene*

cover *(lid)* Deckel (m) *dekel*

cow Kuh (f) *kooh*

crab Krabbe (f) *krabbe*

cramp Muskelkrampf (m) ***moos**kelkrampf*

crazy verrückt *ferrewkt*

cream Sahne (f) *zaane*

  » *(lotion)* Creme (f) *kraym*

  » *(colour)* cremefarben ***kraym**farben*

credit card Kreditkarte (f) *kre**deet**karte*

cricket Cricket (n) *kriket*

crisps Chips (f/pl) *tships*

cross Kreuz (n) *kroyts*

  » **Red Cross** Rotes Kreuz (n) *rohtes kroyts*

to **cross** *(border)* hinüberfahren *hinewberfaaren*

cross-country skiing Langlauf (m) *langlowf*

crossing *(sea)* Überfahrt (f) *ewberfaart*

crossroads Kreuzung (f) *kroytsoong*

crowd Menschenmenge (f) ***menshen**menge*

crowded überfüllt, voll *ewber**fewllt**, foll*

crown Krone (f) *krohne*

cruise Kreuzfahrt (f) *kroytsfaart*

crutch Krücke (f) *krewke*

to **cry** weinen *viynen*

crystal Kristall (n) *kristall*

cucumber Gurke (f) *goorke*

cup Tasse (f) *tasse*

cupboard Schrank (m) *shrank*

cure *(remedy)* Heilmittel (n) *hiylmittel*

to **cure** heilen *hiylen*

curler *(hair)* Lockenwickler (m) ***loken**vikler*

curly lockig *lokig*

curry Curry (m) *kerry*

current *(electricity)* Strom (m) *shtrohm*

curtain Gardine (f), Vorhang (m) *gar**deene**, fohrhang*

curve Kurve (f) *koorve*

cushion Kissen (n) *kissen*

custard Vanillesoße (f) *vanillesohsse*

customs Zoll (m) *tsoll*

cut Schnitt (m) *shnitt*

to **cut** schneiden *shniyden*

  » **to cut oneself** sich schneiden *sish shniyden*

cutlery Besteck (n) *beshtek*

cycling Radfahren (n) ***raat**faaren*

cyclist Radfahrer/in (m/f) ***raat**faarer/in*

cylinder *(car)* Zylinder (m) *tsew**lin**der*

cystitis Blasenentzündung (f) *blaazen-entsewndoong*

D

daily täglich ***tayg**lish*

damage Schaden (m) *shaaden*

to **damage** beschädigen + dat. *be**shay**digen*

damp feucht *foysht*

dance Tanz (m) *tants*
to dance tanzen *tantsen*
danger Gefahr (f) *gefaar*
dangerous gefährlich *gefayrlish*
dark dunkel *doonkel*
darling Liebling (m) *leebling*
darts Dartspiel (n) *dartshpeel*
data (information) Daten (f) *daaten*
date (day) Datum (n), (fruit) Dattel (f)
daatoom, dattel
daughter Tochter (f) *tokter*
daughter-in-law Schwiegertochter (f)
shveegertokter
day Tag (m) *taag*
» day after tomorrow übermorgen
ewbermorgen
» day before yesterday vorgestern
fohrgestern
» day after/before Tag danach/zuvor
taag danaak/tsoofohr
dead tot *toht*
deaf schwerhörig *shverherrig*
dealer Händler/in (m/f) *hendler/in*
dear (loved) liebe/r/s *leebe/r/s*
(expensive) teuer *toyer*
death Tod (m) *toht*
debt Schuld (f) *shoolt*
decaffeinated coffee koffeinfreier
Kaffee (m) *koffayeenfriyer kaffay*
deck Deck (n) *dek*
deckchair Liegestuhl (m) *leegeshtool*
to decide entscheiden *entshiyden*
to declare erklären *erklayren*
deep tief *teef*
deer Hirsch (m), Rotwild (n) *hirsh,*
rohtvilt
defect Fehler (m) *fayler*
defective fehlerhaft *faylerhaft*
definitely bestimmt *beshtimmt*
defrost (food) auftauen *owftowen*
degree (temperature) Grad (m) *graat*
(university) Universitätsabschluss (m)
ooneeverzeetaytsapshlooss
delay Verspätung (f) *fershpaytoong*

delicate fein *fiyn*
delicious lecker, köstlich *leker, kerstlish*
to deliver liefern *leefern*
delivery Lieferung (f) *leeferoong*
demonstration Demonstration (f)
demontratsyohn
denim Jeansstoff (m) *sheens-shtoff*
dentist Zahnarzt (m), Zahnärztin (f)
tsaan-artst, tsaan-erstin
dentures Gebiss (n) *gebiss*
deodorant Deo(dorant) (n) *dayo(dorant)*
to depart (bus, car, train) abfahren *apfaaren*
(plane) abfliegen *apfleegen*
department Abteilung (f) *aptiyloong*
department store Kaufhaus (n)
kowfhows
departure (bus, car, train) Abfahrt (f)
apfaart (plane) Abflug (m) *apfloohg*
departure lounge Abflughalle (f)
apfloohghalle
deposit Anzahlung (f) *antsaaloong*
desert Wüste (f) *vewste*
to describe beschreiben *beshriyben*
description Beschreibung (f)
beshriyboong
design Entwurf (m) *entvoorf*
(dress) Design (n) *deziyn*
to design entwerfen *entverfen*
designer Designer/in (m/f)
dessert Nachtisch (m), Nachspeise (f)
naaktish, naakshpiyze
destination Reiseziel (n) *riyzetseel*
detail Detail (n), Einzelheit (f) *detiy,*
iyntselhiyt
detergent Reinigungsmittel (n)
riynigoongsmittel
to develop entwickeln *entvikeln*
diabetes Diabetes (m) *deeabaytis*
diabetic (adj.) zuckerkrank *tsookerkrank*
to dial wählen *vaylen*
dialling code Vorwahl (f) *fohrvaal*
dialling tone Amtszeichen (n)
amtstsiyshen
diamond Diamant (m) *deeamant*

diarrhoea Durchfall (m) *doorshfall*

diary Tagebuch (n) *taagebookh*

dice Würfel (m) *vewrfel*

dictator Diktator (m) *diktaator*

dictionary Wörterbuch (n) *verrterboohk*

to **die** sterben *shterben*

   died gestorben *geshtorben*

diesel Dieselöl (n) *deezel-erl*

diet Diät (f) *deeayt*

different(ly) verschieden, anders *fersheeden, anders*

difficult schwierig, schwer *shveerig, shvayr*

digital digital *digitaal*

  » **digital camera** Digitalkamera (f) *digitaalkamera*

dining room Esszimmer (n) *esstsimmer*

dinner Abendessen (n) *aabentessen*

dinner jacket Smoking (m) *smohking*

diplomat Diplomat (m) *diplomaat*

direct *(train)* durchgehend *doorshgayend*

direction Richtung (f) *rishtoong*

director Direktor (m), Direktorin (f) *direktohr, direktohrin*

directory *(index)* Verzeichnis (n), *vertsiyshnis*

dirty schmutzig, dreckig *shmootsig, ureckig*

disabled behindert *behindert*

disappointed enttäuscht *enttoysht*

disc Scheibe (f) *shiybe*

  » *(computer)* Disk (f) *(vinyl)* Schallplatte (f) *shallplatte*

disc film Diskfilm (m) *diskfilm*

disc jockey Diskjockey (m) *DJ*

disco(thèque) Disko(thek) (f)

discount Rabatt (m) *rabat*

dish Schüssel (f) *shlewssel*

dishwasher Geschirrspülmaschine (f) *geshirrshpewlmasheene*

disinfectant Desinfektionsmittel (n) *desinfektsyohnsmittel*

dislocated verrenkt *ferrenkt*

disposable wegwerfbar *vegverfbaar*

  » **disposable nappies** Wegwerfwindeln (f/pl) *vegverfvindeln*

distance Entfernung (f) *entfernoong*

distilled water destilliertes Wasser (n) *destilleertes vasser*

district Gebiet (n) *gebeet*

to **dive** tauchen *towken*

diversion Umleitung (f) *oomliytoong*

diving Tauchen (n) *towken*

diving-board Sprungbrett (n) *shproongbrett*

divorced geschieden *gesheeden*

dizzy schwindlig *shvindlig*

to **do** machen, tun *maken, toon*

dock Dock (n) *dok*

doctor Arzt (m), Ärztin (f) *artst, ertstin*

document Dokument (n) *dokooment*

dog Hund (m) *hoont*

doll Puppe (f) *pooppe*

dollar Dollar (m) *dollar*

dome Kuppel (f) *kooppel*

donkey Esel (m) *ayzel*

door Tür (f) *tewr*

double doppelt *doppelt*

double bed Doppelbett (n) *doppelbett*

down *(movement)* hinunter *hinoonter*

download Herunterladen (n) *heroonterlaaden*

downstairs unten *oonten*

drain Abflussrohr (n) *apfloossrohr*

drama Drama (n) *drahma*

draught *(air)* Luftzug (m) *loofttsoog*

draught beer Bier vom Fass (n), Fassbier (n) *beer fom fass, fassbeer*

to **draw** zeichnen *tsiyshnen*

drawer Schublade (f) *shooplaade*

drawing Zeichnung (f) *tsiyshnoong*

dreadful furchtbar *foorshtbaar*

dress Kleid (n) *kliyt*

to **dress, get dressed** sich anziehen *sish antseehen*

dressing *(medical)* Verband (m) *ferbant* *(salad)* Soße (f) *sohsse*

drink Getränk (n) *getrenk*

to drink trinken *trinken*
to drip tropfen *tropfen*
to drive (selbst) fahren *(zelbst) faaren*
  driver Fahrer/in (m/f) *faarer/in*
  driving licence Führerschein (m) *fewrershiyn*
to drown ertrinken *ertrinken*
  drug Droge (f) *drohge*
  » drug addict Drogensüchtiger (m) *drohgensewshtiger*
  drum Trommel (f) *trommel*
  drunk betrunken *betroonken*
  dry trocken *troken*
  (wine) trocken, herb *troken, herb*
  dry-cleaner's chemische Reinigung (f) *shaymishe riynigoong*
  dubbed synchronisiert *zewnkronizeert*
  duck Ente (f) *ente*
  dull (weather) trüb *trewb*
  dumb stumm *shtoomm*
  dummy (baby's) Schnuller (m) *shnooller*
  during während + gen. *vayrent*
  dust Staub (m) *shtowb*
  dustbin Mülleimer (m) *mewliymer*
  dusty staubig *shtowbig*
  duty (tax) Steuer (f) *shtoyer*
  duty-free steuerfrei *shtoyerfriy*
  duvet Federbett (n) *fayderbett*
  DVD DVD (f) *day-fow-day*
  » DVD-player DVD-Spieler (m) *day-fow-day-shpeeler*
  dyslexia Legasthenie (f) *laygastenee*
  dyslexic legasthenisch *laygastaynish*

E

  each jede/r/s *yayde/r/s*
  ear Ohr (n) *ohr*
  earache Ohrenschmerzen (m/pl) *ohrenshmertsen*
  eardrops Ohrentropfen (m/pl) *ohrentropfen*
  earlier früher *frewer*
  early früh *frew*
to earn verdienen *ferdeenen*

  earring Ohrring (m) *ohr-ring*
  earth Erde (f) *erde*
  east Osten (m) *osten*
  » eastern östlich *erstlish*
  Easter Ostern (n) *ohstern*
  easy einfach, leicht *iynfak, liysht*
to eat essen *essen*
  economical ökonomisch *erkonohmish*
  economics Betriebswirtschaft (f) *betreebsvirtshaft*
  economy Wirtschaft (f) *virtshaft*
  the economic miracle Wirtschaftswunder (n) *virtshaftsvoonder*
  edible essbar *essbaar*
  egg Ei (n) *iy*
  eggs Eier (n/pl) *iyer*
  either entweder *entvayder*
  either ... or entweder ... oder *entvayder ...ohder*
  elastic band Gummiband (n) *goommeebant*
  election Wahl (f) *vaal*
  electric elektrisch *elektrish*
  electrician Elektriker/in (m/f) *elektriker/in*
  electricity Elektrizität (f) *elektritsitayt*
  (wiring etc.) Stromanschluss (m) *shtrohmanschlooss*
  electronic elektronisch *elektrohnish*
  email E-Mail (f) *ee-mail*
to email eine E-Mail schreiben *iyne ee-mail shriyben*
to embark (boat) an Bord gehen *an bort gayen*
  embarrassing peinlich *piynlish*
  embassy Botschaft (f) *bohtshaft*
  emergency Notfall (m) *nohtfall*
  emergency telephone (on motorway) Notrufsäule (f) *nohtroohfsoyle*
  empty leer *layr*
to empty (aus)leeren *(ows)layren*
  enamel Emaille (f) *emiy*
  end Ende (n) *ende*
to end enden, aufhören *enden, owfherren*

energy Energie (f) *energee*

engaged *(to be married)* verlobt *ferlohbt*

(occupied) besetzt, beschäftigt *bezetst, besheftigt*

engine Motor (m) *mohtor*

engineer Ingenieur/in (m/f) *inshenyerr*

England England *englant*

English Englisch *english*

to enjoy genießen *geneessen*

enough genug *genoohg*

to enter betreten *betrayten*

(bus, train) einsteigen *iynshtiygen*

entertainment Unterhaltung (f) *oonterhaltoong*

enthusiastic begeistert *begiystert*

entrance Eingang (m) *iyngang*

envelope Briefumschlag (m) *breefoomshlaag*

environment Umwelt (f) *oomvelt*

environmentally friendly umweltfreundlich *oomveltfroyndlish*

equal gleich *gliysh*

equipment Ausrüstung (f) *owsrewstoong*

escalator Rolltreppe (f) *rolltreppe*

especially besonders *bezonders*

essential wesentlich *vayzentlish*

estate agent Immobilienhändler/in (m/f) *immohbeelyenhendler/in*

even *(including)* sogar *zogaar*

(not odd) gerade *geraade*

evening Abend (m) *aabent*

every jede/r/s *yayde/r/s*

everyone alle *alle*

everything alles *alles*

everywhere überall *ewberall*

exact(ly) genau *genow*

examination Prüfung (f) *prewfoong*

exams Prüfungen (f/pl) *prewfoongen*

example Beispiel (n) *biyshpeel*

» **for example** zum Beispiel *tsoom biyshpeel*

excellent ausgezeichnet *owsgetsiyshnet*

except außer + dat. *owsser*

excess baggage Übergepäck (n) *ewbergepek*

to exchange tauschen *towshen*

(money) wechseln *vekseln*

exchange rate Wechselkurs (m) *vekselkoors*

excited aufgeregt *owfgeraygt*

exciting aufregend *owfraygent*

excursion Ausflug (m) *owsfloog*

excuse me Entschuldigen Sie *entshooldigen zee*

executive leitender Angestellter (m), leitende Angestellte (f) *liytender angeshtellter, liytende angeshtellte*

exercise Übung (f) *ewboong*

exhibition Ausstellung (f) *owsshtelloong*

exit Ausgang (m) *owsgang*

to expect erwarten *ervarten*

expensive teuer *toyer*

experience Erfahrung (f) *erfaaroong*

experiment Versuch (m) *ferzoohk*

expert Experte (m) *eksperte*

to explain erklären *erklayren*

explosion Explosion (f) *explosyohn*

export Export (m) *eksport*

to export exportieren *eksporteeren*

express express *ekspress*

extension cable Verlängerungskabel (n) *ferlengeroongskaabel*

external äußere/r/s *oyssere/r/s*

extra zusätzlich *tsoohzetslish*

eye Auge (n) *owge*

eyebrow Augenbraue (f) *owgenbrowe*

eyebrow pencil Augenbrauenstift (m) *owgenbrowenshtift*

eyelash Wimper (f) *vimper*

eyeliner Kajal (n) *kayal*

eyeshadow Lidschatten (m) *leetshatten*

F

fabric Stoff (m) *shtoff*

face Gesicht (n) *gezisht*

» **face cream** Gesichtscreme (f) *gezishtskraym*

» **face powder** Gesichtspuder (m) *gezishtspoohder*

facilities Einrichtungen (f/pl) *iynrishto-ongen*

fact Tatsache (f) *taatzake*

» **in fact** tatsächlich *taatzeshlish*

factory Fabrik (f) *fabrik*

to fail *(exam/test)* durchfallen *doorshfallen*

failure Misserfolg (m) *misserfolg*

to faint ohnmächtig werden *ohnmeshtig verden*

fair *(haired)* blond *blond*

fair Jahrmarkt (m) *yaarmarkt*

» **trade fair** Handelsmesse (f) *handelsmesse*

fairly ziemlich *tseemlish*

faith Glaube (m) *glowbe*

fake Imitation (f) *imeetatsyohn*

to fall *(down/over)* hinfallen *hinfallen*

false falsch *falsh*

familiar vertraut *fertrowt*

family Familie (f) *fameelye*

famous bekannt, berühmt *bekannt, berewmt*

fan *(air)* Ventilator (m) *ventilaator*

(supporter) Fan (m) *fen*

fantastic fantastisch *fantastish*

far *(away)* weit weg *viyt veg*

how far...? wie weit ...? *vee viyt*

is it far? ist es weit? *ist es viyt*

fare Fahrgeld (n) *faargelt*

farm Bauernhof (m), Landwirtschaft *bowernhohf, lantvirtshaft*

farmer Bauer (m) Bäuerin (f) *bower, boyerin*

fashion Mode (f) *mohde*

fashionable/in fashion modisch *mohdish*

fast schnell *shnell*

fat *(adj/noun)* dick; Fett (n) *dik; fett*

fatal tödlich *terdlish*

father Vater (m) *faater*

father-in-law Schwiegervater (m) *shveegerfaater*

fault Fehler (m) *fayler*

faulty fehlerhaft *faylerhaft*

favourite Lieblings... *leeblings...*

» **favourite film** Lieblingsfilm (m) *leeblingsfilm*

fax Fax (n) *faks*

feather Feder (f) *fayder*

to be fed up die Nase voll haben *dee naaze foll haaben*

fee Gebühr (f) *gebewr*

to feed *(inc. baby)* füttern *fewttern*

to feel sich fühlen *sish fewlen*

(ill/well) sich nicht wohl/wohl fühlen *sish nisht vohl/vohl fewlen*

felt-tip pen Filzstift (m) *filtsshtift*

female, feminine weiblich *viyblish*

feminist Feminist/in (m/f) *feminist/in*

fence Zaun (m) *tsown*

ferry Fähre (f) *fayre*

festival Fest (n) *fest*

to fetch holen *hohlen*

fever Fieber (n) *feeber*

(a) few ein paar *iyn paar*

fiancé(e) Verlobter (m), Verlobte (f) *ferlohbter, ferlohbte*

fibre Faser (f) *faazer*

field Feld (n) *felt*

fig Feige (f) *fiyge*

to fight kämpfen *kempfen*

file *(documents)* Aktenordner (m) *aktenordner*

(computer) Datei (f) *datiy*

(nail/DIY) Feile (f) *fiyle*

to fill füllen *fewllen*

filling *(dental)* Füllung (f) *fewlloong*

film Film (m) *film*

» **film star** Filmstar (m) *filmstar*

filter Filter (m) *filter*

finance Finanzen (f/pl) *finantsen*

to find finden *finden*

fine *(OK)* in Ordnung *in ortnoong*

(penalty) Geldstrafe (f) *geltstrafe*

(weather) schön *shern*

finger Finger (m) *finger*

finish Schluss (m) *shlooss*

fire Feuer (n) *foyer*

fire brigade Feuerwehr (f) *foyervayr*
fire extinguisher Feuerlöscher (m) *foyerlersher*
firewood Feuerholz (n) *foyerholts*
firework Feuerwerk (n) *foyerverk*
firm fest *fest*
firm (company) Firma (f) *firma*
first erste/r/s *erste/r/s*
» **first aid** Erste Hilfe (f) *erste hilfe*
» **first aid kit** Verbandskasten (m) *ferbantskasten*
fish Fisch (m) *fish*
to **fish/go fishing** angeln *angeln*
fishing Angeln (n) *angeln*
fishing rod Angelrute (f) *angelroohte*
fishmonger's Fischgeschäft (n) *fishgesheft*
fit (healthy) gesund *gezoont*
to **fit** passen *passen*
» **that fits you well** das passt dir gut *das passt deer gooht*
fitting room Umkleidekabine (f) *oomkliydekabeene*
to **fix** (mend) reparieren *repareeren*
fizzy mit Kohlensäure *mit kohlenzoyre*
flag Fahne (f) *faane*
flash (camera) Blitzlicht (n) *blitzlicht*
flat (apartment) Wohnung (f) *vohnoong*
flat (level) flach *flak*
(empty battery) leer *layr*
flavour Geschmack (m) *geshmak*
flaw Fehler (m) *fayler*
flea market Flohmarkt (m) *flohmarkt*
flight Flug (m) *floohg*
flippers Schwimmflossen (f/pl) *shvimmflossen*
flood Flut (f) *flooht*
floor Boden (m) *bohden*
» **on the first floor** im ersten Stock *im ersten shtok*
» **ground floor** Erdgeschoss (n) *ertgeshoss*
floppy disc Diskette (f) *diskette*
flour Mehl (n) *mayl*

flower Blume (f) *bloohme*
flu Grippe (f) *grippe*
fluent (language) fließend *fleessent*
fluid flüssig *flewssig*
fly Fliege (f) *fleege*
fly sheet Überzelt (n) *ewbertselt*
fly spray Fliegenspray (n) *fleegenshpray*
to **fly** fliegen *fleegen*
fog Nebel (m) *naybel*
foggy neblig *nayblig*
foil Folie (f) *fohlye*
folding chair Klappstuhl (m) *klappshtoohl*
folk music Volksmusik (f) *folksmoohzik*
to **follow** folgen *folgen*
following (next) (nach)folgend *(naak)folgend*
food Essen (n) *essen*
food poisoning Lebensmittelvergiftung (f) *laybensmittelfergiftoong*
foot Fuß (m) *foohss*
» **on foot** zu Fuß *tsoo foohss*
football Fußball (m) *foohssball*
footpath Fußweg (m) *foohssvayg*
for für *fewr*
forbidden verboten *ferbohten*
foreign ausländisch *owslendish*
foreigner Ausländer/in (m/f) *owslender/in*
forest Wald (m) *valt*
to **forget** vergessen *fergessen*
to **forgive** vergeben *fergayben*
fork Gabel (f) *gaabel*
form Form (f) *form*
fortnight vierzehn Tage *feertsayn taage*
fortress Burg (f) *boorg*
forward vorwärts *fohrverts*
forwarding address Nachsendeadresse (f) *naakzendeadressse*
foundation (make-up) Grundierungscreme (f) *groondeeroongskraym*
fountain Brunnen (m) *broonnen*
fox Fuchs (m) *fooks*
foyer Foyer (n) *foayay*

fracture Bruch (m) *brook*

fragile zerbrechlich *tserbreshlish*

frankly ehrlich gesagt *ayrlish gezaagt*

free frei, umsonst *friy, oomzonst*
(available/unoccupied) frei *friy*

freedom Freiheit (f) *friyhiyt*

to freeze frieren *freeren*

freezer (Tief)kühltruhe (f) *(teef)kewltroohe*

frequent häufig *hoyfig*

fresh frisch *frish*

fridge Kühlschrank (m) *kewlshrank*

fried gebraten *gebraaten*

friend Freund/in (m/f) *froynd/in*

friends Freunde (pl) *froynde*

frightened erschrocken *ershroken*

frog Frosch (m) *frosh*

from von + dat. *fon*

front Vorderseite (f) *forderziyte*
» **in front of** vor *fohr*

front door Eingangstür (f) *iyngangstewr*

frontier Grenze (f) *grentse*

frost Frost (m) *frost*

frozen gefroren *gefrohren*

fruit Obst (n), Frucht (f) *ohpst, frookt*

fruit shop Obst- und Gemüsehandlung (f) *ohpst oont gemewzehandloong*

to fry braten *braaten*

frying pan Bratpfanne (f) *braatpfanne*

fuel Brennstoff (m) *brennshtoff*

full voll *foll*
» **full board** Vollpension (f) *follpanzyohn*
» **full up** (booked up) ausgebucht *owsgeboohkt*

to have fun Spaß haben *shpaass haaben*
» **it was fun** es hat Spaß gemacht *es hat shpaass gemakt*

funeral Beerdigung (f) *be-erdigoong*

funfair Jahrmarkt (m) *yaarmarkt*

funny (amazing) lustig *loostig*
(peculiar) komisch *kohmish*

fur Fell (n) *fell*

furniture Möbel (n/pl) *merbel*

further on weiter *viyter*

fuse Sicherung (f) *zisheroong*

fusebox Sicherungskasten (m) *zisheroongskasten*

G

gallery Galerie (f) *galeree*

gambling Spielen (n) *shpeelen*

game (match) Spiel (n) *shpeel*
(hunting) Wild (n) *vilt*

gangway Gang (m) *gang*

garage (for parking) Garage (f) *garaashe*
(for petrol) Tankstelle (f) *tankshtelle*

garden Garten (m) *garten*

gardener Gärtner (m) *gertner*

garlic Knoblauch (m) *knohblowk*

gas Gas (n) *gaaz*
» **gas bottle/cylinder** Gasflasche (f) *gaazflashe*
» **gas refill** Gaskartusche (f) *gaazkartooshe*

gastritis Gastritis (f) *gastreetis*

gate Tor (n) *tohr*
(airport) Flugsteig (m) *floohgshtiyg*

gay (homosexual) homosexuell, schwul *hohmoseksuell, shvool*

gel (hair) Haar-Gel (n) *haar-gel*

general allgemein *allgemiyn*
» **in general** im Allgemeinen *im allgemiynen*

generous großzügig *grohsstsewgig*

gentle sanft *zanft*

gentleman/men Herr (m), Herren (pl) *herr, herren*

genuine echt *esht*

geography Geografie (f) *gayohgrafee*

German Deutsch *doytsh*

Germany Deutschland (n) *doytshlant*

to get bekommen *bekommen*
» **to get off** (bus) aussteigen *ows-shtiygen*
» **to get on** (bus) einsteigen *iyn-shtiygen*
» **to get through** (phone) durchkommen *doorshkommen*

gift Geschenk (n) *geshenk*

gin Gin (m)

girl Mädchen (n) *maydshen*

girlfriend Freundin (f) *froyndin*

to **give** geben *gayben*

» **to give back** zurückgeben *tsoorewkgayben*

glass Glas (n) *glaas*

glasses Brille (f) *brille*

global warming Erderwärmung (f) *ertervermoong*

gloves Handschuhe (m/pl) *hantshoohe*

glue Klebstoff (m) *klaybshtoff*

to **go** gehen *gayen*

» **to go away** weggehen *veggayen*

» **to go down** hinuntergehen *hinoontergayen*

» **to go in** hineingehen *hiniyngayen*

» **to go out** ausgehen *owsgayen*

» **to go round** (visit) besuchen *besooken*

» **let's go!** gehen wir! auf geht's! *gayen veer, owf gayts*

goal Ziel (n) *tseel*

(football) Tor (n) *tohr*

goat Ziege (f) *tseege*

God Gott (m) *gott*

goggles Schutzbrille (f) *shoots-brille*

gold Gold (n) *golt*

golf Golf (n) *golf*

» **golf clubs** Golfschläger (m/pl) *golfshlayger*

» **golf course** Golfplatz (m) *golfplats*

good gut *gooht*

» **good day** guten Tag *goohten taag*

» **good evening** guten Abend *goohten aabent*

» **Good Friday** Karfreitag (m) *karfriytaag*

» **good morning** guten Morgen *goohten morgen*

» **good night** gute Nacht *goohte nakt*

goodbye Auf Wiedersehen, Auf Wiederschauen (S. Germany, Austria)

owf veederzayen, owf veedershowen (casual) Tschüss *tshewss*

goods Waren *vaaren*

government Regierung (f) *regeeroong*

gramme Gramm (n) *gramm*

Grammar Grammatik (f) *grammatik*

grandchildren Enkelkinder (pl) *enkelkinder*

granddaughter Enkelin (f) *enkelin*

grandfather Großvater (m) *grohssfaater*

grandmother Großmutter (f) *grohssmootter*

grandparents Großeltern (pl) *grohsseltern*

grandson Enkel (m) *enkel*

grandstand Haupttribühne (f) *howpttribewne*

grape Weintraube (f) *viyntrowbe*

grapefruit Pampelmuse (f) *pampelmooze*

grass Gras (n) *graas*

grateful dankbar *dankbaar*

greasy fettig *fettig*

great! großartig, prima *grohssartig, preema*

green grün *grewn*

» **green card** Grüne Karte (f) *grewne karte* (environmentally aware) grün *grewn*

greengrocer's Obst- und Gemüsehandlung (f) *ohpst oont gemewzehandloong*

to **greet** grüßen *grewssen*

grey grau *grow*

grilled gegrillt *gegrillt*

grocer's Lebensmittelhändler (m) *laybensmittelhendler*

ground Boden (m) *bohden*

groundsheet Zeltboden (m) *tseltbohden*

ground floor Erdgeschoss (n) *ertgeshoss*

group Gruppe (f) *grooppe*

guarantee Garantie (f) *garantee*

guest Gast (m) *gast*

guest house Pension (f) *panzyohn*

guide Führer/in (m/f) *fewrer/in*
» guided tour Führung (f) *fewroong*
guidebook Reiseführer (m) *riyzefewrer*
guilty schuldig *shooldig*
guitar Gitarre (f) *geetarre*
gun Gewehr (n) *gevayr*
guy rope Zeltschnur (f) *tseltshnoor*

H

habit Gewohnheit (f) *gevohnhiyt*
hail Hagel (m) *haagel*
hair Haar (n), Haare (pl) *haar, haare*
hairbrush Haarbürste (f) *haarbürste*
haircut Haarschnitt (m) *haarshnit*
hairdresser Friseur (m) *frizerr*
hairdryer Fön (m) *fern*
hairgrip Haarklemme (f) *haarklemme*
hairspray Haarspray (n) *haarshpray*
half Hälfte (f) *helfte*
half *(adj)* halb *halp*
half an hour eine halbe Stunde *iyne halbe shtoonde*
half board Halbpension (f) *halppangzyohn*
half past... halb... *halp...*
half price/fare zum halben Preis *tsoom halben priys*
hall *(in house)* Diele (f) *deele*
ham Schinken (m) *shinken*
cured ham geräucherter Schinken (m) *geroysherter shinken*
hamburger Hamburger (m) *hamberrger*
hammer Hammer (m) *hammer*
hand Hand (f) *hant*
» hand luggage Handgepäck (n) *hantgepek*
» hand made handgemacht *hantgemakt*
handbag Handtasche (f) *hanttashe*
handkerchief Taschentuch (n) *tashentook*
handle Griff (m) *griff*
to hang up *(telephone)* auflegen *owflaygen*
hangover Kater (m) *kaater*

to happen passieren *passeeren*
happy glücklich *glewklish*
harbour Hafen (m) *haafen*
» harbour trip Hafenrundfahrt (f) *haafenroontfaart*
hard hart *hart*
(difficult) schwer *shvayr*
hard drive Festplatte (f) *festplatte*
hard shoulder Seitenstreifen (m) *ziytenshtriyfen*
hardware shop Eisenwarengeschäft (n) *iyzenvaarengesheft*
hat Hut (m) *hooht*
to hate hassen *hassen*
to have haben *haaben*
hay Heu (n) *hoy*
hay fever Heuschnupfen (m) *hoyshnoopfen*
he er *er*
head Kopf (m) *kopf*
(boss) Chef/in (m/f) *shef/in*
headache Kopfschmerzen (m/pl) *kopfshmertsen*
headphones Kopfhörer (f/pl) *kopfherrer*
to heal heilen *hiylen*
health Gesundheit (f) *gezoonthiyt*
healthy gesund *gezoont*
health foods Reformkost (f) *reformkost*
to hear hören *herren*
hearing Gehör (n) *geherr*
» hearing aid Hörgerät (n) *herr-gerayt*
heart Herz (n) *herts*
heart attack Herzanfall (m) *hertsanfall*
heat Hitze (f) *hitse*
heater Heizgerät (n) *hiytsgerayt*
heating Heizung (f) *hiytsoong*
heaven Himmel (m) *himmel*
heavy schwer *shvayr*
heel Ferse (f) *ferze*
(shoe) Absatz (m) *apzats*
height Höhe (f) *herhe*
helicopter Hubschrauber (m) *hoopshrowber*
hell Hölle (f) *herlle*
hello Hallo *hallo*

helmet *(motorbike)* Helm (m) *helm*
help Hilfe (f) *hilfe*
» **help!** Hilfe! *hilfe*
to **help** helfen *helfen*
her *(adj and pronoun)* ihr/sie *eer/zee*
» **(to) her** ihr *eer*
herb Kraut (n) *krowt*
herbal tea Kräutertee (m) *kroytertay*
here hier *heer*
here is... hier ist... *heer ist*
hers ihr *eer*
hiccups: to have hiccups Schluckauf haben *shlookowf haaben*
high hoch *hohk*
» **high chair** Babystuhl (m) *baybeeshtoohl*
to **hijack** entführen *entfewren*
hill Hügel (m) *hewgel*
him ihn *een*
» **(to) him** ihm *eem*
to **hire** mieten *meeten*
his *(adj. and pronoun)* sein *ziyn*
history Geschichte (f) *geshishte*
to **hit** schlagen *shlaagen*
to **hitchhike** trampen *trempen*
HIV HIV (n) *haa-ee-fow*
» **HIV positive** HIV positiv *haa-ee-fow pohzeeteef*
hobby Hobby (n) *hobby*
to **hold** halten *halten*
hole Loch (n) *lok*
holiday *(period of time)* Urlaub (m) *oohrlowp*
» **on holiday** im Urlaub *im oohrlowp*
holidays *(school etc)* Ferien (pl) *fayryen*
holy heilig *hiylig*
Holy Week Passionswoche (f) *passyohnsvoke*
home Heimat (f) *hiymaat*
» **at home** zu Hause *tsoo howze*
to **go home** nach Hause gehen *naak howze gayen*
homeopathic homöopathisch *homeopaatish*
to **be homesick** Heimweh haben *hiymfay haaben*

homosexual homosexuell *hohmoseksuell*
honest ehrlich *ayrlish*
honeymoon Flitterwochen (pl) *flittervoken*
to **hope** hoffen *hoffen*
» **I hope so** ich hoffe schon *ish hoffe shohn*
horrible scheußlich *shoysslish*
horse Pferd (n) *pfert*
hose Schlauch (m) *shlowk*
hospital Krankenhaus (n) *krankenhows*
host Gastgeber/in (m/f) *gastgayber/in*
hot heiß *hiyss*
(spicy) scharf *sharf*
hotel Hotel (n) *hotel*
hour Stunde (f) *shtoonde*
half-hour eine halbe Stunde *iyne halbe shtoonde*
house Haus (n) *hows*
housework Hausarbeit (f) *howsarbiyt*
hovercraft Hovercraft (n) *hoverkraaft*
how wie *vee*
» **how far?** wie weit? *vee viyt*
» **how long?** wie lange? *vee lange*
» **how many?** wie viele? *vee feele*
» **how much?** wie viel? *vee feel*
» **how much does it cost?** wie viel kostet das? *vee feel kostet das*
» **how much do they cost?** wie viel kosten sie? *vee feel kosten zee*
human menschlich *menshlish*
» **human being** Mensch (m) *mensh*
hungry hungrig *hoongrig*
to **be hungry** Hunger haben *hoonger haaben*
to **hunt** jagen *yaagen*
hunting Jagd (f) *yaagt*
hurry: to be in a hurry in Eile sein *in iyle ziyn*
to **hurt** weh tun *vay toon*
» **it hurts** es tut weh *es toot vay*
husband Ehemann (m) *ayheman*
hut Hütte (f) *hewtte*

hydrofoil Tragflächenboot (n) *traagfleshenboht*

I

I ich *ish*
ice Eis (n) *iys*
  » *(on roads)* Glatteis (n) *glattiys*
ice cream Eis (n) *iys*
ice rink Schlittschuhbahn (f) *shlittshoohbaan*
icy eisig *iyzig*
idea Idee (f) *eeday*
if wenn *venn*
ill krank *krank*
illness Krankheit (f) *krankhiyt*
to imagine sich vorstellen *sish fohrshtellen*
imagination Vorstellung (f) *fohrshtelloong*
immediately sofort *zofort*
immersion heater Boiler (m) *boyler*
impatient ungeduldig *oongedooldig*
important wichtig *vishtig*
impossible unmöglich *oonmerglish*
impressive beeindruckend *beiyndrookent*
in in + acc. or dat *in*
included inbegriffen *inbegriffen*
income Einkommen (n) *iynkommen*
independent unabhängig *oonabhengig*
indigestion Magenverstimmung (f) *maagenfershtimmoong*
indoors drinnen *drinnen*
industry Industrie (f) *indoostree*
infected infiziert *infitseert*
infection Infektion (f) *infektsyohn*
infectious ansteckend *anshtekend*
inflamed entzündet *entsewndet*
inflammation Entzündung (f) *entsewndoong*
influenza Grippe (f) *grippe*
informal nicht formell *nisht formell*
information Information (f) *informatsyohn*
  » **information desk/office** Auskunftsbüro (n) *owskoonftsbewroh*

injection Spritze (f) *shpritse*
to injure verletzen *ferletsen*
  » **injured** verletzt *ferletst*
injury Verletzung (f) *ferletsoong*
innocent unschuldig *oonshooldig*
insect Insekt (n) *inzekt*
  » **insect bite** Insektenstich (m) *inzektenstish*
  » **insect repellent** Insektenbekämpfungs -mittel (n) *inzektenbekempfoongsmittel*
inside Innere (n) *innere*
to insist bestehen *beshtayen*
inspector Kontrolleur (m) *kontrollerr*
instant coffee Pulverkaffee (m) *poolverkaffay*
instead of statt + dat. *shtatt*
instructor Lehrer/in (m/f) *layrer/in*
insulin Insulin (n) *inzooleen*
insult Beleidigung (f) *beliydigoong*
insurance Versicherung (f) *ferzisheroong*
  » **insurance document** Versicherungskarte (f) *ferzisheroongskarte*
to insure versichern *ferzishern*
  » **insured** versichert *ferzishert*
intelligent intelligent *intelligent*
interest *(money)* Zinsen (pl) *tsinzen*
interested interessiert *interesseert*
interesting interessant *interessant*
international international *internatsyonaal*
internet Internet (n) *internet*
  » **internet connection** Internetverbindung (f) *internetferbindoong*
to interpret dolmetschen *dolmetshen*
interpreter Dolmetscher/in (m/f) *dolmetsher/in*
interval *(theatre etc.)* Pause (f) *powze*
interview Interview (n)
into in + acc. *in*
to introduce vorstellen *fohrshtellen*
invitation Einladung (f) *iynlaadoong*
to invite einladen *iynlaaden*

iodine Jod (n) *yohd*

Ireland Irland *irlant*

Irish (adj.) irisch, (people) Iren *eerish, eeren*

iron (metal) Eisen (n) *iyzen*

(for clothes) Bügeleisen (n) *bewgeliyzen*

to **iron** bügeln *bewgeln*

is (see 'to be') ist *ist*

» **is there...?** gibt es...? *geept es*

Islam Islam (m) *islaam*

Islamic islamisch *islaamish*

island Insel (f) *inzel*

it es *es*

itch Jucken (n) *yooken*

J

jacket Jacke (f) *yake*

jam Konfitüre (f) *konfitewre*

jar Krug (m) *kroohg*

jaw Kiefer (m) *keefer*

jazz Jazz (m)

jeans Jeans (f)

jellyfish Qualle (f) *kvalle*

Jesus Christ Jesus Christus *yayzoos kristoos*

jetty Pier (m), Anlegestelle (f) *peer •anlaygestelle*

jeweller's Juwelier (m) *yooveleer*

Jewish Jüdisch *yewdish*

job Arbeit (f) *arbiyt*

to **jog** joggen *dshoggen*

jogging Joggen (n) *dshoggen*

joke Witz (m) *vits*

journalist Journalist/in (m/f) *shoornalist/in*

journey Reise (f) *riyze*

judge Richter (m) *rishter*

jug Kanne (f) *kanne*

juice Saft (m) *zaft*

to **jump** springen *shpringen*

jump leads Starthilfekabel (n) *shtarthilfekaabel*

jumper Pullover (m) *poollohver*

junction (road) Kreuzung (f) *kroytsoong*

(rail) Gleisanschluss (m) *gliysanshlooss*

just (only) nur *noor*

K

to **keep** behalten *behalten*

(to keep sth. for someone) zurücklegen *tsoorewklaygen*

kettle Kessel (m) *kessel*

key Schlüssel (m) *shlewssel*

» **key ring** Schlüsselring (m) *shlewsselring*

kidney Niere (f) *neere*

to **kill** töten *terten*

kilo(gram) Kilogramm (n) *keelogram*

kilometre Kilometer (m) *keelomayter*

kind (sort) Art (f) *art*

(generous) großzügig *grohsstsewgig*

king König (m) *kernig*

kiss Kuss (m) *kooss*

to **kiss** küssen *kewssen*

kitchen Küche (f) *kewshe*

knee Knie (n) *k-nee*

knickers Slip (m) *slip*

knife Messer (n) *messer*

to **knit** stricken *shtriken*

knitting Stricken (n) *shtriken*

to **knock** klopfen *klopfen*

knot Knoten (m) *k-nohten*

to **know** (someone) kennen *kennen*

(something) wissen *vissen*

» **I don't know** Ich weiß nicht *ish viyss nisht*

L

label Etikett (n) *etiket*

lace Spitze (f) *shpitse*

ladder Leiter (f) *liyter*

lady Dame (pl) *daame*

ladies Damen (f/pl) *daamen*

lager (light beer) Lager (n) *laager*

lake See (m) *zay*

lamb (meat) Lammfleisch (n) *lammfliysh*

lamp Lampe (f) *lampe*

lamp post Laternenpfahl (m), *laternenpfaal*

land Land (n) *lant*

to land landen *landen*

landing *(aeroplane)* Landung (f) *landoong*

  » *(house)* Treppensabsatz (m) *treppenabsats*

  » *(ship)* Anlegen (n) *anlaygen*

landlady Wirtin (f) *virtin*

landlord Wirt (m) *virt*

language Sprache (f) *shpraake*

large groß *grohss*

last letzte/r/s *letste/r/s*

to last dauern *dowern*

late spät *shpayt*

later später *shpayter*

laugh Lachen (n) *laken*

to laugh lachen *laken*

launderette Waschsalon (m) *vashsalong*

laundry Wäsche (f) *veshe*

law *(study subject)* Jura (f), Recht (n) *yoora, resht*

lawyer Rechtsanwalt (m), Rechtsanwältin (f) *reshtsanvalt, reshtsanveltin*

laxative Abführmittel (n) *apfewrmittel*

lazy faul *fowl*

lead Blei (n) *bliy*

  » **lead-free** bleifrei *bliyfriy*

leaf Blatt (n) *blatt*

leaflet Broschüre (f), Prospekt (m) *broshewre, prospekt*

to lean out hinauslehnen *hinowslaynen*

to learn lernen *lernen*

learner Anfänger *anfenger*

least: at least wenigstens, mindestens *vaynigstens, mindestens*

leather Leder (n) *layder*

to leave lassen *lassen*

  (to go away) verlassen *ferlassen*

lecturer Dozent/in (m/f) *dohtsent/in*

left links *links*

left luggage *(office)* Gepäckaufbewahrung (f) *gepekowfbevaaroong*

leg Bein (n) *biyn*

legal legal *legaal*

lemon Zitrone (f) *tsitrohne*

lemonade Limonade (f) *limonaade*

to lend verleihen *ferliyhen*

length Länge (f) *lenge*

lens *(camera)* Linse (f) *linze*

lesbian lesbisch *lesbish*

less weniger *vayniger*

lesson *(instruction)* (Unterrichts-)Stunde (f) *(oonterrishts-)shtoonde*

to let *(allow)* erlauben *erlowben*

  (rent) vermieten *fermeeten*

letter *(to someone)* Brief (m) *breef*

  (of alphabet) Buchstabe (m) *boohkshtaabe*

letterbox Briefkasten (m) *breefkasten*

lettuce Kopfsalat (m) *kopfzalaat*

leukaemia Leukämie (f) *loykaymee*

level *(height, standard)* Niveau (n) *nivoh*

  (flat) flach *flak*

level crossing Bahnübergang (m) *baanewbergang*

library Bibliothek (f) *bibliotayk*

licence *(driving)* Führerschein (m) *fewrershiyn*

  (fishing etc) Lizenz (f) *leetsents*

lid Deckel (m) *dekel*

to lie down sich hinlegen *sish hinlaygen*

life Leben (n) *layben*

lifebelt Rettungsgürtel (m) *rettoongsgewrtel*

lifeboat Rettungsboot (n) *rettoongsboht*

lifeguard *(swimming pool)* Bademeister/in (m/f) *baademiyster/in*

lifejacket Schwimmweste (f) *shvimveste*

lift Fahrstuhl (m) *faarshtool*

light Licht (n) *lisht*

  » **light bulb** Glühbirne (f) *glewbirne*

light *(coloured)* hell *hell*

  (weight) leicht *liysht*

to light *(fire)* anzünden *antsewnden*

lighter *(cigarette)* Feuerzeug (n) *foyertsoyg*

lighter fuel Feuerzeuggas (n) *foyertsoyggaas*

lightning Blitz (m) *blits*

like *(similar to)* wie *vee*

» like this/that so so

» what is ... like? wie ist...? *vee ist*

» what are ... like? wie sind...? *vee zint*

to like *(food, people)* mögen *mergen*

» I like ich mag *ish maag*

to like doing something etwas gerne tun *etvas gerne toohn*

» I like doing that ich tue das gerne *ish toohe das gerne*

likely wahrscheinlich *vaarshiynlish*

limited beschränkt *beshrenkt*

line Linie (f) *leenye*

lion Löwe (m) *lerve*

lip Lippe (f) *lippe*

lipstick Lippenstift (m) *lippenshtift*

liqueur Likör (m) *leekerr*

liquid Flüssigkeit (f) *flewssigkiyt*

list Liste (f) *liste*

to listen (to) zuhören + dat. *tsooherren*

litre Liter (m) *leeter*

litter Abfall (m) *apfall*

little klein *kliyn*

» a little ein wenig, ein bisschen *iyn vaynig, iyn bissshen*

to live leben *layben*

(dwell) wohnen *vohnen*

liver Leber (f) *layber*

living-room Wohnzimmer (n) *vohntsimmer*

loan Kredit (m) *kredeet*

local lokal, örtlich *errtlish*

lock Schloss (n) *shloss*

to lock anschließen *anshleessen*

locker Schließfach (n) *shleessfak*

lonely einsam *iynzam*

long *(inc. hair)* lang *lang*

long-distance Fern- *fairn*

» long-distance call Ferngespräch (n) *fairngeshprayk*

look Blick (m) *blik*

to look (at) ansehen *anzayen*

to look for suchen *zooken*

loose lose *lohze*

lorry LKW (m) (Lastkraftwagen) *el-kaa-vay (lastkraftvaagen)*

to lose verlieren *ferleeren*

lost property office Fundbüro (n) *foontbewroh*

a lot *(of)* viel *feel*

lotion Lotion (f) *lotsyohn*

lottery Lotterie (f) *lotteree*

loud laut *lowt*

lounge Wohnzimmer (n) *vohntsimmer*

(in ship etc.) Salon (m) *zalong*

love Liebe (f) *leebe*

to love lieben *leeben*

low niedrig *needrig*

low-fat fettarm *fettarm*

lower niedriger *needriger*

lucky: to be lucky Glück haben *glewk haaben*

luggage Gepäck (n) *gepek*

lump *(swelling)* Beule (f) *boyle*

lunch Mittagessen (n) *mittaayessen*

M

machine Maschine (f) *masheene*

machinist Maschinist/in (m/f) *masheenist/in*

mad verrückt *ferrewkt*

magazine Zeitschrift (f) *tsiytshrift*

mail Post (f) *post*

main Haupt-

» main station Hauptbahnhof (m) *howptbaanhof*

to make machen, tun *maken, toohn*

make-up Make-up (n)

male männlich *menlish*

man Mann (m) *man*

to manage *(cope)* schaffen *shaffen*

manager Manager/in (m/f)

managing director Geschäftsführer/in (m/f) *geshefts**fewrer**/in*

many viele *feele*

» **not many** nicht viele *nisht **feele***

map Karte (f) *karte*

marble Marmor (m) *marmohr*

margarine Margarine (f) *margar**ee**ne*

market Markt (m) *markt*

married verheiratet *ferh**iy**raatet*

» **to get married** heiraten *h**iy**raaten*

mascara Wimperntusche (f) *vimperntooshe*

masculine männlich *men**lish*

mask (diving) Maske (f) *maske*

mass (church) Messe (f), Gottesdienst (m) *messe, gottesdeenst*

match Streichholz (n) *shtr**iy**sh-holts* (game) Spiel (n) *shpeel*

material Stoff (m), Material (n) *shtoff, mater**yaal***

mathematics Mathematik (f) *matemat**ik***

matter: it doesn't matter das macht nichts *das **makt** nishts*

» **what's the matter?** was ist los? *vas ist **lohs***

mattress Matratze (f) *matra**tse***

» **air mattress** Luftmatratze (f) *looft**matratse***

mature (cheese) reif *r**iy**f*

me mich *mish*

meal Essen (n), Mahlzeit (f) *essen, maalts**iy**t*

mean: what does this mean? was bedeutet das?, was heißt das? *vas bed**oy**tet das, vas h**iy**sst das*

meanwhile in der Zwischenzeit *in der tsv**i**shentsiyt*

measles Masern (pl) *maazern*

» **German measles** Röteln (pl) *rerteln*

to measure messen *messen*

measurement Maß (n) *maass*

meat Fleisch (n) *fl**iy**sh*

» **cold meats** Aufschnitt (m) *owf**shnitt***

mechanic Mechaniker/in (m/f) *mesh**aa**niker/in*

medical medizinisch *medits**ee**nish*

medicine (subject) Medizin (f) *medits**een***

(drug) Medikament (n) *medika**ment***

medieval mittelalterlich *mittelalter**lish***

Mediterranean Mittelmeer (n) *mittelm**ayr***

medium (size) mittelgroß *mittelgr**ohss*** (steak) rosa *r**oh**za* (wine) halbtrocken *h**alp**troken*

meeting Treffen (n) *treffen*

melon Melone (f) *mel**oh**ne*

member Mitglied (n) *mit**gleet***

memory Gedächtnis (n) *ged**esh**tnis*

» **memory card** (for camera, computer) Speicherkarte *shp**iy**sherkarte*

men Männer (pl) *menner*

to mend reparieren *repar**ee**ren*

menu (a la carte) Speisekarte (f) *shp**iy**zekarte*

(set) Menü (n) *men**ew***

message Nachricht (f), Mitteilung (f) *n**aa**krisht, mitt**iy**loong*

metal Metall (n) *met**all***

meter Zähler (m) *ts**ay**ler*

metre Meter (m) *m**ay**ter*

microwave oven Mikrowelle(nherd) (m) *m**ee**krovelle(nhert)*

midday Mittag (m) *mitt**aag***

middle Mitte (f) *mitte*

middle-aged in mittleren Jahren *in mittleren y**aa**ren*

midnight Mitternacht (f) *mitter**nakt***

migraine Migräne (f) *meegr**ay**ne*

mild mild *milt*

mile Meile (f) *m**iy**le*

milk Milch (f) *milsh*

milkshake Milchmixgetränk (n) *milsh**miks**getrenk*

mince Hackfleisch (n) *hak**fliy**sh*

mind: do you mind if...? macht es Ihnen etwas aus, wenn...? *makt es **ee**nen etvas ows, venn...*

» **I don't mind** es macht mir nichts aus *es makt meer **nishts** ows*

mine (of me) mein/e/s *miyne/r/s*
minibus Kleinbus (m) *kliynboos*
mini-disc Mini-Disk (f) *mini-disk*
minister Minister (m) *minister*
minute (time) Augenblick (m), Minute (f) *owgenblik, minoohte*
mirror Spiegel (m) *shpeegel*
miscarriage Fehlgeburt (f) *faylgeboort*
miss Fräulein (n) *froyliyn*
to **miss** (bus etc) verpassen *ferpassen* (nostalgia) vermissen *fermissen*
mist Nebel (m) *naybel*
mistake Fehler (m) *fayler*
» to **make a mistake** einen Fehler machen *iynen fayler maken*
mixed gemischt *gemisht*
mixture Mischung (f) *mishoong*
model Modell (n) *modell*
modem Modem (n) *mohdem*
modern modern *modern*
moisturiser Feuchtigkeitscreme (f) *foyshtigkiytskraym*
moment Moment (m) *moment*
monastery Kloster (n) *klohster*
money Geld (n) *gelt*
month Monat (m) *mohnaat*
monthly monatlich *mohnaatlirh*
monument Denkmal (n) *denkmaal*
moon Mond (m) *mohnt*
moped Moped (n) *mohpet*
more mehr *mayr*
» no **more** nicht mehr *nisht mayr*
morning Morgen (m) *morgen*
mortgage Hypothek (f) *hewpotayk*
mosque Moschee (f) *moshay*
mosquito Stechmücke (f) *shtesh-mewke*
most (of) die meisten *dee miysten*
mother Mutter (f) *mootter*
mother-in-law Schwiegermutter (f) *shveegermootter*
motor Motor (m) *mohtor*
motorbike Motorrad (n) *motohrrat*
motorboat Motorboot (n) *motohrboht*
motor racing Rennsport (m) *rennshport*

motorway Autobahn (f) *owtobaan*
mountain Berg (m) *berg*
mountaineering Bergsteigen (n) *bergshtiygen*
mouth Mund (m) *moont*
to **move** bewegen *bevaygen*
» to **move house** umziehen *oomtseehen*
Mr Herr *herr*
Mrs Frau *frow*
much viel *feel*
not much nicht viel *nisht feel*
mug (cup) Becher (m) *besher*
to **mug** (someone) überfallen *ewberfallen*
to **murder** ermorden *ermorden*
museum Museum (n) *moozayoom*
music Musik (f) *moozeek*
musical Musical (n)
musician Musiker (m) *mooziker*
Muslim Muslim (m), Muslime (f) *mooslim, moosleeme*
must: you must Sie müssen *zee mewssen*
my mein/e *miyn/e*
mystery Rätsel (n) *raytsel*

N

nail Nagel (m) *naagel*
nail clippers/scissors Nagelschere (f) *naagelshayre*
nail file Nagelfeile (f) *naagelfiyle*
nail polish Nagellack (m) *naagellak*
nail polish remover Nagellackentferner (m) *naagellakentferner*
naked nackt *nakt*
name Name (m) *naame*
my name is... ich heiße, mein Name ist... *ish hiysse, miyn naame ist*
what is your name? Wie heißen Sie? *vee hiyssen zee*
napkin Serviette (f) *zervyette*
nappy Windel (f) *vindel*
» **disposable nappy** Wegwerfwindel (f) *vegverfvindel*

» **nappy liner** Windeleinlage (f) *vindeliynlaage*

national national *natsyonaal*

nationality Nationalität (f) *natsyonalitayt*

natural(ly) natürlich *natewrlish*

naughty frech, böse *fresh, berze*

navy Marine (f) *mareene*

navy blue marineblau *mareeneblow*

near nah *naa*

» **nearby** in der Nähe *in der nayhe*

nearest der/die/das Nächste *der/dee/das nekste*

nearly fast *fast*

necessary nötig *nertig*

necklace Halskette (f) *halskette*

to **need** brauchen, benötigen *browken, benertigen*

needle Nadel (f) *naadel*

negative (photo) Negativ (n) *naygateef*

neighbour Nachbar/in (m/f) *nakbaar/in*

neither ... nor ... weder... noch *vayder... nok*

nephew Neffe (m) *neffe*

nervous nervös *nervers*

net Netz (n) *nets*

never nie *nee*

new neu *noy*

» **New Year's Day** Neujahrstag (m) *noy-yaars-taag*

news Nachrichten (f/pl) *naakrishten,*

newspaper Zeitung (f) *tsiytoong*

newspaper kiosk Kiosk (m) *keeosk*

next nächste/r/s *nekste/r/s*

» **week/month/year** Woche/Monat/Jahr *voke, mohnaat, yaar*

next to neben + dat. or acc. *nayben*

nice nett *nett*

niece Nichte (f) *nishte*

night Nacht (f) *nakt*

nightclub Nachtklub (m) *naktcloob*

no nein *niyn*

nobody niemand *neemant*

noise Lärm (m) *lerm*

noisy laut *lowt*

non-alcoholic alkoholfrei *alkohohlfriy*

none kein/e/r *kiyn/e/r*

non-smoking Nichtraucher (m) *nishtrowker*

normal normal *normaal*

» **normally** normalerweise *normaalerviyze*

north Norden (m) *norden*

nose Nase (f) *naaze*

nosebleed Nasenbluten (n) *naazenbloohten*

nostril Nasenloch (n) *naazenlok*

not nicht *nisht*

note (bank) Banknote (f), Geldschein (m) *banknohte, geltshiyn*

nothing nichts *nishts*

» **nothing else** weiter nichts *viyter nishts*

now nun, jetzt *noohn, yetst*

nowhere nirgendwo *nirgentvoh*

nuclear power Kernkraft (f) *kernkraft*

number Nummer (f) *noommer*

nurse Krankenschwester (f), Krankenpfleger (m) *krankenshvester, krankenpflayger*

nursery slope Anfängerhügel (m) *anfengerhewgel*

nut Nuss (f) *nooss*

(DIY) Schraubenmutter (f) *shrowbenmootter*

nylon Nylon (n), Plastik (n) *newlon, plastik*

O

oar Ruder (n) *roohder*

object (thing) Gegenstand (m) *gaygenshtand*

obvious offensichtlich *offenzishtlish*

occasionally gelegentlich, hin und wieder *gelaygentlish, hin oont veeder*

occupied (seat) besetzt *bezetst*

odd merkwürdig *merkvewrdig*

(not even) ungerade *oongeraade*

177

of von + dat. *fon*

of course natürlich *natewrlish*

off *(TV, light)* aus *ows*

(milk) alt *alt*

offended beleidigt *beliygidt*

offer Angebot (n) *angeboht*

» special offer Sonderangebot (n) *zonderangeboht*

office Büro (n) *bewroh*

officer Offizier (m) *offeetseer*, Beamter (m), Beamtin (f) *beamter, beamtin*

» police officer Polizeibeamter *politsiybeamter*

official offiziell *offitsyell*

often oft *oft*

» how often? wie oft? *vee oft*

oil Öl (n) *erl*

OK OK

old alt *alt*

old-fashioned altmodisch *altmohdish*

olive Olive (f) *oleeve*

olive oil Olivenöl (n) *oleevenerl*

on auf + acc. or dat. *owf*

once einmal *iynmaal*

onion Zwiebel (f) *tsveebel*

only nur *noor*

open geöffnet *geerffnet*

to open öffnen *erffnen*

opera Oper (f) *ohper*

operation Operation (f) *operatsyohn*

opinion Meinung (f) *miynoong*

» in my opinion meiner Meinung nach *miyner miynoong naak*

opposite gegenüber + dat. *gaygenewber*

optician Optiker/in (m/f) *optiker/in*

or oder *ohder*

orange *(fruit)* Orange (f), Apfelsine (f) *orangshe, apfelzeene*

(colour) orange *orangsh*

order Bestellung (f) *beshtelloong*

to order bestellen *beshtellen*

ordinary gewöhnlich *gewernlish*

to organise organisieren *organeezeeren*

original(ly) ursprünglich *oohrshprewnglish*

other andere *andere*

others die anderen *dee anderen*

our unser *oonzer*

ours unsere/r/s *oonzere/r/s*

out (of) aus + dat. *ows*

outdoor(s), outside draußen *drowssen*

over über + dat. *ewber*

overcast bedeckt *bedeckt*

to overtake überholen *ewberhohlen*

owe: how much do I owe (you)? Was bin ich (Ihnen) schuldig? *vas bin ish (eenen) shooldig*

owner Besitzer (m) *bezitser*

ozone-friendly ozonfreundlich *otsohnfronydlish*

ozone layer Ozonschicht (f) *otsohnshisht*

P

package tour Pauschalreise (f) *powshaalriyze*

packet Paket (n) *pakayt*

paddle *(canoeing)* Paddel (n) *paddel*

padlock Vorhängeschloss (n) *fohrhengeshloss*

page Seite (f) *ziyte*

pain Schmerz (m) *shmerts*

painful schmerzhaft *shmertshaft*

painkiller Schmerzmittel (n) *shermtsmittel*

paint Farbe (f) *farbe*

to paint streichen *shtriyshen*

(picture) malen *maalen*

painter Maler (m) *maaler*

painting Gemälde (n), Bild (n) *gemaylde, bild*

pair Paar (n) *paar*

palace Palast (m) *palast*

pale blass *blass*

pants Unterhose (f) *oonterhohze*

paper Papier (n) *papeer*

paraffin Paraffin (n) *paraffeen*

paralysed gelähmt *gelaymt*

parcel Paket (n) *pakayt*

pardon? wie bitte? *vee bitte*

parents Eltern (f) *eltern*

park Park (m) *park*

to **park** parken *parken*

parking Parken (n) *parken*
» **parking disc** Parkscheibe (f) *parkshiybe*
» **parking meter** Parkuhr (f) *parkoohr*

parliament Parlament (n) *parlament*

part Teil (m) *tiyl*

parting *(hair)* Scheitel (m) *shiytel*

particular: in particular im Besonderen *im bezonderen*

partly teilweise *tiylviyze*

partner Partner/in (m/f) *partner/in*

party Party (f)
(political) Partei (f) *partiy*

to **pass** *(on road)* überholen *ewberhohlen*
(salt etc.) geben, reichen *gayben, riyshen*
(test, exam) bestehen *beshtayhen*

passenger Passagier (m) *passasheer*
(bus, taxi) Fahrgast (m) *faargast*

passion Leidenschaft (f) *liydenshaft*

passport Pass (m) *pass*

passport control Passkontrolle (f) *passkontrolle*

past Vergangenheit (f) *fergangenhiyt*
» **in the past** in der Vergangenheit *in der fergangenhiyt*
» *(adj.)* nach *naak*

pasta Nudeln (pl), Teigwaren (pl) *noohdeln, tiygvaaren*

pastry Teig (m) *tiyg*

path Weg (m) *vayg*

patient *(hospital)* Patient/in (m/f) *patsyent, patsyentin*

pattern Muster (n) *mooster*

pavement Gehsteig (m), Bürgersteig (m) *gayshtiyg, bewrgershtiyg*

to **pay** bezahlen *betsaalen*
» **to pay cash** bar zahlen *bar tsaalen*

peas Erbsen (pl) *erpsen*

peach Pfirsich (m) *pfirzish*

peanut Erdnuss (f) *ertnooss*

pear Birne (f) *birne*

pedal Pedal (n) *pedaal*

pedal-boat Tretboot (n) *traytboht*

pedestrian Fußgänger (m) *foohssgenger*

pedestrian crossing Fußgängerüberweg (m), Zebrastreifen (m) *foohssgenger- ewbervayg, tsaybra-shtriyfen*

peg Wäscheklammer (f) *vesheklammer*

pen Stift (m) *shtift*

pencil Bleistift (m) *bliyshtift*

penfriend Brieffreund (m) *breeffroynd*

penicillin Penicillin (n) *penicilleen*

pension Rente (f) *rente*

pensioner Rentner (m) *rentner*

people Leute (pl) *loyte*

pepper Pfeffer (m) *pfeffer*
» *(sweet/green/red)* Paprikaschote (f) *paprikashohter*

peppermint Pfefferminze (f) *pfeffermintse*

per pro *proh*

perfect perfekt *perfekt*

performance Vorstellung (f) *fohrshtelloong*

perfume Parfüm (n) *parfewm*

perhaps vielleicht *feeliysht*

period *(menstrual)* Periode (f), Tage (f) *payryohde, taage*
» **period pains** Regelschmerzen (pl), Monatsschmerzen (pl) *raygelshmertsen, mohnaatsshmertsen*

perm Dauerwelle (f) *dowervelle*

permit Erlaubnis (f) *erlowbnis*

to **permit** erlauben *erlowben*

person Person (f) *perzohn*

personal persönlich *perzernlish*

personal stereo Walkman (m)

petrol Benzin (n) *bentseen*

petrol can Benzinkanister (m) *bentseenkanister*

petrol station Tankstelle (f) *tankshtelle*

photocopy Fotokopie (f) *fohtokopee*

to **photocopy** fotokopieren *fohtokopeeren*

photo Foto (n) *fohto*

photographer Fotograf/in (m/f) *fohtograaf*

phrase book Sprachführer (m) *shpraakfewrer*

physics Physik (f) *fewzik*

piano Klavier (n) *klaveer*

to pick (choose) wählen *vaylen*
(flowers etc.) pflücken *pflewken*

picnic Picknick (n) *piknik*

picture Bild (n) *bilt*

piece Stück (n) *shtewk*

pier Pier (m), Anlegestelle (f) *peer, anlaygeshtelle*

pig Schwein (n) *shviyn*

pill Tablette (f) *tablette*
» **the pill** Pille (f) *pille*

pillow Kissen (n) *kissen*

pillowcase Kissenbezug (m) *kissenbetsoog*

pilot Pilot (m) *peeloht*

pilot light Zündflamme (f) *tsewntflamme*

pin Stecknadel (f) *shteknaadel*

pink rosa *rohza*

pipe (smoking) Pfeife (f) *pfiyfe*
(drain) Rohr (n) *rohr*

place Ort (m) *ort*
(seat) Platz (m) *plats*

plain einfach *iynfak*

plan (of town) Stadtplan (m) *shtattplaan*

plane Flugzeug (n) *floohgtsoyg*

plant Pflanze (f) *pflantse*

plaster (sticking) Pflaster (n) *pflaster*

plastic Plastik (n) *plastik*

plastic bag Plastiktüte (f) *plastiktewte*

plate Teller (m) *teller*

platform Bahnsteig (m) *baanshtiyg*

play (theatre) Theaterstück (n) *tayaatershtewk*

to play spielen *shpeelen*

pleasant angenehm *angenaym*

please bitte *bitte*

pleased erfreut *erfroyt*

plenty (of) eine Menge (von) + dat. *iyne menge (fon)*

pliers Zange (f) *tsange*

plug (bath) Stöpsel (m) *shterpsel*
(electrical) Stecker (m) *shteker*

plumber Klempner (m) *klempner*

pneumonia Lungenentzündung (f) *loongenentsewndoong*

pocket (Hosen)Tasche (f) *(hohzen)tashe*

point Punkt (m) *poonkt*
(needle, pin) Spitze (f) *shpitse*

poison Gift (n) *gift*

poisonous giftig *giftig*

pole Pfahl (m) *pfaal*

police Polizei (f) *politsiy*

police car Polizeiauto (n) *politsiyowto*

police station Polizeiwache (f) *politsiyvake*

polish Politur (f) *politoohr*

polite höflich *herflish*

politician Politiker (m) *poleetiker*

political politisch *poleetish*

politics Politik (f) *politik*

polluted verschmutzt *fershmootst*

pollution Umweltverschmutzung (f) *umveltfershmootsoong*

pool (swimming) Schwimmbecken (n) *shvimbeken*

poor arm *arm*

pop (music) Popmusik (f) *popmoozeek*

Pope Papst (m) *paapst*

popular beliebt *beleept*

pork Schweinefleisch (n) *shviynefliysh*

port (harbour) Hafen (m) *haafen*
(wine) Port(wein) (m) *port(viyn)*

portable tragbar *traagbar*

porter Gepäckträger (m) *gepektrayger*

portion Portion (f) *portsyohn*

portrait Portrait (n) *portray*

positive (sure) sicher *sisher*

possible möglich *merglish*
» **as … as possible** so … wie möglich *zoh … vee merglish*

possibly möglicherweise *merglishervize*

post (mail) Post (f) *pohst*

to post abschicken *apshiken*
   postbox Briefkasten (m) *breefkasten*
   postcard Postkarte (f) *postkarte*
   postcode Postleitzahl (f) *postliyttsaal*
   poster Poster (n) *pohster*
   (billboard) Plakat (n) *plakaat*
   postman Postbote (m), Briefträger (m)
      postbohte, breeftrayger
   post office Postamt (n) *postamt*
to postpone aufschieben *owfsheeben*
   pot Topf (m) *topf*
   potato Kartoffel (pl) *kartoffel*
   » potato crisps Kartoffelchips (f)
      kartoffeltships
   pottery Töpferei (f) *terpferiy*
   potty (child's) Töpfchen (n) *terpfshen*
   pound (sterling) Pfund Sterling (n)
      pfoont sterling
to pour gießen *geessen*
   powder Pulver (n) *poolver*
   powdered milk Milchpulver (n)
      milshpoolver
   power Macht (f) *makt*
   (physical strength) Kraft (f) *kraft*
   power cut Stromausfall (m)
      shtrohmowssfall
   pram Kinderwagen (m) *kindervaagen*
to prefer vorziehen *fohrtseehen*
   pregnant schwanger *shvanger*
to prepare vorbereiten *fohrberiyten*
   prescription Rezept (n) *retsept*
   present (gift) Geschenk (n) *geshenk*
   press (newspapers) Presse (f) *presse*
   » press officer Pressesprecher (m)
      presseshpresher
to press drücken *drewken*
   pretty hübsch *hewbsh*
   price Preis (m) *priys*
   priest Geistlicher (m) *giystlisher*
   prime minister Premierminister
      premyayminister
   prince Prinz (m) *prints*
   princess Prinzessin (f) *printsessin*
   print (photo) Abzug (m) *aptsoog*

to print drucken *drooken*
   prison Gefängnis (n) *gefengnis*
   private privat *privaat*
   prize Preis (m) *priys*
   probably wahrscheinlich *vaarshiynlish*
   problem Problem (n) *problaym*
   producer (radio/TV/film) Produzent (m)
      prodootsent
   profession Beruf (m) *beroohf*
   professor Professor (m) *professor*
   profit Gewinn (m) *gevinn*
   programme Programm (n) *programm*
   prohibited verboten *ferbohten*
to promise versprechen *fershpreshen*
   properly richtig, ordentlich *rishtig,
      ordentlish*
   property Eigentum (n) *iygentoohm*
   protestant protestantisch *protestantish*
   public (noun) Öffentlickeit (f)
      erffentlishkiyt
   (adj.) öffentlich *erffentlish*
   public holiday gesetzlicher Feiertag (m)
      gesetslisher fiyertaag
to pull ziehen *tseehen*
to pump up aufpumpen *owfpoompen*
   puncture platter (Reifen) (m) *platter
      (riyfen)*
   pure rein, pur *riyn, poohr*
   purple violett *violett*
   purse Geldbeutel (m), Portemonnaie (n)
      geltboytel, portmonnay
to push schieben *sheeben*
   push-chair Kinderwagen (m)
      kindervaagen
to put down hinstellen *hinshtellen*
to put on (clothes) anziehen *antseehen*
   pyjamas Pyjama (m), Schlafanzug (m)
      shlaafantsoog

Q

   quality Qualität (f) *kvalitayt*
   quarter Viertel (n) *feertel*
   quay Kai (m) *kiy*

queen Königin (f) *kernigin*
question Frage (f) *fraage*
queue Schlange (f) *shlange*
quick(ly) schnell *shnell*
quiet ruhig, leise, still *roohig, liyze, shtill*
quite ziemlich *tseemlish*

R

rabbi Rabbi (m) *rabbi*
rabbit Kaninchen (n) *kaneenshen*
rabies Tollwut (f) *tollvoot*
racecourse Rennbahn (f) *rennbaan*
racing *(horse)* Pferderennsport (m)
    pferderennshport
(motor) Motorsport (m) *mohtorshport*
racket *(tennis)* Schläger (m) *shlayger*
radiator *(heating)* Heizkörper (m)
    hiytskerper
radio Radio (n) *raadio*
radioactive radioaktiv *raadioakteef*
radio station Radiosender (m)
    raadiozender
raft Floß (n) *flohss*
railway Eisenbahn (f) *iyzenbaan*
railway station Bahnhof (m) *baanhohf*
rain Regen (m) *raygen*
    » **it's raining** es regnet *es raygnet*
raincoat Regenmantel (m) *raygenmantel*
to rape vergewaltigen *fergevaltigen*
rare selten *zelten*
(steak) blutig *blootig*
rash *(spots)* Ausschlag (m) *owsshlaag*
raspberries Himbeeren (pl) *himbayren*
rate *(ratio)* Rate (f) *raate*
(tariff) Kurs (m) *koors*
rather *(quite)* ziemlich *tseemlish*
raw roh *roh*
razor Rasierer (m) *razeerer*
razor blade Rasierklinge (f) *razeerklinge*
to reach erreichen *erriyshen*
to read lesen *layzen*
reading Lesen (n) *layzen*
ready fertig *fertig*
real *(authentic)* echt *esht*

really wirklich *virklish*
reason Grund (m) *groont*
receipt Quittung (f) *kvittoong*
receiver *(telephone)* Hörer (m) *herrer*
reception Empfang (m) *empfang*
receptionist Rezeptionist/in (m/f)
    retseptsyonist/in
recipe Rezept (n) *retsept*
to recognise erkennen *erkennen*
to recommend empfehlen *empfaylen*
record Schallplatte (f) *shallplatte*
to record aufnehmen *owfnaymen*
to recover *(from an illness)* sich erholen
    sish erhohlen
red rot *roht*
    » **Red Cross** Rotes Kreuz (n) *rohtes
    kroyts*
reduction Ermäßigung (f) *ermayssigoong*
to refill nachfüllen *naakfewllen*
refrigerator Kühlschrank (m) *kewlshrank*
refugee Flüchtling (m) *flewshtling*
refund Rückerstattung (f)
    rewkershattatoong
to refund zurückerstatten
    tsoorewkershatten
region Region (f), Gebiet (n) *regyohn,
    gebeet*
to register *(luggage etc.)* anmelden
    anmelden
registered *(letter)* eingeschrieben
    iyngeshreeben
registration number
    Kraftfahrzeugkennzeichen (n)
    kraftfaartsoyg-kenntsiyshen
registration documents *(car)*
    Fahrzeugpapiere (pl) *faartsoygpapeere*
relation Verwandter (m) *fervanter*
relatively einigermaßen *iynigermaassen*
religion Religion (f) *religyohn*
to remain bleiben *bliyben*
to remember sich erinnern an + acc. *sish
    erinnern an*
to remove wegnehmen *vegnaymen*
(tooth) ziehen *tseehen*

rent Miete (f) *meete*

to rent mieten *meeten*

to repair reparieren *repareeren*

to repeat wiederholen *veederhohlen*

reply Antwort (f) *antvort*

to reply antworten *antvorten*

report Bericht (m) *berisht*

to report berichten *berishten*

to rescue retten *retten*

reservation *(hotel etc.)* Reservierung (f) *rezerveeroong*

to reserve reservieren, buchen *rezerveeren, boohken*

reserved reserviert *rezerveert*

responsible verantwortlich *ferantvortlish*

to rest sich ausruhen *sish owsroohen*

restaurant Restaurant (n) *restorang*

restaurant-car Speisewagen (m) *shpiyzevaagen*

result Ergebnis (n) *ergaybnis*

retired pensioniert *pangzyoneert*

return Rückkehr (f) *rewkkayr*

(ticket) hin und zurück *hin oont tsoorewk*

to return wiederkommen *veederkommen*

to reverse *(car)* rückwärts fahren *rewkverts faaren*

reverse-charge call R-Gespräch (n) *ayr-geshpraysh*

rheumatism Rheumatismus (m) *roymatismoos*

rice Reis (m) *riys*

rich reich *riysh*

to ride *(horse/bike)* reiten, fahren *riyten, faaren*

right rechts *reshts*

(correct) richtig *rishtig*

» **to be right** Recht haben *resht haaben*

» **you're right** du hast Recht *doo hast resht*

right-hand side rechte Seite (f) *reshte ziyte*

ring *(jewellery)* Ring (m) *ring*

ripe reif *riyf*

river Fluss (m) *flooss*

road Straße (f) *shtraasse*

(main) Hauptstraße *howptshtraasse*

roadworks Straßenarbeiten (pl) *shtraassenarbiyten*

roast Braten (m) *braaten*

to rob berauben *berowben*

robbery Raub (m) *rowb*

roof Dach (n) *dak*

roll *(bread)* Brötchen (n), Semmel (f) *(Austria)* *brertshen, zemmel*

roller *(hair)* Lockenwickler (f) *lokenvikler*

room Zimmer (n) *tsimmer*, *(space)* Raum (m) *rowm*

rope Seil (n) *ziyl*

rose Rose (f) *rohze*

rotten faul, verfault *fowl, ferfowlt*

rough *(surface)* rauh *row*

(sea) stürmisch *shtewrmish*

round rund *roont*

roundabout *(traffic)* Kreisverkehr (m) *kriysferkayr*

row *(theatre etc.)* Reihe (f) *riyhe*

to row rudern *roohdern*

rowing boat Ruderboot (n) *roohderboht*

royal königlich *kerniglish*

rubber Gummi (m) *goommee*

rubbish Müll (m), Abfall (m) *mewl, apfall*

rucksack Rucksack (m) *rooksak*

rude grob, unhöflich *grohb, oonherflish*

ruins Ruine (f) *roo-eene*

ruler *(for measuring)* Lineal (n) *line-aal*

rum Rum (m) *room*

to run rennen, laufen *rennen, lowfen*

rush hour Stoßzeit (f) *shtohss-tsiyt*

rusty rostig *rostig*

S

sad traurig *trowrig*

safe *(strongbox)* Safe (m), Tresor (m) *trezohr*

safe sicher *zisher*

safety pin Sicherheitsnadel (f) *zisherhiytsnaadel*

to sail segeln *zaygeln*

sailboard Surfbrett (n) *serfbrett*

sailing Segeln (n) *zaygeln*

sailing boat Segelboot (n) *zaygelboht*

sailor Matrose (m), Seemann (m) *matrohze, zayman*

saint Heilige (m/f) *hiylige*

salad Salat (m) *zalaat*

sale *(bargains)* Ausverkauf (m), Schlussverkauf (m) *owsferkowf, shloossverkowf*

sales rep Verkaufsvertreter (m) *ferkowfsfertrayter*

salmon Lachs (m) *laks*

salt Salz (n) *zalts*

salty salzig *zaltsig*

same der-/die-/dasselbe *der/dee/dasselbe*

sample Muster (n) *mooster*

sand Sand (m) *zant*

sandals Sandalen (pl) *zandaalen*

sandwich Sandwich (n)

open sandwich belegtes Brot (n) *belaygtes broht*

sandy sandig *zandig*

sanitary towels Damenbinden (pl) *daamenbinden*

sauce Soße (f) *zohsse*

saucepan Kochtopf (m) *kohktopf*

saucer Untertasse (f) *oontertasse*

sauna Sauna (f) *zowna*

sausage Wurst (f) *voorst*

to save *(money)* sparen *shpaaren*

to say sagen *zaagen*

to scald verbrühen *ferbrewhen*

scales Waage (f) *vaage*

scarf Schal (m), Halstuch (n) *shaal, halstoohk*

(head) Kopftuch (n) *kopftoohk*

scene Szene (f) *stsayne*

scenery Landschaft (f) *lantshaft*

scent Duft (m) *dooft*

school Schule (f) *shoolhe*

science Wissenschaft (f) *vissenshaft*

scientist Wissenschaftler/in (m/f) *vissenshaftler/in*

scissors Schere (f) *shayre*

scooter Motorroller (m) *mohtorroller*

score: what's the score? wie steht es? *vee shtayt es*

Scotland Schottland *shottland*

Scottish Schottisch *shottish*

scratch Kratzer (m) *kratser*

to scratch kratzen *kratsen*

screen Bildschirm (m) *biltshirm*

screw Schraube (f) *shrowbe*

screwdriver Schraubenzieher (m) *shrowbentseeher*

sculpture Skulptur (f) *skoolptoohr*

sea Meer (n), See (f) *mayr, zay*

seafood Meeresfrüchte (pl) *mayresfrewhste*

seasick seekrank *zaykrank*

season Jahreszeit (f) *yaarestsiyt*

season ticket Zeitkarte (f) *tsiytkarte*

seat Sitz (m) *zits*

seatbelt Sicherheitsgurt (m) *zisherhiytsgoort*

second zweite/r/s *tsviyte/r/s*

second *(time period)* Sekunde (f) *zekoondé*

secret Geheimnis (n) *gehiymnis*

secretary Sekretär/in (m/f) *zekretayr/in*

section Abschnitt (m) *apshnitt*

to see sehen *zayen*

to seem scheinen *shiynen*

self-catering für Selbstversorger *fewr zelpstverzorger*

self-service Selbstbedienung (f) *zelpstbedeenoong*

to sell verkaufen *ferkowfen*

to send senden *zenden*

senior citizen Rentner/in (m/f) *rentner/in*

sensible vernünftig *fernewnftig*

sentence Satz (m) *zats*

separate(d) getrennt *getrennt*

serious ernst(haft) *ernsthaft*, *(grave)* schlimm *shlimm*

(important) wichtig **vishtig**
to **serve** bedienen **bedeenen**
  service (charge) Bedienung (f)
    bedeenoong
  (church) Gottesdienst (m), Messe (f)
    gottesdeenst, messe
several einige **iynige**
to **sew** nähen **nayen**
  sewing Nähen (n) **nayen**
sex (gender) Geschlecht (n) **geshlesht**
  (intercourse) Sex (m),
    Geschlechtsverkehr (m) **seks,**
    geshleshtsverkayr
shade (not sunny) Schatten (m) **shatten**
shadow Schatten (m) **shatten**
shampoo Shampoo (n) **shampooh**
sharp scharf **sharf**
shave Rasur (f) **razoohr**
to **shave** rasieren **razeeren**
  shaving cream/foam Rasiercreme (f)
    razeerkraym
she sie **zee**
sheep Schaf (n) **shaaf**
sheet Bettlaken (n) **bettlaaken**
shelf Regal (n) **regaal**
shell (egg, nut) Schale (f) **shaale**
shellfish Schalentiere (pl) **shaalenteere**
shelter Schutz (m) **shoots**
shiny glänzend **glentsent**
ship Schiff (n) **shiff**
shirt Hemd (n) **hemt**
shock (electrical) Schlag (m) **shlaag**
  (emotional) Schock (m) **shok**
shocked geschockt **geshokt**
shoe(s) Schuh/e (m, pl) **shooh/e**
shoe polish Schuhcreme (f) **shoohkraym**
shoe repairer's Schuster (m) **shooster**
shoe shop Schuhgeschäft (n)
    shoohgesheft
shop Geschäft (n), Laden (m) **gesheft,**
    laaden
shop assistant Verkäufer/in (m/f)
    ferkoyferin
shopping: to go shopping einkaufen
  gehen **iynkowfen gayen**

shopping centre Einkaufszentrum (n)
    iynkowfstsentroom
short kurz **koorts**
shorts Shorts (pl)
shout Ruf (m) **roohf**
show Aufführung (f), Show (f)
    owffewroong
to **show** zeigen **tsiygen**
shower Dusche (f) **dooshe**
shut geschlossen **geshlossen**
to **shut** schließen **shleessen**
shutter Fensterladen (m) **fensterlaaden**
sick krank **krank**
  » **to be sick** sich übergeben, erbrechen
    sish ewbergayben, erbreshen
  » **I feel sick** mir ist schlecht **meer ist**
    shlesht
sick bag Spucktüte (f) **shpooktewte**
side Seite (f) **ziyte**
sight (vision) Sehvermögen (n)
    zayfermergen
  (tourist) Sehenswürdigkeit (f)
    zayensvewrdigkiyt
sightseeing Besichtigung (f)
    bezishtigoong
sign Schild (f) **shild**
to **sign** unterschreiben **oontershriyben**
signal Zeichen (n) **tsiyshen**
signature Unterschrift (f) **oontershrift**
silent still **shtill**
silk Seide (f) **ziyde**
silver Silber (n) **zilber**
SIM card SIM-Karte (f) **simkarte**
similar ähnlich **aynlish**
simple einfach **iynfak**
since seit + dat. **ziyt**
to **sing** singen **zingen**
single (room) Einzelzimmer
    iyntseltsimmer
  » (ticket) Hinfahrt (f) **hinfaart**
  » (unmarried) ledig, single **lehdig**
sink Spülbecken (n) **shpewlbeken**
sister Schwester (f) **shvester**
sister-in-law Schwägerin (f) **shvaygerin**

to sit (down) sich hinsetzen sish **hin**zetsen

size (clothes, shoes) Größe (f) **grer**sse

skates (ice) Schlittschuhe (pl) **shlitt**shoohe

(roller) Rollschuhe (pl) **roll**shoohe

to skate Schlittschuh laufen **shlitt**shooh **low**fen

ski Ski (m) shee

to ski Ski laufen, Ski fahren shee **low**fen, shee **faa**ren

ski boots Skistiefel (pl) shee**shtee**fel

skiing Skilaufen (n) shee**low**fen

» **downhill skiing** Abfahrtslauf (m) ap**faarts**lowf

» **cross-country skiing** Langlauf (m) **lang**lowf

ski-lift Skilift (m) shee**lift**

skimmed milk Magermilch (f) **maa**germilsh

skin Haut (f) howt

skindiving Tauchen (n) **tow**ken

ski pole Skistock (m) shee**shtok**

skirt Rock (m) rok

ski-run/slope Piste (f) **pis**te

sky Himmel (m) **him**mel

to sleep schlafen **shlaa**fen

sleeper/sleeping-car Schlafwagen (m) **shlaf**waagen

sleeping bag Schlafsack (m) **shlaaf**zak

sleeve Ärmel (m) **er**mel

slice Scheibe (f) **shy**be

sliced geschnitten ge**shnit**ten

slide film Diafilm (m) **dee**afilm

slim dünn, schlank dewnn, shlank

slip (petticoat) Unterrock (m) **oon**terrok

slippery rutschig **root**shig

slow(ly) langsam **lang**zam

small klein klyin

smell Geruch (m) ge**rook**

to smell riechen **ree**shen

(of) nach + dat. naak

(bad/good) schlecht/gut shlesht/gooht

to smile lächeln **le**sheln

smoke Rauch (m) rowk

to smoke rauchen **row**ken

smooth glatt glatt

to sneeze niesen **nee**sen

snorkel Schnorchel (m) **shnor**shel

snow Schnee (m) shnay

snow chains Schneeketten (pl) **shnay**ketten

to snow schneien **shni**yen

» **it's snowing** es schneit es shniyt

so so zoh

(therefore) also **al**zo

soap Seife (f) **zy**fe

sober nüchtern **newsh**tern

social worker Sozialarbeiter/in (m/f) zot**syaal**arbiyter/in

sociology Soziologie (f) zotsyolo**gee**

sock Socke (f) **zo**ke

socket Steckdose (f) **shtek**dohze

soda (water) Soda (n) **zoh**da

soft weich wiysh

soft drink alkoholfreies Getränk (n) al**kohol**friyes ge**trenk**

software Software (f)

soldier Soldat (m) zol**daat**

sold out Ausverkauf (m) **ows**ferkowf

solicitor Rechtsanwalt (m) Rechtsanwältin (f) **reshts**anvalt, **reshts**anveltin

solid fest fest

some einige **iy**nige

somehow irgendwie **ir**gentvee

someone irgendwer **ir**gentvayr

something etwas **et**vas

sometimes manchmal **mansh**maal

somewhere irgendwo **ir**gentvoh

son Sohn (m) zohn

song Lied (n) leed

son-in-law Schwiegersohn (m) **shvee**gerzohn

soon bald balt

» **as soon as possible** so bald wie möglich zoh balt vee **mer**glish

sore (inc. throat) weh, wund vay, voont

sorry: I'm sorry Es tut mir Leid es tooht

meer **liyt**

sort Sorte (f) _zorte_

sound Ton (m) _tohn_

soup Suppe (f) _zooppe_

sour sauer _zower_

south Süden (m) _zewden_

souvenir Souvenir (n)

space Raum (m) _rowm_

spare übrig _ewbrig_

spare time Freizeit (f) _friytsiyt_

spare tyre Ersatzreifen (m) _erzatsriyfen_

sparkle funkeln, sprühen _foonkeln, shprewen_

sparkling wine Schaumwein (m) _showmviyn_

to **speak** sprechen _shpreshen_

special besondere/r/s _bezondere/r/s_

» **special offer** Sonderangebot (n) _zonderangeboht_

specialist Spezialist/in (m/f) _shpetsyalistin_

speciality Spezialität (f) _shpetsyalitayt_

spectacles Brille (f) _brille_

speed Tempo (n), Geschwindigkeit (f) _tempo, geshvindigkiyt_

speed limit Geschwindigkeitsbegrenzung (f) _geshvindigkiytsbegrentsoong_

to **spend** _(money)_ ausgeben _owsgayben_ _(time)_ verbringen _ferbringen_

spice Gewürz (n) _gevewrts_

spicy würzig _vewrtsig_

spinach Spinat (m) _shpinaat_

spirits Spirituosen (f) _shpirituohzen_

splinter Splitter (m) _shplitter_

to **spoil** verderben _ferderben_

sponge _(bath)_ Schwamm (m) _shvamm_

spoon Löffel (m) _lerffel_

sport Sport (m) _shport_

spot Punkt (m) _poonkt_, _(place)_ Stelle (f) _shtelle_

to **sprain** verstauchen _fershtowken_

sprained verstaucht _fershtowkt_

spray Spray (n) _shpray_

spring _(season)_ Frühling (m) _frewling_

square Platz (m) _plats_, _(shape)_ Quadrat (n) _kvadraat_

stadium Stadion (n) _shtaadyon_

stain Fleck (m) _flek_

stainless steel rostfreier Stahl (m) _rostfriyer shtaal_

stairs Treppe (f) _treppe_

stalls _(theatre)_ Parkett (n) _parkett_

stamp _(postage)_ Briefmarke (f) _breefmarke_

stand _(stadium)_ Tribüne (f) _tribewne_

to **stand** _(be placed)_ stehen _(bear)_ aushalten _shtayen, owshalten_

» **to stand up** aufstehen _owfshtayen_

stapler Heftmaschine (f) _heftmasheene_

star Stern (m) _shtern_

start Start (m), Beginn (m) _shtart, beginn_

to **start** beginnen, anfangen _beginnen, anfangen_

starter _(food)_ Vorspeise (f) _fohrshpiyze_

state Staat (m) _shtaat_

station Bahnhof (m), Station (f) _baanhohf, shtatsyohn_

stationer's Schreibwarenhandlung (f) _shriypvaarenhandloong_

statue Statue (f) _shtaatooe_

to **stay** _(live)_ wohnen _vohnen_ _(remain)_ bleiben _bliyben_

steak Steak (n) _stayk_

to **steal** stehlen _shtaylen_

steam Dampf (m) _dampf_

steamer Dampfer (m) _dampfer_

steel Stahl (m) _shtaal_

steep steil _shtiyl_

step _(footstep)_ Schritt (m) _shritt_ _(stairs)_ Treppe (f) _treppe_

stepbrother Stiefbruder (m) _shteefbroohder_

stepchildren Stiefkinder (pl) _shteefkinder_

stepfather Stiefvater (m) _shteeffaater_

stepmother Stiefmutter (f) _shteefmootter_

stepsister Stiefschwester (f) *shteefshvester*

stereo *(sound system)* Stereoanlage (f) *shtayreoh-anlaage*

sterling: pound sterling Pfund Sterling (n) *pfoont sterling*

steward *(air)* Steward (m)

stewardess *(air)* Stewardess (f)

stick Stock (m) *shtok*

to **stick: it's stuck** es klemmt *es klemmt*

sticking plaster Heftpflaster (n) *heftpflaster*

sticky klebrig *klaybrig*

sticky tape Klebeband (n) *klaybeband*

stiff steif *shtiyf*

still *(yet)* noch *nok*

still *(non-fizzy)* ohne Kohlensäure *ohne kohlenzoyre*

sting Stich (m) *shtish*

to **sting** stechen *shteshen*

stock cube Suppenwürfel (m) *zooppenvewrfel*

stock exchange Börse (f) *berrze*

stolen gestohlen *geshtohlen*

stomach Magen (m) *maagen*

stomach ache Magenschmerzen (pl) *maagenshmertsen*

stomach upset verdorbener Magen (m) *ferdorbener maanen*

stone Stein (m) *shtiyn*

stop *(bus)* Haltestelle (f) *halteshtelle*

to **stop** halten *halten*

stop! halt!, stop! *halt, shtop*

stopcock Abstellhahn (m) *apshtellhaan*

story Geschichte (f) *geshishte*

stove Herd (m) *hert*

straight gerade *geraade*

straight on immer geradeaus *immer geraadeows*

strange merkwürdig, seltsam *merkvewrdig, zeltzam*

strap Riemen (m) *reemen*

straw *(drinking)* Strohhalm (m) *shtrohhalm*

strawberries Erdbeeren (pl) *ertbayren*

stream Strom (m), Fluss (m) *shtrohm,*

flooss

street Straße (f) *shtraasse*

stretcher Bahre (f) *baare*

strike Streik (m) *shtriyk*

» **on strike** streiken *shtriyken*

string Schnur (f) *shnoor*

striped gestreift *geshtriyft*

strong stark *shtark*

student Student/in (m/f) *shtoodent/in*

studio *(radio/TV)* Studio (n) *shtoohdyo*

to **study** studieren *shtoodeeren*

stupid dumm *doomm*

style Stil (m) *shteel*

styling mousse Schaumfestiger (m) *showmfestiger*

subtitle Untertitel (m) *oonterteetel*

suburb Vorort (m) *fohrort*

to **succeed** Erfolg haben *erfolg haaben*

success Erfolg (m) *erfolg*

such solch *zolsh*

suddenly plötzlich *plertslish*

sugar Zucker (m) *tsooker*

sugar lump Zuckerwürfel (m) *tsookervewrfel*

suit *(man's)* Anzug (m) *antsoog* *((woman's) Kostüm (n) kostewm*

suitcase Koffer (m) *koffer*

summer Sommer (m) *zommer*

sun Sonne (f) *zonne*

to **sunbathe** sonnenbaden *zonnenbaaden*

sunburn Sonnenbrand (m) *zonnenbrant*

sunglasses Sonnenbrille (f) *zonnenbrille*

sunny sonnig *zonnig*

sunshade Sonnenschirm (m) *zonnenshirm*

sunstroke Sonnenstich (m) *zonnenshtish*

suntan creme Sonnencreme (f) *zonnenkraym*

» **suntan oil** Sonnenöl (n) *zonnenerl*

supermarket Supermarkt (m) *zoopermarkt*

supper Abendbrot (n) *aabentbroht*

supplement Zuschlag (m) *tsooshlaag*

suppose: I suppose so Ich nehme es an *ish nayme es an*

suppository Zäpfchen (n) *tsepfshen*

sure sicher *zisher*

surface Oberfläche (f) *ohberfleshe*

to **surf** *(Internet)* surfen

surname Nachname (m) *naaknaame*

surprise Überraschung (f) *ewberrashoong*

surprised überrascht *ewberrasht*

surrounded by umgeben von + dat. *oomgayben fon*

to **sweat** schwitzen *shvitsen*

sweater Pullover (m) *poolohver*

to **sweep** fegen, kehren *faygen, kayren*

sweet süß *zewss*

sweetener Süßstoff (m) *zewss-shtoff*

sweets Süßigkeiten (pl) *sewssigkiyten*

swelling Schwellung (f) *shvelloong*

to **swim** schwimmen *shvimmen*

swimming pool Schwimmbecken (n) *shvimmbeken*

swimming trunks Badehose (f) *baadehohze*

swimsuit Badeanzug (m) *baadeantsoohg*

switch Schalter (m) *shalter*

to **switch off** ausschalten *owsshalten*

to **switch on** einschalten *iynshalten*

swollen geschwollen *geshvollen*

symptom Symptom (n) *zimptohm*

synagogue Synagoge (f) *zinagohge*

synthetic synthetisch *zintaytish*

system System (n) *zistaym*

T

table Tisch (m) *tish*

tablet Tablette (f) *tablette*

table tennis Tischtennis (n) *tishtennis*

tailor Schneider (m) *shniyder*

to **take** nehmen *naymen*

(photo, exam) machen *maken*

(time) dauern *dowern*

taken *(seat)* besetzt *bezetst*

to **take off** *(clothes)* ausziehen *owstseehen*

(plane) abfliegen *apfleegen*

to **talk** reden *rayden*

tall groß *grohss*

tampon Tampon (f) *tampong*

tap Wasserhahn (m) *vasserhaan*

tape *(adhesive)* Klebeband (n) *klaybebant*

(cassette) Kassette (f) *kassette*

tape measure Bandmaß (n) *bantmaass*

taste Geschmack (m) *geshmak*

to **taste** schmecken *shmeken*

tax Steuer (f) *shtoyer*

taxi Taxi (n) *taksi*

taxi rank Taxistand (m) *taksishtand*

tea Tee (m) *tay*

teabag Teebeutel (m) *tayboytel*

to **teach** unterrichten, lehren *oonterrishten, layren*

teacher Lehrer/in (m/f) *layrer/in*

team Team (n)

teapot Teekanne (f) *taykanne*

tear *(rip)* Riss (m) *riss*

(cry) Träne (f) *trayne*

» **in tears** in Tränen aufgelöst *in traynen owfgelerst*

teaspoon Teelöffel (m) *taylerffel*

teat *(for baby's bottle)* Sauger (m) *zowger*

technical technisch *teshnish*

technology Technologie (f) *teshnolohgee*

teenager Teenager (m)

telegram Telegramm (n) *telegramm*

telephone Telefon (n) *telefohn*

telephone card Telefonkarte (f) *telefohnkarte*

telephone directory Telefonbuch (n) *telefohnboohk*

telephone box Telefonzelle (f) *telefohntselle*

to **telephone** anrufen *anroofen*

television Fernsehen *fernzayen*

to **tell** erzählen *ertsaylen*

temperature Temperatur (f)

*tempera***toohr**

to have a temperature Fieber haben **feeber haaben**

temporary provisorisch **provizohrish**

tender zart **tsart**

tennis Tennis (n) **tennis**

tennis court Tennisplatz (m) **tennisplats**

tent Zelt (n) **tselt**

tent peg Hering (m) **hayring**

tent pole Zeltstange (f) **tseltshtange**

terminal *(airport)* Terminal (m)

terminus Endstation (f) **entshtatsyohn**

terrace Terrasse (f) **terrasse**

terrible schrecklich **shreklish**

terrorist Terrorist/in (m/f) **terrorist/in**

text message SMS (f) es-em-es

than als **als**

thank you (very much) (vielen) Dank *(feelen)* dank

that (one) das (da) **das (daa)**

the der, die, das **der, dee, das**

theatre Theater (n) **tayaater**

their ihr **eer**

theirs ihr **eer**

them sie **zee**

» to them ihnen **eenen**

then dann **dann**

there dort, da **dort, daa**

» there is/are es gibt **es geept**

therefore deshalb **deshalp**

these diese **deeze**

they sie **zee**

thick dick **dik**

thief Dieb/in (m/f) **deeb/in**

thin dünn **dewnn**

thing Sache (f), Ding (n) **sake, ding**

to think denken **denken**

(believe) glauben **glowben**

I (don't) think so Ich glaube (nicht) **ish glowbe nisht**

third dritt **dritt**

thirsty durstig **doorstig**

this (one) das (hier) **das heer**

those diese, jene **deeze, yayne**

thread Faden (m) **faaden**

threat Drohung (f) **drohoong**

through durch + acc. **doorsh**

to throw werfen **verfen**

to throw away wegwerfen **vegnaymen**

thumb Daumen (m) **dowmen**

thunder Donner (m) **donner**

ticket *(travel)* Fahrkarte (f) **faarkarte** *(theatre etc.)* Eintrittskarte (f) **iyntrittskarte**

ticket office Fahrkartenschalter (m) **faarkartenshalter**

tide *(high/low)* Hochwasser (n), Niedrigwasser (n) **hohkvasser, needrigvasser**

tidy ordentlich **ordentlish**

tie Schlips (m) **shlips**

tight *(clothes)* eng **eng**

tights Strumpfhose (f) **shtroompfhohze**

till *(until)* bis **bis**

time Zeit (f) **tsiyt**, *(once etc.)* das eine Mal **das iyne maal**, *(on clock)* Uhr (f) **oohr**

timetable *(train)* Fahrplan (m) **faarplaan**

tin Dose (f) **dohze**

tin foil Alufolie (f) **aaloofohlye**

tinned Dosen- **dohzen**

tin opener Dosenöffner (m) **dohzenerffner**

tip *(in restaurant etc.)* Trinkgeld (n) **trinkgelt**

tired müde **mewde**

tissues Taschentücher (pl) **tashentewsher**

to zu + dat. **tsooh** *(with named places)* nach + dat. **naak**

toast Toast (m)

tobacco Tabak (m) **tabak**

tobacconist's Tabakladen (m) **tabaklaaden**

toboggan Schlitten (m) **shlitten**

today heute **hoyte**

toiletries Toilettenartikel (m/pl) **toalettenartikel**

toilet Toilette (f) *toalette*

toilet paper Toilettenpapier (n) *toalettenpapeer*

toll Gebühr (f) *gebewr*

tomato Tomate (f) *tomaate*

tomorrow morgen *morgen*

tongue Zunge (f) *tsoonge*

tonight heute Nacht, heute Abend *heute nakt, hoyte aabent*

too zu *tsooh*

(as well) auch *owk*

tool Werkzeug (n) *verktsoyg*

toolkit Werkzeugkasten (m) *verktsoygkasten*

tooth Zahn (m) *tsaan*

toothache Zahnschmerzen (pl) *tsaanshmertsen*

toothbrush Zahnbürste (f) *tsaanbewrste*

toothpaste Zahnpasta (f) *tsaanpasta*

toothpick Zahnstocher (m) *tsaanshtoker*

top *(mountain)* Gipfel (m) *gipfel*

» **on top of** oben auf + acc. or dat. *ohben owf*

torch Taschenlampe (f) *tashenlampe*

torn zerrissen *tserrissen*

total Endsumme (f) *entsoomme*

totally total *totaal*

to touch berühren *berewren*

tough *(difficult)* schwer *shvayr*

tour Fahrt (f) *faart*

to tour eine Tour machen *iyne toor maken*

tourism Tourismus (m) *toorismoos*

tourist Tourist/in (m/f) *toorist/in*

tourist office Reisebüro (n) *riyzebewroh*

towards nach + dat. *naak*

towel Handtuch (n) *hanttoohk*

tower Turm (m) *toorm*

town Stadt (f) *shtatt*

» **town centre** Stadtzentrum (n) *shtattsentroom*

» **town hall** Rathaus (n) *raathows*

» **town plan** Stadtplan (m) *shtattplaan*

tow rope Abschleppseil (n) *apshleppziyl*

toy Spielzeug (n) *shpeeltsoyg*

track Bahn (f) *baan*

traditional traditionell *traditsyonell*

traffic Verkehr (m) *ferkayr*

traffic jam Stau (m) *shtow*

traffic lights Ampel (f) *ampel*

trailer Anhänger (m) *anhenger*

train Zug (m) *tsoog*

» **by train** mit dem Zug *mit daym tsoog*

trainers Turnschuhe (pl) *toornshoohe*

tram Straßenbahn (f) *shtraassenbaan*

tranquilliser Beruhigungsmittel (n) *beroohigoongsmittel*

to translate übersetzen *ewberzetsen*

translation Übersetzung (f) *ewberzetsoong*

to travel reisen *riyzen*

travel agency Reisebüro (n) *riyzebewroh*

traveller's cheques Reisechecks (pl) *riyzesheks*

travel sickness Reisekrankheit (f) *riyzekrankhiyt*

tray Tablett (n) *tablett*

treatment Behandlung (f) *behandloong*

tree Baum (m) *bowm*

trip Fahrt (f) *faart*

trousers Hose (f) *hohze*

trout Forelle (f) *forelle*

true wahr *vaar*

» **that's true** das ist wahr *das ist vaar*

to try versuchen *fersoohken*

to try on anprobieren *anprobeeren*

T-shirt T-Shirt (n)

tube *(pipe)* Rohr (n) *rohr*

(underground) U-Bahn (f) *ooh-baan*

tuna Thunfisch (m) *toohnfish*

tunnel Tunnel (m) *toonnel*

turn: it's my turn ich bin dran *ish bin dran*

to turn drehen *drayen*

to turn off abbiegen *abbeegen*

turning *(side road)* Abfahrt (f) *apfaart*

twice zweimal *tsviymaal*

twin beds zwei Einzelbetten *tsviy*

*iynt*selbetten

twins Zwillinge (pl) *tsvillinge*

twisted *(ankle)* verrenkt *ferrenkt*

type *(sort)* Typ (m) *tewp*

to type tippen *tippen*

typical typisch *tewpish*

U

USB lead USB-Kabel *ooh-es-bay kaabel*

ugly häßlich *hesslish*

ulcer Geschwür (n) *geshvewr*

umbrella Regenschirm (m) *raygenshirm*

uncle Onkel (m) *onkel*

uncomfortable unbequem *oonbekvaym*

under unter + acc. or dat. *oonter*

underground *(tube)* U-Bahn (f)
    ooh-baan

underpants Unterhose (f) *oonterhohze*

underpass Unterführung (f)
    oonterfewroong

to understand verstehen *fershtayen*

underwater Unterwasser *oontervasser*

underwear Unterwäsche (f) *oonterveshe*

to undress ausziehen *ows-tseehen*

unemployed arbeitslos *arbiytslohs*

unemployment Arbeitslosigkeit
    arbiytslohzigkiyt

[unusually] [illegible] *[illegible]*

unhappy unglücklich *oonglewklish*

uniform Uniform (f) *ooniform*

university Universität (f) *ooniversitayt*

unleaded petrol bleifreies Benzin (n)
    bliyfriyes bentseen

unpleasant unangenehm *oonangenaym*

to unscrew aufschrauben *owfshrowben*

until bis *bis*

unusual ungewöhnlich *oongevernlish*

unwell unwohl *oonvohl*

up auf *owf*

  » up the hill bergauf *bergowf*

  » up the road die Straße rauf *dee
    shtraasse rowf*

upper obere/r/s *ohbere/r/s*

upstairs oben *ohben*

---

urgent dringend *dringent*

urine Urin (m) *ooreen*

us uns *oons*

to use benutzen *benootsen*

useful nützlich *newtslish*

useless nutzlos *nootslohs*

usually gewöhnlich *gevernlish*

V

vacant frei *friy*

vacuum cleaner Staubsauger (m)
    shtowbzowger

valid gültig *gewltig*

valuable wertvoll *vertfoll*

valuables Wertsachen (pl) *vertzaken*

van Lieferwagen (m) *leefervaagen*

vanilla Vanille (f) *vanille*

vase Vase (f) *vaaze*

VAT Mehrwertsteuer (f)
    mayrvert-shtoyer

veal Kalbfleisch (n) *kalpfliysh*

vegan Veganer/in (m/f) *vaygaaner/in*

vegetables Gemüse (n) *gemewze*

vegetarian Vegetarier/in (m/f)
    vegetaarier

(adj.) vegetarisch *vegetaarish*

vehicle Fahrzeug (n) *faartsoyg*

very sehr *zavr*

vest Unterhemd (n) *oonterhemt*

vet Tierarzt (m), Tierärztin (f). *teerartst,
    teerertstin*

video Video (n) *video*

view Aussicht (f) *ows-sisht*

village Dorf (n) *dorf*

vinegar Essig (m) *essig*

vineyard Weinberg (m) *viynberg*

virgin Jungfrau (f) *yoongfrow*

  » Virgin Mary Jungfrau Maria (f)
    yoongfrow mareea

visa Visum (n) *veezoom*

to visit besuchen *bezooken*

  (tourist site) besichtigen *bezishtigen*

visitor Besucher/in (m/f) *bezooker/in*

vitamin Vitamin (n) *vitameen*

voice Stimme (f) *shtimme*

volleyball Volleyball (m)

voltage Spannung (f) *shpannoong*

W

wage Lohn (m) *lohn*

waist Taille (f) *tallye*

to wait (for) warten (auf) + acc. *varten (owf)*

waiter Ober (m) Kellner (m) *ohber, kellner*

waiting room Warteraum (m) *varterowm*

waitress Kellnerin (f) *kellnerin*

Wales Wales *vales*

to walk, go for a walk einen Spaziergang machen *iynen shpatseergang maken*

walking stick Spazierstock (m) *shpatseershtok*

wall (inside) Wand (f) *vant*
(outside) Mauer (f) *mower*

wallet Brieftasche (f) *breeftashe*

to want wollen *vollen*

would like möchte *mershte*

war Krieg (m) *kreeg*

warm warm *varm*

to wash waschen *vashen*

washable waschbar *vashbaar*

wash-basin Waschbecken (n) *vashbeken*

washing Wäsche (f) *veshe*

washing machine Waschmaschine (f) *vashmasheene*

washing powder Waschpulver (n) *vashpoolver*

washing-up Abwasch (m) *apvash*

washing-up liquid Spülmittel (n) *shpewlmittel*

wastepaper basket Papierkorb (m) *papeerkorb*

watch (clock) Armbanduhr (f) *armbantoohr*

to watch zuschauen *tsoohshowen*
  » to watch TV fernsehen *fernzayen*

water Wasser (n) *vasser*

water melon Wassermelone (f) *vassermelohne*

waterfall Wasserfall (m) *vasserfall*

waterproof wasserfest *vasserfest*

water-skiing Wasserskilaufen (n) *vassersheelowfen*

wave Welle (f) *velle*

way (path) Weg (m) *vayg*
  » that way in der Richtung *in der rishtoong*
  » this way in dieser Richtung *in deezer rishtoong*

way in Eingang (m) *iyngang*

way out Ausgang (m) *owsgang*

wax Wachs (n) *vaks*

we wir *veer*

weather Wetter (n) *vetter*

weather forecast Wettervorhersage (f) *vetterforhayrzaage*

web (internet) Internet (n)

web designer Webdesigner/in (m/f)

wedding Hochzeit (f) *hoktsiyt*

week Woche (f) *voke*

weekday Werktag (m) *verktaag*

weekend Wochenende (n) *vokenende*

weekly wöchentlich *vershentlich*

to weigh wiegen *veegen*

weight Gewicht (n) *gevisht*

well gut *gooht*

well done (steak) durch *doorsh*

Welsh walisisch *valeezish*

west Westen (m) *vesten*

western westlich *vestlish*
(film) Western (m)

wet nass *nass*

wetsuit Taucheranzug (m) *towkerantsoog*

what? was? *vas*

wheel Rad *raat*

wheelchair Rollstuhl (m) *rollshtoohl*

when (whenever) wenn *venn*
(with past tense) als *als*

where wo *voh*

which welche/r/s *vel*she/r/s

whisky Whisky (m)

white weiß *viyss*

who *(relative)* der, die, das *der, dee, das*

who? wer? *vayr*

whole vollständig *foll*shtendig

why? warum? *va*room

wide breit *briyt*

widow Witwe (f) *vit*ve

widower Witwer (m) *vit*ver

wife Ehefrau (f) *ay*hefrow

wild wild *vilt*

to win gewinnen *ge*vinnen

» **who won?** wer hat gewonnen?
    *vayr hat ge*vonnen

wind Wind (m) *vint*

windmill Windmühle (f) *vint*mewle

window Fenster (n) *fenster*

» *(shop)* Schaufenster (n) *show*fenster

to windsurf windsurfen *vint*surfen

windy windig *vin*dig

wine Wein (m) *viyn*

wing Flügel (m) *flew*gel

winter Winter (m) *vin*ter

with mit + dat. *mit*

without ohne + acc. *ohne*

woman Frau (f) *frow*

wonderful wunderbar *voon*derbar

wood Holz (n) *holts*

wool Wolle (f) *volle*

word Wort (n) *vort*

work Arbeit (f) *arbiyt*

to work *(job)* arbeiten *arbiyten*

   (function) funktionieren
      *foonktsyo*neeren

world *(noun)* Welt (f) *velt*

worried besorgt *be*zorgt

worse schlimmer *shlimmer*

worth: it's not worth it das ist es nicht
   wert *das ist es nisht vert*

would like *(see 'to want')* möchten
      *mer*shten

wound Wunde (f) *voon*de

to wrap (up) verpacken *ferpaken*

wrong falsch *falsh*

to write schreiben *shriyben*

   writer Schriftsteller/in (m/f)
      *shrift*shteller/in

   writing paper Briefpapier (n)
      *breef*papeer

X

X-ray Röntgenaufnahme (f)
   *rernt*shenowfnaame

Y

yacht Jacht (f) *yakt*

to yawn gähnen *gaynen*

   year Jahr (n) *yaar*

   » **leap year** Schaltjahr (n) *shalt*yaar

yellow gelb *gelb*

yes ja *yaa*

yesterday gestern *gestern*

yet noch *nok*

yoghurt Joghurt (m) *yoh*goort

you *(formal)* Sie *zee*

   (informal singular) du *dooh*

   (informal plural) ihr *eer*

young jung *yoong*

your Ihr, dein, euer *eer, diyn, oyer*

yours Ihre/r/s, deine/r/s, eure/r/s
      *eer*e/r/s, *diyn*e/r/s, *oyr*e/r/s

youth Jugend (f) *yoogent*

   youth hostel Jugendherberge (f)
      *yoog*entherberge

Z

zip Reißverschluss (m) *riyss*fershlooss

zoo Zoo (m), Tiergarten (m) *teer*garten

zoology Zoologie (f) *tsoh-oh-lo*gee

German – English dictionary

Words for drinks and food are given in the **menu reader**, page 89. See also the **'You may see...'** lists in the individual subject sections of the phrase book.

A

abbiegen to turn off
Abend (m) evening
Abendbrot (n) supper
Abendessen (n) dinner *(evening meal)*
aber but
abfahren to depart *(bus, car)*
Abfahrt (f) departure *(bus, car)*
Abfahrtslauf (m) downhill skiing
Abfall (m) rubbish
Abfertigungsschalter (m) check-in desk
abfliegen to depart *(plane)*
Abflug (m) departure *(plane)*
Abflussrohr (n) drain
Abführmittel (n) laxative
Abholung (f) collection *(post, rubbish)*
absagen to cancel
abschicken to post, send off
abschleppen to tow
Abschleppseil (n) tow rope
Abschleppwagen (m) breakdown truck
Abschnitt (m) section
Abstellhahn (m) stopcock
Abteil (n) compartment
Abteilung (f) department
Abwasch (m) washing-up
Adresse (f) address
Agentur (f) agency
ähnlich similar
Aids (n) AIDS
Alkohol (m) alcohol
alkoholfrei non-alcoholic
Alkoholiker (m) alcoholic *(person)*
alkoholisch alcoholic *(content)*
alle all
Allee (f) avenue

allein alone
alles everything
allgemein general
als as, when *(with past tense)*; than
also so, well, therefore
alt old
Alter (m) age
altmodisch old-fashioned
Alufolie (f) aluminium foil
Ampel (f) traffic lights
Amtszeichen (n) dialling tone
an at, on
andere other
anders different(ly)
Anfang (m) beginning
anfangen to begin
Anfänger (m) beginner, learner
Angebot (n) offer
angebrannt burnt *(food)*
angeln to fish, go fishing
Angelrute (f) fishing rod
angenehm pleasant
Angst (f) fear
Anhänger (m) fan *(supporter)*; trailer *(car)*
ankommen arrive
Anlegestelle (f) jetty, pier
anmelden to register
anprobieren to try on
Anruf (m) *(phone)* call
anrufen to call
ansehen to look at
ansteckend infectious
Antenne (f) aerial
Antibiotikum (n) antibiotic
Antiquität (f) antique

antiseptisch antiseptic
Antwort (f) answer
antworten to answer
Anzahlung (f) deposit
anziehen to put on
anziehen, sich to dress, get dressed
Anzug (m) suit
anzünden to light *(fire)*
Apfel (m) apple
Arbeit (f) job, work
arbeiten to work
arbeitslos unemployed
Arbeitslosigkeit (f) unemployment
Architekt (m) architect
Arm (m) arm
arm poor
Armband (n) bracelet
Armbanduhr (f) watch
Ärmel sleeve
Artikel (m) article
Arzt (m), Ärztin (f) doctor
Asche (f) ash
Aschenbecher (m) ashtray
Aspirin (n) aspirin
Assistent (m) Assistentin (f) assistant
Asthma (n) asthma
Atmosphäre (f) atmosphere
auch also
auf on, on top, up
auf Wiederschauen goodbye *(Austria)*
auf Wiedersehen goodbye
Aufführung (f) performance
aufgeregt excited
auflegen to hang up *(telephone)*
aufnehmen to record
aufregend exciting
Aufschnitt (m) cold meats
aufstehen to stand up, get up
auftauen to defrost
Auge (n) eye
Auktion (f) auction
aus out, from *(light etc.)* off
Auseinandersetzung (f) argument
Ausflug (m) trip, excursion

Ausgang (m) exit
ausgeben to spend *(money)*
ausgebucht full up *(booked up)*
ausgehen to go out
ausgezeichnet excellent
Auskunft (f) information
Ausland (n) abroad
Ausländer (m), Ausländerin (f) foreigner
ausländisch foreign
auspacken to unpack
ausruhen, sich to rest, relax
Ausrüstung (f) equipment
ausschalten to turn out, switch off
außer except
außerdem besides
Aussicht (f) view
aussprechen to pronounce
Ausstattung (f) equipment
aussteigen to get off *(bus)*, to get
    out *(car)*
Ausstellung (f) exhibition
Ausverkauf (m) sale *(bargains)*
ausziehen, sich to get undressed
Auto (n) car
Autobahn motorway
automatisch automatic
Autovermietung (f) car hire
Autowäsche (f) car wash

B

Baby (n) baby
Babyflasche (f) baby's bottle
Babynahrung (f) baby food
Babytücher (pl) baby wipes
Bäckerei bakery shop
Bad (n) bath
Badeanzug (m) bathing costume
Badehose (f) swimming trunks
Bademeister (m) attendant *(bathing)*,
    lifeguard
baden to bathe
Badezimmer (n) bathroom
Bahn (f) track, way
Bahnhof (m) station

Bahnsteig (m) platform
bald soon
Ball (m) ball *(tennis, football etc.)*
Ballet (n) ballet
Banane (f) banana
Band (n) ribbon
Banknote (n) bank note
Bargeld (n) cash
» bar bezahlen to pay cash
Bart (m) beard
Batterie (f) battery
Bauarbeiter (m) builder
bauen to build
Bauernhof (m) farm
Baum (m) tree
Baumwolle (f) cotton
bedeckt overcast
bedeuten to mean, signify
bedienen to serve
Beerdigung funeral
Beere berry
beginnen to begin
behalten to keep
Behandlung (f) treatment
behindert disabled, handicapped
Beilage (f) side dish, side salad
Bein (n) leg
Beispiel (n) example
bekannt famous
bekommen to get
beliebt popular
benutzen to use
Benzin (n) petrol
Benzinkanister (m) petrol canister
bequem comfortable
Berater (m) consultant
Berg (m) mountain
Bergsteigen (n) mountaineering
berichten to report
Beruf (m) career, profession
Beruhigungsmittel (n) sedative
berühren to touch
beschädigen damage
beschäftigt busy

beschränkt limited
beschreiben to describe
Beschreibung (f) description
besetzt taken, engaged, occupied
besichtigen to visit *(tourist sites)*
Besichtigung sightseeing
Besitzer (m), Besitzerin (f) owner
besonders special, particular
besorgt worries
besser better
bestätigen to confirm
Beste (n) the best
Besteck (n) cutlery
bestellen to order
Bestellung (f) order
bestimmt definitely
Besuch visit
besuchen to go round, visit
Besucher (m), Besucherin (f) visitor
Betrag (m) amount *(money)*
Betriebswirtschaft (f) economics
betrunken drunk
Bett (n) bed, berth
Bettdecke (f) blanket
Bettuch (n) sheet
bevor before
bezahlen to pay
beziehungsweise (bzw.) respectively
Bibel (f) the Bible
Bibliothek (f) library
Biene bee
Bier (n) beer
Bier vom Fass (n) draught beer
Bild (n) picture
Bildschirm (m) screen
billig cheap
Bindehautentzündung (f) conjunctivitis
Birne (f) pear
bis until
bitte please; not at all
Blase blister; bladder
blau blue
blauer Fleck (m) bruise
Blei (n) lead

bleiben to remain
Bleichmittel (n) bleach
bleifrei lead free
bleifreies Benzin (n) leadfree petrol
Bleistift (m) pencil
blind blind
Blinddarmentzündung (f) appendicitis
Blitz (m) lightning
blond fair-haired
Blume (f) flower
Bluse (f) blouse
Blut (n) blood
bluten to bleed
Boden (m) ground, floor
Bogen (m) arch
Bohne (f) bean
Bordkarte (f) boarding card
Börse (f) stock exchange
Botschaft (f) embassy
braten to fry
Bratpfanne (f) frying pan
brauchen to need
braun brown
Braut (f) bride
Bräutigam (m) bridegroom
brechen to break
brennen to burn
Brennstoff (m) fuel
Brief (m) letter
Brieffreund (m), Brieffreundin (f)
    penfriend
Briefkasten (m) letterbox
Briefmarke (f) stamp (postage)
Briefpapier (n) writing paper
Brieftasche (f) wallet
Briefträger (m), Briefträgerin (f)
    postman, postwoman
Briefumschlag (m) envelope
Brille (f) glasses
bringen to bring
britisch British
Broschüre (f) leaflet
Brot (n) bread
Brötchen (n) bread roll

Brücke (f) bridge
Bruder (m) brother
Brunnen (m) fountain, well
Buch (n) book
buchen to book, reserve
Buchhandlung (f) bookshop
Bucht (f) bay
Buchung (f) booking
Büffet (n) buffet
Bügeleisen (n) iron (for clothes)
Buntstift (m) crayon
Büroangestellter (m) office clerk
Burg (f) castle, fortress
Büro (n) office
Bürste (f) brush
Bus (m) bus
Busbahnhof (m) bus station
Busfahrer (m) bus driver
Büstenhalter, BH (m) bra
Butangas (n) butane gas
Butter (f) butter

C

Camping (n) camping
Campingplatz (m) campsite
CD (f) CD
Chalet (n) Chalet
Champagner (m) champagne
Chef (m) head (boss)
Chips (pl) potato crisps
Computer (m) Computer
Cousin (m) cousin (male)
Creme (f) lotion, cream

D

da there
Dach (n) roof
Damen Ladies (toilets)
Damenbinden (pl) sanitary towels
Dampf (m) steam
danke thank you
dann then
das the, this, that, which (neuter)
Daten (pl) data

Datum (n) date *(date)*
dauern to last, take time
Dauerwelle (f) perm
Daumen (m) thumb
Deckel (m) lid
dein/e your *(adj.) (informal)*
dein/e/r yours *(informal)*
Demonstration (f) demonstration
denken to think
Denkmal (n) monument
denn for, as
Deodorant (n) deodorant
der the, who, which *(masculine)*
der-/die-/dasselbe the same
deshalb therefore, for that reason
Desinfektionsmittel (n) disinfectant
destilliertes Wasser (n) distilled water
Detail (n) detail
deutsch German
Deutschland Germany
Diät (f) diet
dich you *(informal)*
dick thick, fat
die the, who, which (feminine)
Dieb (m) thief
dies this
diese these
Diesel (n) diesel
digital digital
Digitalkamera (f) digital camera
dir (to) you
Direktor (m), Direktorin (f) director
Disk (f) disk
Diskothek (f) discothèque
Dokument (n) document
Dollar (m) dollar
dolmetschen to interpret
Dom (m) cathedral
Donner (m) thunder
Doppelbett (n) double bed
doppelt double
Dorf (n) village
dort there
Dose (f) can, tin

Dosenmilch (f) tinned milk
Dosenöffner (m) can opener
Dozent (m), Dozentin (f) lecturer
Drahtseilbahn (f) cable car
Drama (n) drama
draußen outside
drehen to turn
dringend urgent
dritte/r third
Droge (f) drug
Drogensüchtiger (m) drug addict
drücken to press
drucken to print
DSL, Breitband (n) broadband
du you *(familiar)*
dumm stupid
dunkel dark
dünn thin
durch through
Durchfall (m) diarrhoea
durchgehend direct *(train)*
durchkommen to get through
Durst thirst
durstig thirsty
Dusche (f) shower

E

echt genuine, real
Ecke (f) corner
egal: es ist mir egal I don't mind
Ehe (f) marriage
» (Ehe)Frau (f) wife
» (Ehe)Mann (m) husband
ehrgeizig ambitious
ehrlich gesagt frankly
ehrlich honest
Ei (n), Eier (pl) egg(s)
eigentlich in fact
Eigentum (n) property
Eimer (m) bucket
ein one, a
einchecken to check in
eindrucksvoll impressive
eine one, a *(feminine)*

einfach simple, plain
einfache Fahrt (f) single *(ticket)*
Eingang (m) entrance
einige some
einigermaßen relatively
einkaufen gehen to go shopping
Einkaufszentrum (n) shopping centre
Einkommen (n) income
Einladung (f) invitation
einmal once
Einrichtungen (f/pl) facilities
eins one *(number)*
einschalten to switch on
einschiffen embark *(boat)*
einsteigen to enter, get on *(bus, train)*
Eintritt (m) admission
Eintrittsgeld (n) admission charge
Eintrittskarte (f) ticket *(theatre etc.)*
Einzelbett (n) single bed
einzeln one by one
Einzelzimmer (n) single room
Eis (n) ice
Eisen (n) iron *(metal)*
Eisenbahn (f) railway
eisig icy
Elektriker (m) electrician
Elektrizität (f) electricity
elektronisch electronic
Eltern (pl) parents
Empfang (m) reception
empfehlen to recommend
Ende (n) end
Endstation (f) last stop, terminus
Energie (f) energy
eng narrow, tight
Englisch English
Enkel (m) grandson
Enkelin (f) granddaughter
Enkelkinder (pl) grandchildren
Ente (f) duck
Entfernung (f) distance
entführen to hijack
entschließen, sich to decide
entschuldigen Sie excuse me

entweder either
» entweder ... oder either ... or
entwerfen to design
entwickeln to develop
Entwurf (f) design
Entzündung (f) inflammation
er he
» er/sie hat he/she has
Erbse (f) pea
Erdbeben (n) earthquake
Erdbeeren (f) strawberry
Erde (f) earth
Erdgeschoss (n) ground floor
erholen, sich to recover
Erdnuss (f) peanut
Erfahrung (f) experience
Erfolg (m) success
erfreut pleased
Ergebnis (n) result
erinnern an, sich to remember
erkältet sein to have a cold
Erkältung (f) cold, flu
erlauben to let *(allow)*
Erlaubnis (f) permission
Ermäßigung (f) reduction, discount
ermorden to murder
ernst serious
erreichen to reach
Ersatzreifen (m) spare tyre
Erste Hilfe (f) first aid
erste/r/s first
erste/zweite Weltkrieg (m) the First/
    Second World War
erster Weihnachtstag (m) Christmas
    Day
Erwachsene (m, f) adult
erwarten to expect
erzählen to tell
es it
es macht nichts it doesn't matter
es regnet it's raining
es sei denn unless
es tut mir Leid I'm sorry
es tut mir weh it hurts

Esel (m) donkey
essbar edible
Essen (n) food
essen to eat
Essig (m) vinegar
Esszimmer (n) dining room
Etikett (n) label
etwas something
etwas gerne tun to like doing something
euch (to) you *(informal)*
euer/e your *(adj.) (informal)*
eure/r/s yours *(familiar)*
Euro (m) euro
eventuell perhaps
Examen (n) examination
Experte (m) expert
Export (m) export
express express

F

Fabrik (f) factory
Faden (m) thread
Fähre (f) ferry
fahren to drive
Fahrer (m) driver
Fahrgeld (n) fare
Fahrkarte (f) ticket *(travel)*
Fahrkartenschalter (m) ticket office
Fahrplan (m) timetable *(travel)*
Fahrrad (n) bicycle
Fahrstuhl (m) lift
Fahrt (f) trip, journey, tour
Fahrzeug (n) vehicle
falsch wrong
Familie (f) family
fantastisch fantastic
Farbe (f) colour
farbecht colour fast
farbenblind colour blind
Faser (f) fibre
fast nearly
faul lazy
Fax (n) fax
Feder (f) feather

Federbett (n) duvet
Fehler (m) fault, flaw, mistake, error
» einen Fehler machen to make a
mistake
fehlerhaft faulty
Fehlgeburt (f) miscarriage
feige cowardly
Feigling (m) coward
Feld (n) field
Felsen (m) rock
Fenster (n) window
Ferien (pl) holidays *(school)*
» Ferienhaus (n) holiday house
» Ferienwohnung (f) holiday apartment
Fern- long-distance
» Ferngespräch (n) long-distance call
Fernglas (n) binoculars
Fernsehen (n) television, TV
fernsehen to watch television
Fernsehprogramm (n) television
programme
Ferse (f) heel *(foot)*
fertig ready
Fest (n) festival, party
fest firm, solid
Festplatte (f) hard drive
Fett (n) fat
fettarm low-fat
fettig greasy
feucht damp
Feuer (n) fire
Feuerlöscher (m) fire extinguisher
Feuerwehr (f) fire brigade
Feuerwerk (n) firework
Feuerzeug (n) lighter *(cigarette)*
Fieber (n) fever, temperature
finden to find
Finger (m) finger
Firma (f) firm *(company)*
Fisch (m) fish
flach level *(flat)*
Flasche (f) bottle
Flaschenöffner (m) bottle opener
Fleisch (n) meat

Fliege (f) fly
fliegen to fly
fließend fluent *(language)*
Flohmarkt (m) flea market
Flüchtling (m) refugee
Flug (m) flight
Flügel (m) wing
Fluggesellschaft (f) airline
Flughafen (m) airport
Flugzeug (n) aeroplane, aircraft
Fluss (m) river
flüssig liquid
Flüssigkeit (f) liquid
folgen to follow
Fön (m) hair-drier
fönen to blow-dry *(hair)*
Form (f) shape
formell formal
Formular (n) form
fortgeschritten advanced
Foto (n) photo
Fotograf (m) photgrapher
Frage (f) question
fragen to ask
Frau (f) woman
Frau Mrs
Fräulein Miss
frech cheeky
frei free *(available, unoccupied)*
Freiheit (f) freedom
Fremde (m) (f) stranger
Freund (m) friend, boyfriend
Freundin (f) friend, girlfriend
Frieden (m) peace
Friedhof (m) cemetery
frisch fresh
Friseur (m) hairdresser
Frucht (f) fruit
früh early
früher earlier
Frühling (m) spring
Frühstück (n) breakfast
Führerschein (m) driving licence
Führung (f) guided tour

fühlen, sich to feel
fühlen, sich unwohl/wohl to feel ill/well
füllen to fill
Füllung (f) filling
funktionieren to work *(function)*
für for
Fuß (m) foot
Fußball (m) football
Fußgänger (m) pedestrian
Fußweg (m) footpath
füttern to feed

G

Gabel (f) fork
Galerie (f) gallery
Gang (m) corridor, gangway
ganz bestimmt yes, absolutely
Garage (f) garage
Garantie (f) guarantee
Garderobe (f) cloakroom
Gardine (f) curtain
Garten (m) garden
Gasflasche (f) gas bottle
Gaskartusche (f) gas refill
Gast (m) guest
Gastgeber (m), Gastgeberin (f) host, hostess
Gebäude (n) building
geben to give
Gebiet (n) district, region
Gebiss (n) denture
Gebühr (f) charge, fee
Geburtstag (m) birthday
Gedächtnis (n) memory
Gefahr (f) danger
gefährlich dangerous
Gefängnis (n) prison
gefroren frozen
gegen against
Gegenstand (m) object *(thing)*
gegenüber opposite
Geheimnis (n) secret
gehen to go
Gehirn (n) brain

Gehirnerschütterung (f) concussion

Gehör (n) hearing

gehören to belong (to)

Gehsteig (m) pavement

Geistlicher (m) priest

gekochtes Ei (n) boiled egg

gelähmt paralysed

gelb yellow

Geld (n) money

Geldautomat (m) cash point machine, ATM

Geldbeutel (m) purse

Geldstrafe (f) fine

gelegentlich occasionally

Gemälde (n) painting

gemeinsam together

genau exact(ly)

genießen to enjoy

genug enough

geöffnet open

Gepäck (n) luggage

Gepäckaufbewahrung (f) left luggage

gerade straight, even (not odd)

geräucherter Schinken (m) cured ham

Gericht (n) court (lawcourt) meal (food)

Geschäft (n) shop, business
 » geschäftlich on business

Geschäftsführer (m), Geschäftsführerin (f) managing director

Geschäftsreise (f) business trip

Geschenk (n) gift, present

Geschichte (f) history (past); story (tale)

geschieden divorced

Geschirrspülmaschine (f) dishwasher

Geschirrtuch (n) tea towel

geschlossen closed

Geschmack (m) flavour, taste

geschnitten cut, sliced

Geschwindigkeit (f) speed

Geschwindigkeitsbegrenzung (f) speed limit

Geschwister (pl) brothers and sisters

Gesellschaft (f) society, company (business)

gesetzlicher Feiertag (m) public holiday

Gesicht (n) face

Gesichtscreme (f) face cream

Gesichtspuder (m) face powder

gesperrt closed (road)

gestern yesterday

gestohlen stolen

gestreift striped

gesund fit (healthy)

Gesundheit (f) health

Getränk (n) drink

getrennt separated

Gewehr (n) gun

Gewerkschaft (f) trade union

Gewicht (n) weight

Gewinn (m) profit

gewinnen to win

Gewitter thunderstorm

Gewohnheit (f) habit

gewöhnlich usual, common

Gewürz (n) spice

gibt es...? is there...?

gießen to pour

Gift (n) poison

giftig poisonous

Gipfel (m) summit, top

Gitarre (f) guitar

Glas (n) glass

Glaube (m) belief

glauben to believe

gleich equal

Gleiche (m, n, f) the same

Gleisanschluss (m) junction (rail)

Glocke (f) bell

Glück (n) luck

Glück haben to be lucky

glücklich happy

Glühbirne (f) light bulb

Golf (n) golf

Golfplatz (m) golf course

Golfschläger (m) golf club

Gott God

Götterspeise (f) jelly

Gottesdienst (m) church service
Grad (n) degree
Gramm (n) gram
Grammatik (f) grammar
grau grey
Grenze (f) frontier, border
Griff (m) handle
Grippe (f) flu
grob coarse
groß big, tall
großartig great!
Großbuchstaben (pl) upper-case letters
Größe (f) size
Großeltern (pl) grandparents
größer bigger
Großmutter (f) grandmother
Großvater (m) grandfather
großzügig generous
grün green
Grund (m) reason
Gruppe (f) group
gültig valid
Gummi (m) rubber
Gummiband (n) rubber band
günstig convenient
Gurke (f) cucumber
Gürtel (m) belt
gut good, well
gute Nacht good night
guten Abend good evening, hello
guten Morgen good morning
guten Tag hello

H

Haar (n), Haare (pl) hair
Haarbürste (f) hair brush
Haarklemme (f) hair grip
Haarschnitt (m) haircut
Haarspülung (f) conditioner
haben to have
Hackfleisch (n) mince (meat)
Hafen (m) harbour
Hafenrundfahrt (f) harbour trip
Hahn (m) tap; cock

Hähnchen (m) chicken
halb half (adj.)
Halbpension (f) half board
Hälfte (f) half
Hallo! hello!
Halspastillen (pl) throat lozenges
Halt! stop !
halten to hold, stop
Haltestelle (f) stop (bus)
Hand (f) hand
Handcreme (f) hand cream
Handelsmesse (f) trade fair
handgearbeitet handmade
Handgepäck (n) hand luggage
Händler (m) dealer
Handschuh (m) glove
Handtasche (f) handbag
Handtuch (n) towel
Handy (n) mobile (phone)
hart hard
hässlich ugly
häufig frequent
Haupt... main
Hauptstadt (f) capital city
Hauptstraße (f) high (main) street
Haus (n) house
Hausarbeit (f) housework
Hausfrau (f) housewife
Haut (f) skin
Heftpflaster (n) sticking plaster
heilig holy
Heiligabend Christmas Eve
Heimat (f) home
Heimweh haben to be homesick
heiraten to get married
heiß hot
heißen to be called
Heizkörper (m) radiator
Heizung (f) heating
helfen to help
hell light (coloured)
helles Bier (n) lager
Helm (m) helmet
Hemd (n) shirt

herausnehmen to take out, remove
Herbst (m) autumn
Herd (m) stove, cooker
Herein! come in!
hereinkommen to come in
Hering (m) herring
Herr (m) man, gentleman
Herr Mr
herum around
Herz (n) heart
Herzanfall (m) heart attack
Heuschnupfen (m) hay fever
heute today
heute Abend this evening, tonight
hier here
hier ist... here is...
Hilfe (f) help
Hilfe! help!
Himbeere (f) raspberry
Himmel (m) sky, heaven
hin und wieder occasionally
hin und zurück return *(ticket)*
hinauslehnen to lean out
hineingehen to enter
hinstellen to put down
hinten at the back
hinter behind
Hintern (m) bottom
hinunter down *(movement)*
Hirsch (m) deer
Hitze (f) heat
HIV HIV
» HIV-positiv HIV-positive
Hobby (n) hobby
hoch high
Hochwasser (n) high tide; flood
Hochzeit (f) wedding
hoffen to hope
höflich polite
Höhe (f) height
Höhle (f) cave
holen to fetch
Hölle (f) hell
Holz (n) wood

homöopathisch homeopathic
homosexuell homosexual
hören to hear
Hörer (m) receiver *(telephone)*
Hörgerät (n) hearing aid
Hose (f) trousers
Hotel (n) Hotel
Hubschrauber (m) helicopter
Hügel (m) hill
Hund (m) dog
Hunger (m) hunger
Hunger haben to be hungry
hungrig hungry
Husten (m) cough
husten to cough
Hut (m) hat

I

ich I
ich heiße ... my name is ...
ich nehm es an I suppose so
ihm (to) him
ihn him
ihnen (to) them
Ihnen (to) you *(formal)*
ihr (to) her
ihr/e her, their *(adj.)*
Ihr/e your *(adj.) (formal)*
ihre/r/s hers, theirs
Ihre/r/s yours *(formal)*
im Allgemeinen in general
im Ausland abroad
im ersten Stock on the first floor
im Urlaub on holiday
immer always
immer geradeaus straight on
immer wieder again and again
in Eile sein hurry; to be in a hurry
in in
inbegriffen included
Infektion (f) infection
Informatik (f) computer science
Information (f) information
Ingenieur (m), Ingenieurin (f) engineer

innere inner
innerhalb within
ins Ausland fahren to go abroad
ins Internet gehen to log on
Insekt (n) insect
» Insektenspray (n) insect repellent
» Insektenstich (m) insect bite
Insel (f) island
insgesamt altogether
Institut (n) college, institute
Insulin (n) insulin
intelligent intelligent
interessant interesting
Internet (n) internet
Internet-Café Internet café
Internetverbindung (f) Internet
   connection
Ire, Irin Irishman, Irishwoman
irgendwie somehow
irgendwo somewhere
Irland Ireland
Islam Islam
ist es weit? is it far?

J

Jacke (f) jacket
Jagd (f) hunt
jagen to hunt
Jahr (n) year
Jahreszeit (f) season
Jahrhundert (n) century
Jahrmarkt (m) fair
Jeans (pl) jeans
Jeansstoff (m) denim
jede/r/s each
jemand someone
jene those
Jesus Christus Jesus Christ
jetzt now
Jod (n) iodine
Journalist (m) journalist
jüdisch Jewish
Jugend (f) youth
Jugendherberge (f) youth hostel

jung young
Junge (m) boy
Jungfrau (f) virgin
» Jungrauf Maria Virgin Mary
Jura law (study subject)
Juwelier (m) jeweller

K

Kabine (f) cabin
Kaffee (m) coffee
kalt cold
Kamera (f) camera
Kamillentee (m) camomile tea
Kamin (m) fireplace
Kamm (m) comb
kämpfen to fight
Kaninchen (n) rabbit
Kanister (m) petrol can
Kanne (f) jug
Kanu (n) canoe
Kapelle (f) chapel
kaputt broken
Karfreitag (m) Good Friday
kariert checked (pattern)
Karriere (f) career
Karte (f) map
Kartoffel (f) potato
Kartoffelchips (pl) potato crisps
Käse (m) cheese
Käsekuchen (m) cheese cake
Kasse (f) cash point
Kassette (f) cassette
Kassettenrekorder (m) cassette recorder
Katalog (m) catalogue
Kater (m) tom(cat); hangover
Kathedrale (f) cathedral
Katze (f) cat
kaufen to buy
keine/r/s no, none
Keks (m) biscuit
Keller (m) cellar
Kellner (m) waiter
Kellnerin (f) waitress
kennen to know (someone)
Kernkraft (f) nuclear power

Kerze (f) candle
Kessel (m) kettle
Kette (f) chain
Kiefer (m) jaw
Kilogramm (n) kilogram
Kind (n) child
Kinder (pl) children
Kinderbett (n) cot
Kinderwagen (m) pram
Kino (n) cinema
Kiosk (m) kiosk
Kirche (f) church
Kirsche (f) cherry
Kissen (n) cushion, pillow
Kiste (f) box
Klappstuhl (m) folding chair
klar clear
Klasse (f) class
Klavier (n) piano
Klavier spielen to play the piano
Klebeband (n) sticky tape
klebrig sticky
Klebstoff (m) glue
Kleid (n) dress
Kleider (pl) clothes
klein little
Kleinbus (m) minibus
Kleingeld (n) change
klemmt: es klemmt it's stuck
Klempner (m) plumber
klettern to climb
Klima (n) climate
Klimaanlage (f) air-conditioning
klopfen to knock
Kloster (n) monastery
klug clever
Knäckebrot (n) crisp bread
Knoblauch (m) garlic
Knöchel (m) ankle
Knopf (m) button
Koch (m) cook
Kochtopf (m) saucepan
koffeinfreier Kaffee (m) decaffeinated coffee

Koffer (m) suitcase
Kohl (m) cabbage
Kohlensäure (f) carbon dioxide
Kollege (m) colleague
komisch funny, peculiar
kommen to come
kommerziell commercial
Komödie (f) comedy
kompliziert complicated
Komponist (m) composer
Konditorei (f) cake shop
Konferenz (f) conference
Konfitüre (f) jam
König (m) king
Königin (f) queen
können to be able
könnte could
Konsulat (n) consulate
Kontaktlinsen (pl) contact lenses
Kontaktlinsenreiniger (m) contact lense cleaner
Konto (n) bank account
Kontrolle (f) control *(passport)*
Kontrolleur (m), Kontrolleurin (f) ticket inspector
Konzert (n) concert, concerto
Kopf (m) head
Kopfhörer (m) headphones
Kopfkissen (n) pillow
Kopfkissenbezug (m) pillow case
Kopfsalat (m) lettuce
Kopfschmerzen (f) headache
Kopftuch (n) head scarf
Korb (m) basket
Korken (m) cork
Korkenzieher (m) corkscrew
Körper (m) body
Kosmetik (f) cosmetics
kosten to cost
Kostüm (n) suit *(lady's)*
Kraftfahrzeugkennzeichen (n) registration number
krank ill
Krankenhaus (n) hospital

Krankenpfleger (m), Krankenschwester (f) nurse
Krankenwagen (m) ambulance
Krankheit (f) illness
kratzen to scratch
Kratzer (m) scratch
Kraut (n) herb
Kräutertee (m) herbal tea
Krawatte (f) tie
Krebs (m) cancer
Kredit (m) loan
Kreditkarte (f) credit card
Kreis (m) circle
Kreisverkehr (m) roundabout
Kreuz (n) cross
Kreuzfahrt (f) cruise
Kreuzung (f) crossroads
Krieg (m) war
Krone (f) crown
Krücke (f) crutch
Küche (f) kitchen
Kuchen (m) cake
Kugelschreiber (m) ballpoint pen
Kuh (f) cow
kühl cool
Kühlschrank (m) fridge
Kunst (f) art
Künstler (m), Künstlerin (f) artist
künstlich artificial
Kupfer (n) copper
Kuppel (f) cupola
Kurs (m) course
Kurve (f) curve, bend
kurz short
Kusine (f) cousin *(female)*
Kuss (m) kiss
küssen to kiss
Küste (f) coast

L

lächeln to smile
lachen to laugh
Lachs (m) salmon
Ladegerät (n) charger

Laden (m) shop
Lamm (n) (lamb)
Lampe (f) lamp
Land (n) country, land
Landesvorwahl (f) country code
Landschaft (f) countryside, scenery
lang long *(inc. hair)*
Länge (f) length
Langlauf (m) cross-country skiing
langsam slow(ly)
langweilig boring
Laptop (m) Laptop
Lärm (m) noise
lassen to leave
Lätzchen (n) bib
laut loud, noisy
Lawine (f) avalanche
leben to live
lebendig alive
Lebensmittelvergiftung (f) food poisoning
Leber (f) liver
lecker delicious
Leder (n) leather
ledig single *(unmarried)*
leer empty
legal legal
Lehrer (m), Lehrerin (f) instructor, teacher
leicht easy, light *(weight)*
Leichtathletik (f) athletics
leider unfortunately
Leiter (f) ladder
lernen to learn
lesbisch lesbian
lesen to read
letzte/r/s last
leuchtend bright
Leute (f) people
Licht (n) light
Licht anmachen to switch on the light
Lidschatten (m) eye shadow
lieben to love
Lieblings... favourite

Lied (n) song
liefern to deliver
Lieferung (f) delivery
Lieferwagen (m) delivery van
Liegestuhl (m) deckchair
Liegewagen (m) couchette
Limonade (f) lemonade
Linie (f) line
links left
Linse (f) lens *(camera)*
Lippe (f) lip
Liste (f) list
Liter (m) litre
Lizenz (f) licence *(fishing etc.)*
LKW (Lastkraftwagen) (m) lorry
Loch (n) hole
Löffel (m) spoon
Lohn (m) wage
lokal local
los: was ist los? What's the matter?
Lotion (f) lotion
Löwe (m) lion
Luft (f) air
Luftmatratze (f) air mattress
Luftpost (f) air mail
Lungenentzündung (f) pneumonia
lustig funny *(amusing)*

M

machen to do, make
macht das Ihnen etwas aus, wenn...?
   do you mind if...?
Mädchen (n) girl
Magen (m) stomach
» Magenschmerzen (pl) stomach ache
» Magenverstimmung (f) indigestion
Magermilch (f) skimmed milk
Make-up (n) make-up
Maler (m), Malerin (f) painter
man one *(pronoun)*
manchmal sometimes
Mandel (f) almond
Mann (m) man, husband
männlich male, masculine

Mantel (m) coat
Margarine (f) margarine
Marine (f) navy
Marke (f) brand
Markt (m) market
Maschine (f) machine
Masern (pl) measles
Maske (f) mask *(diving)*
Maß (n) measurement
Mathematik (f) mathematics
Mauer (f) wall
Maus (f) mouse
Mechaniker (m) mechanic
Medikament (n) medicine *(drug)*
Medizin (f) medicine
medizinisch medical
Meer (n) sea
Mehl (n) flour
mehr more
Mehrfachstecker (m) adaptor
   (electrical)
Mehrwertsteuer (f) VAT
mein/e my *(adj.)*
mein/e/s mine (of me)
Meinung (f) opinion
Melone (f) melon
Mensch (m) human being
menschlich human
merkwürdig odd
Messe (f) mass (church); trade fair
messen to measure
Messer (n) knife
Metall (n) metal
Meter (m) metre
Metzgergei (f) butcher's
mich me
Miete (f) rent
mieten to hire, rent
Migräne (f) migraine
Mikrowelle (f) microwave
Milch (f) milk
mindestens at least
Minister (m) minister
Minute (f) minute *(time)*

mir (to) me
Mischung (f) mixture
Misserfolg (m) failure
mit with
» mit dem Auto by car
» mit dem Bus by bus
» mit dem Zug by train
» mit Kohlensäure fizzy
Mitglied (n) member
Mittag (m) midday
Mittagessen (n) lunch
Mitte (f) middle
Mittel (n) means
mittelalterlich medieval
Mittelmeer (n) Mediterranean
Mitternacht (f) midnight
Möbel (n/pl) furniture
Mode (f) fashion
Modell (n) model
Modem (n) modem
mögen to like
möglich possible
möglicherweise possibly
Möglichkeiten (pl) facilities, possibilities
Möhre (f) carrot
Monat (m) month
monatlich monthly
Mond (m) moon
Moped (n) moped
Morgen (m) morning
» morgen früh tomorrow morning
» morgen tomorrow
Moschee (f) mosque
Moslem (m) Muslim
Motor (m) engine
Motorboot (n) motorboat
Motorrad (n) motorbike
müde tired
Müll (m) rubbish
Mülleimer (m) dustbin
Mund (m) mouth
Münze (f) coin
Museum (n) museum
Musik (f) music

Musiker (m), Musikerin (f) musician
müssen: Sie müssen/du musst... must; you must
Muster (n) pattern, sample
mutig brave
Mutter (f) mother

N

nach Hause gehen to go home
nach to, towards; after
Nachbar (m), Nachbarin (f) neighbour
nachfüllen to refill
Nachmittag (m) afternoon
Nachname (n) surname
Nachricht (f) message
Nachrichten (pl) news
nächste/r/s next
Nacht (f) night
Nachtclub (m) nightclub
Nachthemd nightdress
Nadel (f) needle
Nagel (m) nail
nah near
nähe: in der Nähe nearby
nähen to sew
Name (m) name
Nase (f) nose
Nasenbluten (n) nosebleed
nass wet
national national
Nationalität (f) nationality
Naturkost (f) health foods
natürlich natural(ly)
Naturschutz (m) conservation
Nebel (m) fog
neben next to
neblig foggy
Neffe (m) nephew
Negativ (n) negative
nehmen to take, catch *(train etc.)*
nein no
nervös nervous
nett kind *(generous)*, nice
Netz (n) net
Netzkarte (f) all-zone travel card

neu new
Neujahrstag (m) New Year's Day
nicht not
» nicht formell informal
» nicht mehr no more
» nicht viel not much
» nicht viele not many
Nichte (f) niece
Nichtraucher (m) non-smoker
nichts nothing
nie never
niedrig low
Niedrigwasser (n) low tide
niemand nobody
Niere (f) kidney
niesen to sneeze
nirgendwo nowhere
Niveau (n) level
noch still, yet
Norden (m) north
normalerweise normally
Notfall (m) emergency
nötig necessary
Notrufsäule (f) emergency telephone
    (on motorway)
nüchtern sober
Nudeln (pl) pasta
Nummer (f) number
nur just, only
Nuss (f) nut
nützlich useful
nutzlos useless

O

ob whether, if
oben on top of, above, upstairs
Ober (m) waiter
Obst (n) fruit
Obst- und Gemüsehandlung (f)
    greengrocer's
obwohl although
offensichtlich obviously
öffentlich public *(adj.)*
Öffentlichkeit (f) public

offiziell official
öffnen to open
oft often
ohne without
Ohr (n) ear
Ohrenschmerzen (pl) earache
Ohrentropfen (pl) eardrops
Ohrring (m) earring
Öl (n) oil
Oma (f) granny
Onkel (m) uncle
online buchen to book online
online online
Opa (m) grandpa
Oper (f) opera
Operation (f) operation
ordentlich tidy
Ordnung: in Ordnung all right, OK, fine
organisieren to organize
Ort (m) place
örtlich local
Osten (m) east
Ostern Easter
östlich eastern
Ozonschicht (f) ozone layer

P

Paar (n) pair, couple
Paket (n) packet, parcel
Pampelmuse (f) grapefruit
Panne (f) breakdown
Papier (n) paper
Papierkorb (m) wastepaper bin
Papiertaschentücher (pl) tissues
Paprikaschote (f) pepper *(vegetable)*
Papst (m) pope
Park (m) park
Parkscheibe (f) parking disc
Parlament (n) parliament
Partei (f) party *(political)*
Pass (m) passport
Passagier (m) passenger
passen to fit
Passkontrolle (f) passport control

Patient (m) patient
Pauschalreise (f) package tour
Pause (f) interval *(theatre etc.)*
PC (m) PC
peinlich embarrassing
Pension (f) guest house
pensioniert retired
perfekt perfect
persönlich personal(ly)
Pfeffer (m) pepper *(spice)*
Pfefferminze (f) peppermint
» Pfefferminztee (m) peppermint tea
Pfeife (f) pipe
Pferd (n) horse
Pfirsich (m) peach
Pflanze (f) plant
Pflaster (n) (sticking) plaster
Photoapparat (m) camera
Pier (m) jetty
Plastiktüte (f) plastic bag
Platten (m) puncture
Platz (m) place, seat *(in theatre etc.)*,
    square *(in town)*
Plombe (f) filling *(dental)*
plötzlich suddenly
Politik (f) politics
Polizei (f) police
Polizeiwache (f) police station
Pommes frites (pl) chips
Post (f) mail
Postkarte (f) post card
Postleitzahl (f) post code
Presse (f) press
prima! great!
privat private
pro per
Problem (n) problem
Produzent (m), Produzentin (f) producer
    (radio, television)
Prospekt (m) brochure, leaflet
Prost! cheers!
provisorisch temporarily
prüfen to check
Prüfung (f) exam

Pullover (m) sweater
Pulver (n) powder
Punkt (m) point
putzen to clean
Putzfrau (f) cleaning lady
Putzmittel (n) detergent

Q

Quadrat (n) square
Qualität (f) quality
Qualle (f) jellyfish
Quittung (f) receipt

R

Rabatt (m) discount
Rabbiner (m) rabbi
Rad (n) wheel
Radfahren (f) cycling
Rand (m) border
rasieren to shave
Rasierer (m) razor
Rasierklinge (f) razor blade
Rathaus (n) town hall
rau rough
rauchen to smoke
Raucher (m) smoker
Raum (m) room, space
Rechnung (f) bill
rechts right
Rechtsanwalt (m), Rechtsanwältin (f)
    lawyer
reden to talk
Reformkost (f) health food
Regelschmerzen (f) period pains
Regen (m) rain
Regenschirm (m) umbrella
Regierung (f) government
regnerisch rainy
reich rich
reif mature
Reihe (f) row
rein clean, pure
Reinigung (f) drycleaners
Reinigungsmittel (n) detergent
Reis (m) rice

Reise (f) journey
Reisebüro (n) travel agent
Reiseführer (m) guidebook
reisekrank travel sick
Reisescheck (m) travellers' cheque
Reiseziel (n) destination
reiten to ride
Rente (f) old age pension
Rentner (m), Rentnerin (f) pensioner
reparieren to fix *(mend)*
reservieren to book, to reserve
Reservierung reservation
retten to save, rescue
Rettungsboot (n) lifeboat
Rettungsgürtel (m) lifebelt
Rezept (n) recipe, prescription
richtig right, correct
Richtung (f) direction
riechen to smell
Rock (m) skirt
roh raw
Rohr (n) pipe
Rollstuhl (m) wheel chair
Rolltreppe (f) escalator
Röntgenbild (n) X-ray
rosa pink
Rost (m) rust
rot red
Röteln (f) German measles
Rowdy (m) yob
Rückerstattung (f) refund
Rückkehr (f) return
Rucksack (m) rucksack
Rückseite (f) the back *(reverse side)*
rückwärts backwards
rudern to row
rufen to call
ruhig calm, quiet
rund round
Rundfunkstation (f) radio station
rutschig slippery

S

Sache (f) thing

Saft (m) juice
Sahne (f) cream
Salat (m) salad
Salz (n) salt
sammeln to collect
Sammlung (f) collection
sauber machen to clean
sauer acid, sour
saurer Regen (m) acid rain
Schaden (m) damage
Schaf (n) sheep
schaffen to manage *(cope)*
Schal (m) scarf
schälen to peel
Schallplatte (f) record *(disc)*
Schalter (m) counter *(post office, ticket office etc.)*
Schalentiere (f) shellfish
Schaufenster (n) shop window
Schauspieler (m) actor
Scheck (m) cheque
Scheibe (f) slice, disc *(parking)*
scheiden: sich scheiden lassen to get a divorce
Schein (m) note *(bank)*
scheinen to seem, appear
Schere (f) scissors
scheußlich horrible
schicken to send
schieben to push
Schiff (n) ship, boat
Schild (n) sign
Schinken (m) ham
schlafen to sleep
Schlafsack (m) sleeping bag
Schlafwagen (m) sleeper
Schlafzimmer (n) bedroom
schlagen to hit
Schlange (f) queue, snake
schlecht bad
schließen to close
Schließfach (n) locker
schlimm bad, serious
Schlips (m) tie

Schlitten (m) toboggan
Schlittschuhbahn (f) ice rink
Schlittschuhe (pl) skates *(ice)*
Schloss (n) castle, palace; lock
Schluckauf (m) hiccups
Schluss (m) finish
Schlüssel (m) key
Schlüsselring (m) key ring
schmecken to taste
» schmeckt es Ihnen? does it taste all right?
Schmerz (m) pain
schmerzhaft painful
Schmerzmittel (n) painkiller
Schmetterling (m) butterfly
schmutzig dirty
Schnee (m) snow
Schneeketten (pl) snow chains
schneiden to cut
schneien to snow
schnell fast
Schnur (f) string
Schnurrbart (m) moustache
Schokolade (f) chocolate
schon already
schön pretty, nice, fine *(weather)*
Schornstein (m) chimney
Schrank (m) cupboard
Schraube (f) screw
Schraubenzieher (m) screwdriver
Schreck (m) fright
schrecklich awful, dreadful
schreiben write
Schreibwarenhandlung (f) stationer's
Schriftsteller (m), Schriftstellerin (f) writer
Schublade (f) drawer
Schuh (m) shoe
Schuld (f) debt
schuldig guilty
Schule (f) school
Schüssel (f) bowl, dish
Schuster (m) shoe mender
Schutz (m) shelter, protection

Schutzbrille (f) goggles
Schwager (m) brother-in-law
Schwägerin (f) sister-in-law
Schwamm (m) sponge
schwanger pregnant
schwarz black
schwarzfahren fare dodging
schwarzweiß black and white
Schwein (n) pig
Schweinefleisch (n) pork
schwer difficult
schwerhörig deaf
Schwester (f) sister
Schwiegermutter (f) mother-in-law
Schwiegersohn (m) son-in-law
Schwiegertochter (f) daughter-in-law
Schwiegervater (m) father-in-law
schwierig difficult
Schwimmbad (n) swimming pool
schwimmen to swim
Schwimmflossen (f) flippers
Schwimmweste (f) lifejacket
schwindelig dizzy
schwitzen to sweat
schwül muggy
See (f) sea
See (m) lake
seekrank seesick
segeln to sail
sehen to see
Sehenswürdigkeit (f) tourist attraction
sehr very
Seide silk
Seife (f) soap
Seil (n) rope
sein to be
sein/e his *(adj. and pronoun)*
seit since
Seite (f) side, page
Sekt (m) German equivalent to Champagne
Selbstbedienung (f) self-service
Selbstversorger: für Selbstversorger self-catering

selten seldom, rare

seltsam strange

Semmel (f) bread roll *(Austria)*

Senf (m) mustard

Serviette (f) napkin

Sessel (m) armchair

Sessellift (m) chair lift

sicher certain, sure, positive, safe

Sicherheitsgurt (m) seat belt

Sicherheitsnadel (f) safety pin

Sicherung (f) fuse

Sicherungskasten (m) fusebox

sie she, her, they, them *(pronoun)*

Sie you *(polite)*

Sieb (n) sieve

Silvester New Year's Eve

SIM-Karte (f) SIM card

singen to sing

Sitz (m) seat

Ski laufen to ski

Skischuhe (pl) ski boots

Skulptur (f) sculpture

Slip (m) knickers

Smoking (m) dinner jacket

SMS schicken to text

» SMS (f) text message

so bald wie möglich as soon as possible

Socke (m) sock

sofort immediately

Software (f) software

sogar even

Sohn (m) son

solche/r/s such

Sommer (m) summer

Sonderangebot (n) special offer

Sonne (f) sun

Sonnenbrand (m) sunburn

Sonnenbrille (f) sunglasses

Sonnenschirm (m) sunshade

Sonnenstich (m) sunstroke

sonst otherwise

Soße (f) sauce

sowieso anyway

Spannung (f) tension

sparen to save *(money)*

Spaß machen to be fun

spät late

später later

spazieren gehen to go for a walk

Spaziergang (m) walk

Speicherkarte (f) memory card

speichern to save *(comp)*

Speisekarte (f) menu *(à la carte)*

Speisewagen (m) dining car

sperren to block

Spiegel (m) mirror

Spiel (n) game

Spielen (n) gambling

spielen to play

Spielzeug (n) toy

Spinat (m) spinach

Sprache (f) language

Sprachführer (m) phrase book

sprechen to speak

springen to jump

Spritze (f) injection

Spülbecken (n) sink

Spülmittel (n) washing-up liquid

Staat (m) state

Stadion (n) stadium

Stadt (f) town, city

Stadtplan (m) street map

Stadtzentrum (n) town centre

Stahl (m) steel

Starthilfekabel (n) jump leads

statt instead of

Staub (m) dust

staubig dusty

stechen to sting *(insect)*

Stechmücke (f) mosquito

Steckdose (f) socket

Stecker (m) plug *(electrical)*

stehen to stand

stehlen to steal

steil steep

Stein (m) stone

sterben to die

Stern (m) star

Steuer (f) tax, duty
Stiefel (pl) boots
Stiefmutter (f) stepmother
Stift (m) pen
Stil (m) style
still quiet, silent
Stimme (f) voice
stimmen: das stimmt that's true
Stockwerk (n) floor, storey
Stoff (m) fabric, material
Stoßzeit (f) rush hour
Strand (m) beach
Straße (f) street
Straßenbahn (f) tram
Straßenarbeiten (f) roadworks
Streifen (m) stripe
streuen to scatter
stricken to knit
Strohhalm (m) straw
Strom (m) current *(electricity)*
Stromausfall (m) power cut
Strümpfe (pl) stockings
Strumpfhose (f) tights
Stück (n) piece, bit
Stückchen (n) little bit
Student (m) student
Stuhl (m) chair
Stunde (f) hour
» eine halbe Stunde half an hour
suchen to look for
süchtig addicted
Summe (f) total, sum
Supermarkt (m) supermarket
Surfbrett (n) surfboard
süß sweet
Süßigkeiten (pl) sweets
Symptom (n) symptom
synchronisiert dubbed
System (n) system
Szene (f) scene

T

Tabak (m) tobacco
Tag (m) day
Tage (pl), Regel (f) period
Tagebuch (n) diary
täglich daily
Taille (f) waist
Tal (n) valley
tanken to fill up with petrol
Tankstelle (f) garage *(for petrol)*
Tante (f) aunt
Tanz (m) dance
Tasche (f) bag, pocket
Taschenlampe (f) torch
Taschenmesser (n) penknife
Taschenrechner (m) calculator
Taschentücher (pl) tissues
Tasse (f) cup
Tastatur (f) keyboard
tauchen to dive
technisch technical
Tee (m) tea
Teebeutel (m) tea bag
Teekanne (f) teapot
Teelöffel (m) teaspoon
Teig (m) dough
Teil (n) part, piece
Telefon (n) telephone
Telefonkarte (f) telephone card
Telefonladen (m) telephone shop
Telefonzelle (f) telephone box
Teller (m) plate
Temperatur (f) temperature
Tennisplatz (m) tennis court
Teppich (m) carpet
Termin (m) date, appointment
Terrorist (m) terrorist
teuer expensive
Theater (n) theatre
Theaterstück (n) play *(theatre)*
Thermometer (n) thermometer
tief deep
Tiefkühltruhe (f) freezer
Tier (n) animal

Tierarzt (m), Tierärztin (f) vet
Tiergarten (m) zoo
tippen to type
Tisch (m) table
Tochter (f) daughter
Tod (m) death
tödlich fatal
Toilette (f) toilet
toll lovely, wonderful
Tollwut (f) rabies
Tomate (f) tomato
Ton (m) sound
Tonbandgerät (n) tape recorder
Topf (m) pot
Tor (n) gate; goal *(football)*
tot dead
Tourismus (m) tourism
traditionell traditional
tragbar portable
tragen to carry
Tragetasche (f) carrier bag
Tragflächenboot (n) hydrofoil
trampen to hitchhike
Tränen (pl) tears
traurig sad
Treffen (m) meeting
treffen, sich to meet
Treppe (f) stairs
trinken to drink
Trinkgeld (n) tip
trocken dry
tschüss goodbye *(casual)*
Tuch (n) cloth
tun to do, make
Tür (f) door
Turm (m) tower
Turnschuhe (pl) trainers
Tüte (f) bag
typisch typical

U

über over, above; via
überall everywhere
Überfahrt (f) crossing *(sea)*

überfallen to attack, mug
Übergepäck (n) excess luggage
überholen to overtake
übermorgen the day after tomorrow
Überraschung (f) surprise
übersetzen to translate
Übersetzung (f) translation
Überzelt (n) fly sheet
übrig spare
Übung (f) exercise
Uhr (f) clock, time
Umkleidekabine (f) changing room
Umleitung (f) diversion
umsonst free
umsteigen to change *(trains)*
Umwelt (f) environment
» umweltfreundlich environmentally
    friendly
» Umweltverschmutung (f) pollution
umziehen to change *(clothes);* to move
    house
unabhängig independent
unangenehm unpleasant
unbequem uncomfortable
und and
Unfall (m) accident
ungeduldig impatient
ungefähr roughly, about
ungewöhnlich unusual
unglücklich unhappy, unlucky
unhöflich rude
Universität (f) university
unmöglich impossible
uns us, to us
unschuldig innocent
unser our
unser/r/s ours
unten downstairs, below
unter under, underneath
Unterführung (f) underpass
Untergeschoss (n) basement
Unterhaltung (f) conversation,
    entertainment
Unterhemd (n) vest

Unterhose (f) underpants
Unterkunft (f) accommodation
Unterricht (m) lesson *(instruction)*
unterrichten to teach, instruct
unterschreiben to sign
Unterschrift (f) signature
Untertasse (f) saucer
Untertitel (m) subtitle
Unterwäsche (f) underwear, lingerie
unvorsichtig careless
unwohl unwell
Urlaub (m) holiday *(period of time)*
ursprünglich original(ly)
USB-Kabel (n) USB lead

V

Vanillesoße (f) custard
Vater (m) father
Vegetarier (m) vegetarian
Verbandskasten (m) first aid kit
Verbindung (f) connection *(travel, computer)*
verboten forbidden, prohibited
verbringen spend *(time)*
verderben to go off *(food)*
verderben to spoil, ruin
verdienen to earn
vereinbaren to agree
vergessen to forget
vergewaltigen to rape
Vergnügungspark (m) amusement park
verhaftet: Sie sind verhaftet you're under arrest
Verhütungsmittel (n) contraceptive
verkaufen to sell
Verkäufer (m), Verkäuferin (f) shop assistant
Verkehr (m) traffic
Verkehrsampel (f) traffic light
Verlängerungskabel (m) extension lead
verlassen to leave
verleihen to lend
verletzen to injure
verletzt injured

Verletzung (f) injury
verlieren to lose
verlobt engaged *(to be married)*
Verlobte (m/f) fiancé(e)
vermeiden to avoid
vermieten to let *(rent)*
vermissen to miss *(nostalgia)*
vernünftig sensible, reasonable
verpacken to wrap (up)
verpassen to miss *(bus etc.)*
verschieden different
versichert insured
Versicherung (f) insurance
Versicherungskarte (f) insurance document
Verspätung (f) delay
versprechen to promise
verstauchen to sprain
verstehen to understand
verstopft blocked
Verstopfung (f) constipation
Versuch experiment, attempt
versuchen to try
Vertrag (m) contract
vertraut familiar
verursachen to cause
Verwandte (m/f) relation
Verzeichnis (n) directory *(index)*
viel (von) a lot (of), much
viele many
vielen Dank thank you very much
vielleicht perhaps
vierzehn Tage a fortnight
Visum (n) visa
Vogel (m) bird
Volk (n) people, nation
voll full
Vollkornbrot (n) wholemeal bread
Vollpension (f) full board
von from, by
vor before, in front of
vorbereiten to prepare
Vorderseite (f) front
vorgestern the day before yesterday